DISCO, PUNK, NEW WAVE, HEAVY METAL, AND MORE

MUSIC IN THE 1970s AND 1980s

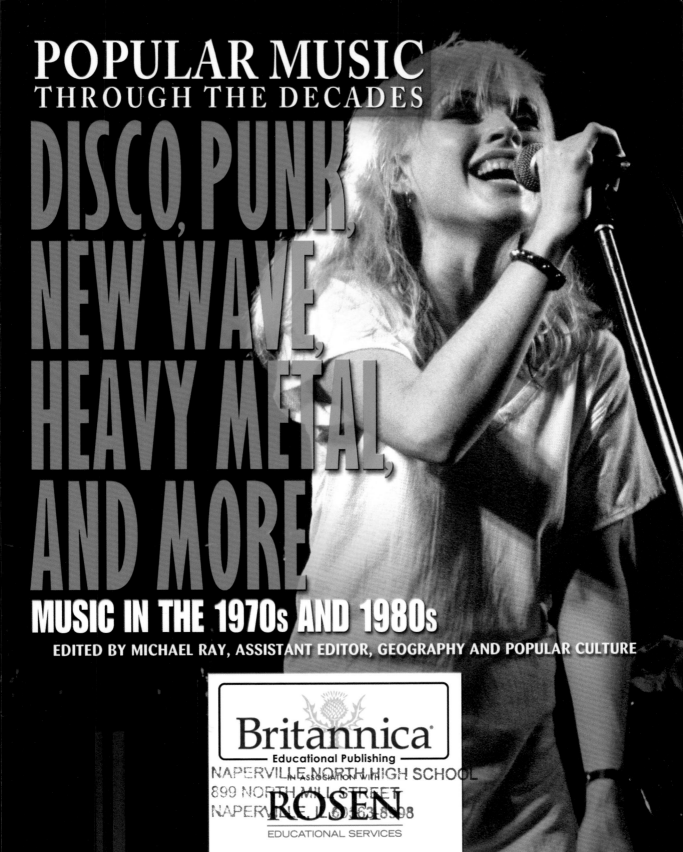

POPULAR MUSIC
THROUGH THE DECADES

DISCO, PUNK, NEW WAVE, HEAVY METAL, AND MORE

MUSIC IN THE 1970s AND 1980s

EDITED BY MICHAEL RAY, ASSISTANT EDITOR, GEOGRAPHY AND POPULAR CULTURE

Britannica®
Educational Publishing

IN ASSOCIATION WITH

ROSEN
EDUCATIONAL SERVICES

Published in 2013 by Britannica Educational Publishing
(a trademark of Encyclopædia Britannica, Inc.) in association with Rosen Educational Services, LLC

29 East 21st Street, New York, NY 10010.

Distributed exclusively by Rosen Educational Services.
For a listing of additional Britannica Educational Publishing titles, call toll free (800) 237-9932.

First Edition

Britannica Educational Publishing
J.E. Luebering: Senior Manager
Adam Augustyn: Assistant Manager
Marilyn L. Barton: Senior Coordinator, Production Control
Steven Bosco: Director, Editorial Technologies
Lisa S. Braucher: Senior Producer and Data Editor
Yvette Charboneau: Senior Copy Editor
Kathy Nakamura: Manager, Media Acquisition
Michael Ray, Assistant Editor, Geography and Popular Culture

Rosen Educational Services
Hope Lourie Killcoyne: Executive Editor
Nelson Sá: Art Director
Cindy Reiman: Photography Manager
Karen Huang: Photo Researcher
Brian Garvey: Designer, Cover Design
Introduction by Michael Ray

Library of Congress Cataloging-in-Publication Data

Disco, punk, new wave, heavy metal, and more : music in the 1970s and 1980s/edited by Michael Ray.—1st ed.
    p. cm.—(Popular music through the decades)
"In association with Britannica Educational Publishing, Rosen Educational Services."
Includes bibliographical references and index.
ISBN 978-1-61530-908-5 (library binding)
1. Popular music—1971-1980—History and criticism. 2. Popular music—1981-1990—History and criticism. I. Ray, Michael.
ML3470.D57 2013
781.6309'047—dc23

2012032630

Manufactured in the United States of America

On the cover, p. iii: Singer Deborah Harry of the new wave band Blondie performing at the Roundhouse in London, 1978. *Denis O'Regan/Hulton Archive/Getty Images*

Pages 1, 11, 38, 55, 66, 105, 118, 126, 136, 143, 148, 165, 178 Ethan Miller/Getty Images (Fender Stratocaster guitar), iStockphoto.com/catrinka81 (treble clef graphic); interior background image iStockphoto.com/hepatus; back cover © iStockphoto.com/Vladimir Jajin

CONTENTS

15

19

37

46

Chapter 4: The Sounds of So-Cal: Country Rock

51

70

153

167

176

Introduction

Given the variety of musical trends that rose and fell throughout the 1970s, one could say that the '70s didn't so much begin as the '60s ended. The "peace and love" atmosphere of the Woodstock era came to a violent conclusion at the Altamont festival in Livermore, California, on December 6, 1969. The free concert, organized by the Rolling Stones as a token of appreciation for their fans, was marred by violence on a widespread scale. Much of it was instigated by the Oakland chapter of the Hell's Angels, an outlaw biker gang that had been hired by the Stones to provide security for the event. While the consequences of this decision became apparent relatively quickly, the Stones initially had few concerns. Just a few months earlier, they had contracted a U.K. chapter of the Angels to provide security for a free concert in London's Hyde Park. What's more, the Angels had been a presence in the Bay Area scene for years. They were associated with American writer and '60s counterculture icon Ken Kesey's Merry Pranksters (who provided the Angels with LSD) and had served as unofficial security guards at previous concerts.

At Altamont, however, things turned ugly quickly. Beatings were frequent and indiscriminate. Marty Balin of the Jefferson Airplane was struck unconscious when an Angel with a pool cue assaulted him. Parts of the crowd took to the stage in an effort to escape the ongoing melee. The show reached its tragic, and perhaps unsurprising, climax during the Stones' set, when a pair of Angels stabbed a member of the audience to death. But this was not the only death to herald the dawn of the '70s.

Rock's decade of decadence began with the figurative and sometimes literal demise of numerous pioneers of the '60s. The Beatles broke up in early 1970, and their final album, *Let It Be*, was, in essence, released posthumously. Guitar legend Jimi Hendrix died of a drug overdose in September of that year. Janis Joplin died less than three weeks later. The Doors' lead singer Jim Morrison died in Paris the following summer. In its relatively short history, rock had already witnessed the passing of its share of luminaries, but the loss of Hendrix, Joplin, and Morrison in such quick succession was a shock. In later years, fans would speak of a "Forever 27" curse, as each artist died before his or her 28th birthday (the "Forever 27" club would ultimately claim additional members, such as Kurt Cobain and Amy Winehouse).

But in rock, artists can achieve some measure of life after death. Hendrix, Joplin, and Morrison each left an enduring legacy, and even the survivors of the '60s did not emerge from the decade untouched. The Rolling Stones were a changed band; the death of founding member Brian Jones (himself an inductee of the "Forever 27" club) in July 1969 and the Altamont fiasco signaled a shift for both the Stones and bands to come. No longer would Mick Jagger serve as rock's dark jester, the band's brushes with the law becoming a thing of the past. The Stones of the '70s were a corporate juggernaut, a well-oiled rock machine designed to fill stadiums. Indeed, the Rolling Stones proved to be one of the most successful touring bands of all time, with a career that would ultimately span more than half a century. Notable, however, was a claim by Keith Richards that he had not set foot inside Jagger's dressing room over the last 20 years of that time. Thus, it was with one of the biggest

surviving acts of the '60s that the mood of the '70s was set. Flower power was a thing of the past. "Turn on, tune in, drop out"—the mantra of American psychologist, author, and LSD-advocate Timothy Leary—could now be concluded with "cash in."

This is not to say that the '70s were a decade devoid of artistic merit. On the contrary, vibrant new talents were emerging in the center of the rock spotlight as well as at its fringes. Led Zeppelin took the psychedelic-blues fusion that had characterized the early Rolling Stones and melded it with a wild mixture of European and Eastern influences. Singer Robert Plant and guitarist Jimmy Page built on the Jagger and Richards dynamic to such a degree that their individual styles would provide a formula for entire genres that were to follow. Page's guitar work was virtuosic without being excessive, and Plant's vocals, which ranged from a virtual whisper to an animalistic howl, set the standard for generations of hard rock and heavy metal bands. Plant would also serve as the visual archetype for the heavy metal front man, exhibiting unbridled sensuality and sporting a wild mane of hair.

Seizing upon the success of Zeppelin and incorporating influences from the burgeoning glam rock scene, Queen burst into the limelight with anthemic singles powered by Brian May's stellar guitar work

Two seminal musicians who bridged the divide from late '60s to '70s rock—Robert Plant and Jimmy Page of Led Zeppelin—performing live onstage at Earls Court Arena in London, May 1975. *Dick Barnatt/Redferns/Getty Images*

and front man Freddie Mercury's nimble vocals. While Plant exemplified the rock star as sex symbol, Mercury was a consummate showman, exhibiting a stage persona that was equal parts substance and spectacle. Beneath Mercury's flamboyant exterior was a skilled songwriter and multi-instrumentalist who possessed the uncanny ability to command a crowd of tens of thousands of people. Neither Led Zeppelin nor Queen were afforded the level of critical examination that was applied to the Beatles or the Stones, but both bands were enormously popular, and each crafted a body of work that remains surprisingly fresh today.

On the other side of the Atlantic, a young man from New Jersey had just broken free of the East Coast bar band circuit. Initially working in the singer-songwriter idiom, Bruce Springsteen soon made his mark as a rock-and-roll everyman who sang with the voice of working-class America. Although he would go on to sell tens of millions of albums, Springsteen would retain his blue-collar image with heartfelt lyrics, occasional nods to American roots music, and marathon-length live performances that displayed the breadth of his talents as a performer and a bandleader.

Outside of Springsteen, the title "bandleader" was one that had been applied rarely, if at all, in the world of rock. One spoke of frontmen or lead singers—bandleaders were the stuff of the swing era. But the E Street Band, Springsteen's longtime backing group, were a motley crew of diverse personalities and styles, an intensely talented collection of individuals united by the force of Springsteen's will and musicianship. Springsteen himself articulated the E Street ethic on the occasion of the death of his longtime friend and bandmate Clarence Clemons in 2011. Clemons, popularly known as the Big Man, was a striking presence both musically and visually. Standing almost six and a half feet tall and always impeccably dressed (in contrast to Springsteen's work shirts and jeans), Clemons played saxophone and, perhaps more importantly, was a fixture in Springsteen's live show. In his eulogy for Clemons, Springsteen stated, "Clarence doesn't leave the E Street Band when *he* dies. He leaves when *we* die."

The Eagles expressed a similar sentiment in their 1976 hit "Hotel California," but it had far darker implications. Southern California's drink- and drug-fueled scene inspired the line, "You can check out any time you like, but you can never leave." The song captured the hedonism and cynicism of the era, wrapped in a tightly produced, country rock package. While both the message and the medium resonated with white baby boomers, an entirely different sort of sound was emerging from stages in Ohio and Oklahoma and from nightclubs in New York and Miami.

Funk had its roots in 1950s jazz, but by the '70s, a collection of bands had transformed it into something decidedly funkier. The Ohio Players donned sequined jumpsuits, frequently traded vocal duties, and supplemented an upbeat R&B sound with a robust horn section. Parliament-Funkadelic was a massive funk collective, its live show resembling nothing short of a psychedelic tent revival featuring a cast of dozens. Other artists flirted with funk while remaining firmly planted in the soul or R&B idioms.

Developing on a parallel track but drawing from somewhat different influences, disco emerged from the underground club scene to become one of the defining musical genres of the decade. Popularized in the

1977 film *Saturday Night Fever*, disco was the product of Philly soul, Latin rhythms, and Europop electronic instrumentation. While disco would see the emergence of the DJ as an artist in his or her own right, a number of producers and performers would come to embody the disco era. The Bee Gees, a trio that adopted a disco sound relatively late in their career, scored some of the genre's biggest hits, and their work on the *Saturday Night Fever* soundtrack made it one of the top-selling albums of all time. Donna Summer teamed with legendary producer Giorgio Moroder on a string of singles, and Summer earned the nickname "the Queen of disco." The Village People's camp theatrics were designed as a direct appeal to the gay community that had long formed an important part of the club scene. Partially recruited through an advertisement that read "Macho Types Wanted: Must Dance and Have a Moustache," the Village People appeared to be a collection of hypermasculine clichés—a construction worker, a cowboy, a leather-clad biker, etc.—but their songs were thinly (or not so thinly) veiled references to gay culture. The group amassed a series of dance hits, and they became one of the most successful disco acts to cross over onto the mainstream pop charts.

Of course, the Village People were far from the first group to be created primarily for visual effect. The Monkees were a wholly made-to-order band, but they happened to be supported by an exceptional crew of songwriters, and their resulting catalog was far stronger than one might expect from four telegenic strangers with limited musical abilities. It might seem surprising that a similar process would result in a band that would become the centerpiece of the British punk movement, but "surprising" is the norm when it comes to the history of the Sex Pistols. Formed by British rock impresario Malcolm McLaren as a marketing tool to promote his clothing shop, Sex, the Sex Pistols took the do-it-yourself attitude to new extremes. They unleashed a raw, guitar-heavy sound combined with socially conscious lyrics and a look that would define the punk aesthetic. It has been said that only a handful of people purchased the debut album from the Velvet Underground, but every one of those people formed a band. The Sex Pistols triggered a similar creative spark in their early fans, and nowhere was that more apparent than at the Pistols' now-legendary show at the Manchester Lesser Free Trade Hall in June 1976. Among the audience members were Stephen Patrick Morrissey, who would later become the lead vocalist of the Smiths; the Buzzcocks, who were the show's organizers; Bernard Albrecht and Peter Hook, founding members of Joy Division; and Mark E. Smith of the Fall. When the Pistols returned the following month, they had already gained a reputation among Britain's music elite. In attendance at the second show were Tony Wilson, a Granada Television personality who would later cofound Factory Records and Ian Curtis, who would cross paths with Sumner and Hook and eventually sign on as their lead singer. These two shows are condensed into a single event in the movie *24 Hour Party People*, a fictionalized history of the Manchester scene as Wilson saw it from the '70s through the '90s.

The historical sweep of *24 Hour Party People* covers the progression from punk to postpunk and new wave, and nowhere is that evolution more pronounced than with those three lads from the Sex Pistols' shows. Albrecht, Hook, and Curtis initially recorded as Warsaw, and their sound was unabashedly punk. Changing their name to Joy Division and adding the precise, almost machine-like, drumming of Stephen Morris, the group's sound was altered dramatically. Producer Martin Hannett spurred the band to new heights, and Hook's distinctive bass lines combined with Curtis's vocals to create one of the most recognizable sounds of the era. After Curtis's death, Albrecht stepped in as lead singer and the band, reborn as New Order and adopting a more electronic sound, became one of the most successful dance acts of the '80s.

On both sides of the Atlantic, punk rejected rock's conventions while embracing its excesses. New wave artists eschewed both, turning to the sounds and styles of bygone ages, while at the same time integrating new technology, such as synthesizers. Adam and the Ants adopted eyeliner and the look of 18th-century dandy highwaymen while playing ska-influenced pop. The B-52s crafted clever party music with a generous helping of camp, topped with beehive hairdos. The Police explored virtually every kind of Western popular music in an effort to accompany Sting's aggressively literary lyrics. The Go-Go's resurrected the girl group formula to produce a string of breezy hits. The Smiths paired guitar wizard Johnny Marr with so-called "miserabilist" Morrissey, and the result was both catchy and bookish. Although the new wave would ultimately recede, as punk-derived alternative rock acts moved to the fore in the early '90s, the genre would experience something of a revival in the 21st century. Bands such as the Strokes, Interpol, the Killers, the Postal Service, and Metric consciously drew upon the legacy of new wave, interpreting it for a new generation of fans. They, and others, proved the maxim that, in rock, everything old can be new again.

CHAPTER 1

Life After Woodstock

Woodstock, the legendary rock festival that was billed as "Three Days of Peace and Music," virtually defined a generation. The amateur promoters who organized the event, however, were left nearly bankrupt, as only a small minority of the 400,000 concert attendees had actually purchased tickets. Although the event itself was a financial bust, the promoters had the foresight to secure the film and recording rights for the performances. Michael Wadleigh's subsequent documentary *Woodstock* (1970) put the promoters back in the black, demonstrating that, properly marketed, a celebration of youth counterculture and freedom could remain a valuable commodity for decades to come. Without overly romanticizing the Age of Aquarius, it had become clear by 1970 that rock and roll was not only here to stay, it was big business.

ROCK GOES MAINSTREAM

The 1970s began as the decade of the rock superstar. Excess became the norm for bands such as the Rolling Stones, not just in terms of their private wealth and well-publicized decadence but also in terms of stage and studio effects and costs. The sheer scale of rock album sales gave musicians— and their ever-growing entourage of managers, lawyers, and accountants—the upper hand in negotiations with record

Guitarist Ron Wood and singer Mick Jagger of the Rolling Stones onstage in Knebworth, outside London, Aug. 21, 1976. Michael Putland/Hulton Archive/Getty Images

companies, and for a moment it seemed that the greater the artistic self-indulgence the bigger the financial return. By the end of the decade, though, the 25-year growth in record sales had come to a halt, and a combination of economic recession and increasing competition for young people's leisure spending (notably from the makers of video games) brought the music industry, by this point based on rock, its first real crisis. The Anglo-American music market consolidated into a shape that did not change appreciably for the next three decades, while new sales opportunities beyond the established transatlantic route began to be pursued more intently.

The 1970s, in short, was the decade in which a pattern of rock formats and functions was settled. The excesses of rock superstardom elicited both a return to DIY (do-it-yourself) rock and roll (in the roots sounds of performers such as Bruce Springsteen and in the punk movement of British youth) and a self-consciously camp take on rock stardom itself (in the glam rock of the likes of Roxy Music, David Bowie, and Queen). The continuing needs of dancers were met by the disco movement (originally shaped by the twist phenomenon in the 1960s), which was briefly seized by the music industry as a new pop mainstream following the success of the film *Saturday Night Fever* in 1977. By the early 1980s, however, disco settled back into its own world of clubs, deejays, and recording studios and its own crosscurrents from African American, Latin American, and gay subcultures. African American music developed in parallel to rock, drawing on rock technology sometimes to bridge black and white markets (as with Stevie Wonder) and sometimes to sharpen their differences (as in the case of funk). Rock, in other words, was routinized, as both a moneymaking and a music-making practice.

ROCK ON THE AIRWAVES

Inevitably, as teenagers grew up, the Top 40 formula began to wear thin. In the late 1960s, so did rock. A new generation sought freedom, and on the radio it came on the FM band with underground, or free-form, radio. Disc jockeys were allowed—if not encouraged—to choose their own records, usually rooted in rock but ranging from jazz and blues to country and folk music as well. Similar latitude extended to nonmusical elements, including interviews, newscasts, and impromptu live performances. While free-form evolved into album-oriented rock (or AOR, in industry lingo), other formats catered to an increasingly splintered music audience. Initially labeled as "chicken rock" when it emerged in the early 1970s ("chicken" as in, "people who are afraid of real rock"), adult contemporary (A/C) found a large audience of young adults who wanted their rock quieter. A/C blended the lighter elements of pop and rock with what was called "middle of the road" (MOR) rock, an adult-oriented format that favoured big bands and pop singers such as Tony Bennett, Peggy Lee, and Nat King Cole.

On both sides of the Atlantic, rock-and-roll radio had matured. Commercial broadcasters took a page from the pirates who had ruled the airwaves in the '60s, transforming stagnating Top 40 stations into an array of specialized, genre-specific channels. In the United States, syndicated programs such as the *King Biscuit Flower Hour* showcased performances from both established and up-and-coming artists, while call-in shows such as *Rockline* and *Innerview* explored the stories behind the songs. Live concerts aired by the British Broadcasting Corporation (BBC) drew a following in both Britain and the United States, and programs featuring specific artists became highly sought after by "tape traders," who participated in a transatlantic barter system of live recordings (of both the legal and bootleg variety).

THE DECLINE OF PIRATE RADIO

Pirate radio stations, the unlicensed broadcasters that operated outside the national boundaries of their signal's target audience, would forever hold a special place in the history of rock-and-roll radio, and the "outlaw DJ" would become one of rock's more enduring archetypes. By the 1970s, however, large-scale pirate operations were in decline. North American "border blasters" faced financial difficulties and increasingly restrictive treaties that limited their signal strength. A 1986 broadcasting agreement between the United States and Mexico effectively ended the border radio era in North America, and an increasingly competitive FM market forced Radio Luxembourg's AM signal to go dark in 1991. They also faced direct competition from commercial broadcasters as the rapid expansion on the FM band saw many stations offering "pirate quality" playlists with high-fidelity sound that could not be matched by the pirates' AM signal. In Britain, many of the offshore disc jockeys had migrated to the London studios of Radio 1 (the BBC's popular music network). British DJ Johnny Walker (born Peter Dingley), for example, became popular on Radio Caroline and later shifted to BBC's Radio 1; in the mid-1970s, he even worked on American

WMMS

Radio stations, as a rule, reflect and serve the local community. In Cleveland, Ohio, where Alan Freed rocked and ruled in the early 1950s, it was WMMS-FM that came to represent the city in the 1970s. Central to the success of WMMS was deejay Kid Leo (Lawrence J. Travagliante), who ultimately became the station's program director. By the time Kid Leo joined WMMS in 1973 (after graduating from Cleveland State University), the station had been rocking for five years. By 1976 he had helped take the station to the top of the city's radio ratings. Kid Leo combined a belief in rock's blue-collar appeal and an irreverent attitude on the air with a zeal for obtaining—and playing—new recordings by major acts before anyone else had them. WMMS won numerous industry awards and *Rolling Stone* magazine polls as the nation's favourite radio station.

radio. Doing it the other way around, British expatriate John Peel began in American radio in the 1960s, later joining pirate Radio London and then transferring to Radio 1.

CAPITAL RADIO

The launch of London's Capital Radio in October 1973 signaled a new era in British broadcasting. However, if those who had campaigned for a legitimate commercial radio network in the United Kingdom were expecting

the flagship of Independent Local Radio to rehoist the Jolly Roger, they were soon disabused by the slick, seamless—and advertiser-friendly—format of daytime programming that relegated non-Top 40 musical "specialisms" to the evenings and weekends, alongside current affairs, drama, and the weekly concert of classical music that the station's license demanded. Capital nevertheless made rapid inroads into Radio 1's listenership and created the breakfast-show (a morning drive-time program) blueprint—first with Kenny Everett and then with Chris Tarrant—that virtually all British stations have followed.

WNEW

Once underground, or free-form, radio proved itself capable of attracting listeners and advertising revenue in significant numbers, radio corporations jumped onto the bandwagon. None was as successful as Metromedia, which owned the West Coast pioneers KSAN in San Francisco and KMET in Los Angeles. The company soon switched its New York City FM station, WNEW, from an all-female deejay format to free-form, which as it matured under corporate umbrellas became known as progressive rock radio. Sister stations WMMR in Philadelphia, Pennsylvania, and WMMS in Cleveland, Ohio, soon followed suit.

WNEW attracted one major name from Top 40—Scott Muni, who had replaced Alan Freed at WAKR in Akron, Ohio, in the early 1950s on his way to WMCA and WABC in New York City. WNEW's on-air staff also included Bill ("Rosko") Mercer, who had been part of a short-lived freeform experiment at WOR-FM; Dave Herman, who had been a progressive pioneer at WMMR; Allison Steele, "The Nightbird"; and Carol Miller, also from WMMR, whose daily Led

Zeppelin feature was engagingly titled "Get the Led Out." In 1969 *Billboard* noted that some 60 progressive stations were on the air. The two top stations, according to the magazine, were WNEW and KSAN.

DJ CULTURE

For some, the disc jockey's role had evolved irreversibly from the dream career of a music enthusiast with an unstoppable desire to share his or her tastes with the widest possible audience to an apprenticeship for would-be TV entertainers for whom the records mattered less than their on-air personalities. This was especially true in Britain, where DJs such as Kenny Everett, Noel Edmonds, and Chris Evans successfully made the jump from radio to a host of other media. For others, there remained no higher praise than the label "tastemaker," and the challenge of remaining abreast of the latest trends in music was one to which they would happily rise.

JOHN PEEL

Throughout his four-decade career, John Peel (born John Robert Parker Ravenscroft, August 30, 1939, Heswall, Cheshire, England—died October 25, 2004, Cuzco, Peru) was one of the most influential tastemakers in rock music. Peel was renowned for discovering and championing emerging artists and for his connossieurship of groundbreaking offbeat music and performers.

The son of a cotton merchant, he grew up in upper-middle-class comfort near Liverpool, for whose powerhouse football (soccer) team he developed a lifelong obsession. After attending boarding school and a stint in the military, he emigrated to the United States in 1960—to Dallas, Texas, where, still using his given last name, Ravenscroft, he worked at the Cotton Exchange and then sold insurance. In 1961 he landed his first (unpaid) job as a disc jockey, at station WRR. Thereafter, as the British Invasion, led by the Liverpudlian Beatles, swept the United States, he capitalized on his Scouse accent (the distinctive dialect of the Merseyside region), and, though he had left England before the advent of "Merseybeat," became its authentic ambassador on local American airwaves.

After working at radio stations in Dallas, Oklahoma City, and San Bernadino, California, he returned to the United Kingdom in 1967 to host his late-night, hippytrippy *Perfumed Garden* on Radio London. While his fellow deejays cultivated wild and crazy personalities, Ravenscroft, having adopted the last name Peel as a pirate mask, was droll and unflappable but ever

John Peel, 1968. Central Press/Hulton Archive/ Getty Images

the iconoclast. Still, when the BBC established Radio 1 in September 1967 in response to the challenge of pirate radio, Peel was one of the new network's original recruits. From then until the early 21st century, Peel was the advocate for new and often challenging music, playing recordings to which a less adventurous broadcaster or less committed music enthusiast would likely not have given airtime. In the process he became enamoured of everything from art rock to punk, post-punk, and beyond, introducing his audience to previously "unknown" artists such as David Bowie, Joy Division, the Smiths, Billy Bragg, and countless performers who flooded his mailbox with demo tapes. Meanwhile, he remained steadfastly loyal to an eclectic array of personal favourites that included Captain Beefheart, oddball poet-singer Ivor Cutler, unconventional songwriter Kevin Coyne, abrasive rockers the Fall, Northern Ireland's Undertones (whose "Teenage Kicks" was Peel's all-time favourite song), the ethereal Cocteau Twins, and PJ Harvey. Yet the same breadth of taste that tested the boundaries of what could be broadcast on the BBC could also find room for a good-time group like the Faces—Peel famously mimed the mandolin part from Rod Stewart's "Maggie May" (1971) on *Top of the Pops*—and an unlikely love affair with the Eurovision Song Contest, the annual competition sponsored by state-run European television stations to determine the best new pop song.

Never particularly adept technologically (he occasionally played records at the wrong speed), Peel was nevertheless seemingly ageless and effortlessly hip. He was a perennial choice as *NME* magazine's favourite deejay of the year, and his year-end "best-of" playlist, the Festive 50, conferred significant cachet for those who found their way onto it, much as his longtime involvement with the Glastonbury Festival helped ensure its status as one of the world's premiere rock festivals. Likewise, being chosen to record a live Peel Session for his show was a sign of arrival. Those thousands of sessions—many of which were released as commercial recordings—originated as a work-around response to needle time, a longtime requirement of British broadcasting that limited the amount of airtime that could be devoted to playing records. Even after the repeal of this requirement, Peel Sessions remained the signature and mainstay of his program. Peel was made an Officer of the Order of the British Empire (OBE) in 1998. He died of a heart attack while on vacation in South America in 2004. On the anniversary of his last appearance on BBC, the network annually presents an annual celebration, John Peel Day.

B. MITCHEL REED

In a career that spanned four decades, B. Mitchel Reed (born Burton Mitchell Goldberg, June 10, 1926, Brooklyn, New York, U.S.—died March 16, 1983, Los Angeles, California) roamed the wide world of radio formats and established himself as a standout in both Top 40 and its flip side, free-form FM rock. He began his radio career as a jazz announcer in Baltimore, Maryland, in the early 1950s, but his first fame came as a fast-talking deejay at KFWB in Los Angeles and WMCA in New York City ("I'm not talking too fast," he once said, "you're listening too slow"). By the time he moved to the pre-Top 40 KFWB, he was calling himself "the Boy on a Couch" and telling stories from sessions with his psychoanalyst between jazz cuts. When the station shifted to a rock-and-roll format, Reed became the rapid-fire "B.M.R.," helping turn "Color Radio" into a success.

After five years at KFWB Reed accepted an offer from WMCA, duplicated his success in New York City, and returned to California. There he helped pioneer underground radio— first at KPPC in Pasadena, then most prominently at KMET, the "Mighty Met," in Los Angeles. Reed decelerated his delivery to a jazz tempo and took a warm, conversational approach. Just as listeners had accepted his switch from mellow to manic in the late 1950s, so they welcomed his reversal a decade later. KMET went on to give KHJ, "Boss Radio," its first strong challenger. A new generation of rock music and a new form of radio had arrived on stereo FM.

CHARLIE GILLETT

British radio broadcaster and author Charlie Gillett (born February 20, 1942, Morecambe, Lancashire, England—died March 17, 2010, London, England) championed world music after having earlier helped to popularize in Britain classic American rock and roll in a career as an influential host of radio programs. Gillett also wrote a well-respected serious history of rock and roll, *The Sound of the City: The Rise of Rock and Roll* (1970). He originated and hosted (1972–78) the BBC Radio London show *Honky-Tonk*, which in its early years focused on American music and later was credited with launching the careers of British musicians Elvis Costello and Graham Parker and the band Dire Straits. In the mid-1970s Gillett partnered with Gordon Nelki to create the record label and publishing company Oval Music; its successes included "Lucky Number" by Lene Lovich (1979), "19" by Paul Hardcastle (1985), and "Would You...?" by Touch and Go (1998). In 1980 Gillett became a disc jockey for the commercial station Capital Radio in London, where in 1983 he launched the world music showcase *A Foreign Affair*. In 2000 he released *World 2000*, the first in a series of 10 double-CD compilations of world music, the last of which, *Otro Mundo*, came out in 2009.

LARRY LUJACK

"I'm just plain fantastic—the best damn rock-and-roll DJ of our time or any other time!" wrote Larry Lujack (born Larry Blankenburg, June 6, 1940, Quasqueton, Iowa, U.S.), a Chicago radio kingpin in the 1960s and '70s, in his autobiography, *Super Jock* (1975). Lujack had the ratings to back up his braggadocio. Sweeping in from Seattle (with a brief, unhappy stop in Boston) in 1967, he bounced between Chicago's dueling rock stations, WLS and WCFL, which made him the object of high-priced bidding wars until his retirement 20 years later. Lujack was the anti-deejay, offering sarcasm and insults instead of happy talk. But he also prided himself on preparation, so that his comments would be topical, and he matched the rock and roll he played with a brash, high energy.

CHAPTER 2

The Makings of a Classic

The label "classic rock" is one that can only be applied at a distance. Contemporary musicians certainly would not have identified themselves as existing in such a category. But within the confines of commercial radio, the blues-infused, album-oriented rock of the 1970s has been gathered under a broad umbrella that covers a diverse range of performers, from the proto-heavy metal of Led Zeppelin to the pop wizardry of Fleetwood Mac.

LED ZEPPELIN

The British rock band Led Zeppelin was extremely popular in the 1970s. Although their musical style was diverse, they came to be well known for their influence on the development of heavy metal. The members were Jimmy Page (born January 9, 1944, Heston, Middlesex, England), Robert Plant (born August 20, 1948, West Bromwich, West Midlands), John Paul Jones (born John Baldwin, January 3, 1946, Sidcup, Kent), and John Bonham (born May 31, 1948, Redditch, Hereford and Worcester—died September 25, 1980, Windsor, Berkshire).

Initially called the New Yardbirds, Led Zeppelin was formed in 1968 by Jimmy Page, the final lead guitarist for the legendary British blues band the Yardbirds. Bassist and keyboard player Jones, like Page, was a veteran studio musician;

Led Zeppelin, c. 1970 (from left to right): John Paul Jones, Jimmy Page, John Bonham, and Robert Plant. Michael Ochs Archives/Getty Images

vocalist Plant and drummer Bonham came from little-known provincial bands. The group was influenced by various kinds of music, including early rock and roll, psychedelic rock, blues, folk, Celtic, Indian, and Arabic music. Although acoustic and folk-based music was part of the band's repertoire from its inception, it was the bottom-heavy, loud, raw, and powerful electric style that gained them their following and notoriety early on; their first two albums included many of the songs that prompted Led

Zeppelin's categorization as a precursor of heavy metal. The heaviness of songs such as "Dazed and Confused" and "Whole Lotta Love" was created by Bonham's enormous drum sound and through Page's production techniques, in which he emphasized drums and bass, resulting in a sonic spaciousness that has kept the records sounding fresh years after they were made. Page and Jones also wrote most of the band's music, while Plant contributed lyrics and some musical ideas. Although Page was responsible for the majority of their signature riffs (the short, repeated musical ideas that often structure a song), Jones wrote the riff for the celebrated "Black Dog" and several other songs. Jones also contributed much to the arrangement of songs. Page's guitar solos were based primarily on melodic ideas derived from the blues scale ("Heartbreaker" is a good example), and he is especially known for creating multiple, simultaneous guitar parts—a kind of guitar orchestra—in such songs as "Achilles Last Stand" and "The Song Remains the Same." Page is considered one of rock's guitar heroes, but, because he was more interested in creating a distinctive mood and sound on a recording than in displaying his virtuosity, he frequently chose not to include a guitar solo in Zeppelin songs.

Plant's voice rounded out Led Zeppelin's sound. Exaggerating the vocal style and expressive palette of blues singers such as Howlin' Wolf and Muddy Waters, Plant created the sound that has defined much hard rock and heavy metal singing: a high range, an abundance of distortion, loud volume, and emotional excess ("Whole Lotta Love" is a classic example). Plant was, however, capable of a broader stylistic range, including tender ballads ("The Rain Song") and songs showing the influence of Indian and Arabic vocal styles ("Kashmir").

Led Zeppelin's best-known song is "Stairway to Heaven"; its gentle acoustic beginning eventually builds to an exhilarating climax featuring a lengthy electric guitar solo. This combination of acoustic and electric sections was typical for Page, who from the band's beginning was interested in juxtaposing what he called "light and shade." The song appeared on the band's fourth and most famous album, released untitled, which showed only four runic symbols (intended to represent the band members) on the cover and had the mystical, mythological lyrics to "Stairway" printed on the inner sleeve. The sense of mystery and ritual that this created became an important part of the band's image. They kept their distance from the press and were uninterested in catering to the singles market. Moreover, "Stairway" and several other songs were of epic length by rock standards, and concert improvisations stretched some songs to triple the length of their studio versions.

Thanks in part to their manager, Peter Grant, the band enjoyed phenomenal commercial success throughout the 1970s. While Led Zeppelin never received the kind of critical acclaim or mainstream acceptance accorded the Beatles or the Rolling Stones, their influence on rock music has been prodigious. They are regularly cited as the progenitors of both hard rock and heavy metal. Their sound has been imitated by bands from Black Sabbath to Nirvana. They also inspired hard rock bands to include acoustic elements in their music and were among the first to experiment with Indian and North African music. Page's style—both his solos and riffs—has served as an important model for most rock guitarists, and Bonham is often cited as the model for metal or hard rock drumming.

Led Zeppelin disbanded in 1980 after Bonham's accidental death. The group re-formed for short, one-off performances in 1985 (the Live Aid benefit), 1988 (Atlantic Records' 40th anniversary concert), and 1995 (the band's induction into the Rock and Roll Hall of Fame). Much more momentous was the group's full-blown concert in London in December 2007 to honour Atlantic's cofounder Ahmet Ertegun, at which Bonham's son, Jason, played the drums.

QUEEN

The British rock band Queen fused heavy metal, glam rock, and camp theatrics to become one of the most popular groups of the 1970s. Queen crafted an elaborate blend of layered guitar work by virtuoso Brian May and overdubbed vocal harmonies enlivened by the flamboyant performance of front man and principal songwriter Freddie Mercury. The members were Mercury (born Farrokh Bulsara, September 5, 1946, Stone Town, Zanzibar [now in Tanzania]—died November 24, 1991, Kensington, London, England), Brian May (born July 19, 1947, Twickenham, Middlesex), John Deacon (born August 19, 1951, Leicester, Leicestershire), and Roger Taylor (born July 26, 1949, King's Lynn, Norfolk).

Members of two bands composed of university and art-school students combined to form Queen in London in 1971. Incorporating elements of both heavy metal and glam rock, the band debuted on record with *Queen* (1973), which was followed by *Queen II* (1974). Despite an impressive blend of majestic vocal harmonies and layered virtuosic guitar work, Queen initially failed to attract much notice beyond the United Kingdom. Aided by producer Roy Thomas Baker, Queen shot up the international charts with its third album, *Sheer Heart Attack* (1974). *A Night at the Opera* (1975), one of pop music's most expensive productions, sold even better. Defiantly eschewing the use of synthesizers, the band constructed a sound that was part English music hall, part Led Zeppelin, epitomized by the mock-operatic "Bohemian Rhapsody." The song spent nine weeks atop the British singles chart, and its accompanying promotional film helped the music industry recognize

Queen. PRNewsFoto/Hollywood Records/AP Images

its future in video. Spectacular success followed in 1977 with "We Are the Champions" and "We Will Rock You"—which became ubiquitous anthems at sporting events in Britain and the United States. *The Game* (1980), featuring "Crazy Little Thing Called Love" and "Another One Bites the Dust," was Queen's first number one album in the United States. Their popularity waned for a period in the 1980s; however, a stellar performance at the charity concert Live Aid in 1985 reversed their fortunes commercially. Mercury died of AIDS in 1991, and the band issued its final album in 1995. Queen was inducted into the Rock and Roll Hall of Fame in 2001.

TRAFFIC

The British rock group Traffic was known for incorporating lengthy jazzlike improvisation into rock-music structures. Principal members included singer-keyboardist Steve Winwood (born May 12, 1948, Birmingham, Warwickshire, England), flautist-saxophonist Chris Wood

FREDDIE MERCURY

Farrokh Bulsara, who became one of rock's most dynamic front men as Freddie Mercury, was born to Parsi parents who had emigrated from India to Zanzibar, where his father worked as a clerk for the British government. As a child, Bulsara was sent to a boarding school in Panchgani, Maharashtra state, India. Artistically inclined from an early age, he formed a band there in which he played the piano. When Zanzibar became part of the independent country of Tanzania in 1964, Bulsara moved with his family to Feltham, England. He later studied graphic art and design at Ealing Technical College and School of Art (now part of the University of West London), graduating in 1969.

Influenced by the hard-edged, blues-based style of rock acts such as Cream and Jimi Hendrix, Bulsara began singing with bands in London. He also became friends with guitarist Brian May and drummer Roger Taylor of the band Smile, and in 1970, when Smile's lead singer quit, Bulsara replaced him. He soon changed the group's name to Queen and his own to Freddie Mercury. Bassist John Deacon joined the following year. By the early 1980s Queen had become an international phenomenon, drawing particular attention for its elaborately staged performances in enormous venues. Strutting the stage in outrageous costumes, Mercury effortlessly commanded audiences in the tens of thousands. In 1985 Mercury released the solo record *Mr. Bad Guy*, which took musical inspiration from disco. Mercury later appeared on the sound track of Dave Clark's science-fiction musical *Time* (1986) and teamed with Spanish soprano Montserrat Caballé for the semi-operatic album *Barcelona* (1988).

In 1991 Mercury, who had engaged in relationships with both men and women, announced that he had been diagnosed with

AIDS. He died a day later from complications related to the disease. Until shortly before his death, Mercury had continued to record with Queen, and he was posthumously featured on the band's final album, *Made in Heaven* (1995).

(born June 24, 1944, Birmingham—died July 12, 1983, Birmingham), guitarist Dave Mason (born May 10, 1946, Worcester, Worcestershire), and drummer Jim Capaldi (born August 2, 1944, Evesham, Worcestershire—died January 28, 2005, London).

Founded in 1967 and charting one of the most tumultuous careers in rock history, Traffic underwent substantial shifts in both musical style and membership. The group's first incarnation was a psychedelic pop collective whose members lived together in Berkshire, England, and collaborated on the composition of most songs on their debut album, *Mr. Fantasy* (1967), which reached the British Top Ten. Mason departed briefly, returning just long enough to write half of the songs on *Traffic* (1968)—a hit in both the United Kingdom and the United States—before leaving again. Shortly thereafter, Winwood (who had already experienced fame as a teenager with the Spencer Davis Group) broke up the band and formed Blind Faith with former Cream members Eric Clapton and Ginger Baker. In 1970, midway through recording a solo album, Winwood reconvened with Wood and Capaldi, releasing *John Barleycorn Must Die* as Traffic. The 1970s version of Traffic, built on this core trio, moved away from pop songcraft and forged a sound built on free-form improvisation, earning continued commercial success with *The Low Spark of High Heeled Boys* (1971), *Shoot Out at the Fantasy Factory* (1973), and *When the Eagle Flies* (1974). Both on tour and in the studio, the group added and subtracted a number of additional musicians during these years before finally disbanding in 1975.

Winwood enjoyed a successful solo career in the 1980s. He and Capaldi reunited under the Traffic name in 1994 to record *Far From Home*. The pair also staged a successful concert tour. Traffic was inducted into the Rock and Roll Hall of Fame in 2004.

BRUCE SPRINGSTEEN

American singer, songwriter, and bandleader Bruce Springsteen (born September 23, 1949, Freehold, New Jersey, U.S.) became the archetypal rock performer of the 1970s and '80s.

Springsteen grew up in Freehold, a mill town where his father worked as a labourer. His rebellious and artistic side led him to the nearby Jersey shore, where his imagination was sparked by the rock band scene and the boardwalk life, high and low. After an apprenticeship in bar bands on the mid-Atlantic coast, Springsteen turned himself into a solo singer-songwriter in 1972 and auditioned for talent scout John Hammond, Sr., who immediately signed him to Columbia Records. His first two albums, released in 1973, reflect folk rock, soul, and rhythm-and-blues influences, especially those of Van Morrison, Bob Dylan, and Stax/Volt Records. Springsteen's voice, a rough baritone that he used to shout on up-tempo numbers and to more sensual effect on slower songs, was shown to good effect here, but his sometimes spectacular guitar playing, which ranged from dense power chord effects to straight 1950s rock and roll, had to be downplayed to fit the singer-songwriter format.

With his third album, *Born to Run* (1975), Springsteen transformed into a full-fledged rock and roller, heavily indebted to Phil Spector and Roy Orbison. The album, a diurnal song cycle, was a sensation even before it hit the shelves; indeed, the week of the album's release, Columbia's public relations campaign landed Springsteen on the covers of both *Time* and *Newsweek*. But it sold only middling well, and three years passed before the follow-up, the tougher and more somber *Darkness on the Edge of Town* (1978), appeared. With "Hungry Heart," from *The River* (1980), Springsteen finally scored an international hit single.

By then, however, he was best known for his stage shows, three- and four-hour extravaganzas with his E Street Band that blended rock, folk, and soul with dramatic intensity and exuberant humour. The band, a crew of mixed stereotypes— from rock-and-roll bandit to cool music professional—was more like a gang than a musical unit, apparently held together by little other than faith in its leader. Springsteen and saxophonist Clarence Clemons, a huge black man, seemed sometimes to be playing out scenes from Huckleberry Finn, using the stage as their raft. Springsteen's refusal, after *Born to Run*, to cooperate with much of the record company's public relations and marketing machinery, coupled with his painstaking recording process and the draining live shows, helped earn his reputation as a performer of principle as well as of power and popularity. Yet to this point Springsteen was probably more important as a regional hero of the Eastern Seaboard from Boston to Virginia, where his songs and attitudes metaphorically summed up a certain rock-based lifestyle, than as a figure of national or international importance.

Nebraska (1982), a stark set of acoustic songs, most in some way concerned with death, was an unusual interlude. It was *Born in the U.S.A.* (1984) and his subsequent 18-month world tour that cinched Springsteen's reputation as the preeminent writer-performer of his rock-and-roll period.

The album produced seven hit singles, most notably the title track, a sympathetic portrayal of Vietnam War veterans widely misinterpreted as a patriotic anthem. Springsteen's social perspective has been distinctly working-class throughout his career, a point emphasized both by his 1995 album, *The Ghost of Tom Joad*, which, inspired by John Steinbeck's *The Grapes of Wrath*, concerned itself with America's economically and spiritually destitute, and by his 1994 hit single (his first in eight years), the AIDS-related "Streets of Philadelphia," from the film *Philadelphia*, for which he won both an Academy Award and a Grammy Award.

Springsteen and the E Street Band, 2007. PRNewsFoto/SIRIUS Satellite Radio/AP Images

The other side of Springsteen's work is reflected in the albums that he produced in the period beginning with *Tunnel of Love* (1987) and including *Human Touch* and *Lucky Town* (released simultaneously in 1992). The songs on these albums are intensely personal reflections on intimate relationships. In general, they have not been as popular.

Bridging all this is the five-record set *Bruce Springsteen and the E Street Band Live 1975–1985* (1986), which captures as much of his highly visual stage show of that period as can be rendered in a solely audio form. (His work in music video has been judged far less good, showing his tendency to be somewhat stilted on TV despite his being a naturally gifted stage performer.)

The breakup of the E Street Band in 1989 and general trends in pop music fashion curbed Springsteen's popularity. In 1998 he put together a box set, *Tracks*, consisting for the most part of leftover material that had failed to make the cut on his albums with the band. This grandiose gesture established him as prolix beyond all but a couple of peers. Sales of *Tracks* were trivial compared with those for *Live*.

In 1999 Springsteen reunited the E Street Band. They appeared with him when he alone was inducted into the Rock and Roll Hall of Fame in early 1999, then spent a year touring with him, resulting in a live album (*Live in New York City* [2001]) but only a handful of new songs. On September 21, 2001, Springsteen performed the national debut of his song "My City of Ruins" on a television special. It was written about Asbury Park but took on a different tone in the wake of the September 11 attacks. That tone continued on *The Rising*, his 2002 album with the E Street Band and new producer Brendan O'Brien, which weighed the consequences of the attacks and their aftermath. Beginning on the Rising tour, Springsteen became an adamant critic of the U.S. government, especially regarding the Iraq War. These developments culminated in his participation in the 2004 Vote for Change tour in support of Democratic presidential candidate John Kerry. Springsteen toured with the band, but he went solo on the plane with Kerry for the final week of the campaign. Springsteen's 2005 solo tour, following the release of the *Devils and Dust* album and coinciding with a 30th anniversary celebration of *Born to Run*, explored the full depth of his song catalog—it was *Tracks* with a one-man band—and continued his opposition to the Bush administration's policies.

We Shall Overcome: The Seeger Sessions (2006) took a turn unanticipated by even the closest Springsteen observers. He made the recording over a period of 10 years with a folk-roots band and a horn section. It featured traditional American folk songs ("Oh, Mary, Don't You Weep," "Froggie Went A-Courtin'," and "John Henry") as well as songs associated with its inspiration, Pete Seeger ("My Oklahoma Home," "How Can I Keep from Singing," and "Bring 'Em Home"). Springsteen's tour of the United States and Europe in 2006 featured a 20-piece band.

Magic (2007), another E Street Band album produced by O'Brien, spoke sometimes metaphorically and sometimes explicitly in opposition to the war and government intrusions on civil liberties. Springsteen continued his commentary through a worldwide tour with the E Street Band in 2007 and 2008. He ranks with that small number of artists whose work has grown rather than remained static or regressed with the approach of the end of middle age. This continued to be true even after the April 2008 death of the E Street Band organist and accordionist Danny Federici from melanoma. The band's playing acquired a darker urgency of tone. The later stages of the Magic tour featured arguably the most assertive, inspired playing Springsteen and the group had ever done. Their guiding principle, that the way to play was as if every night might be the last, was no longer an abstraction.

Springsteen seemed freed by this recognition. *Working on a Dream*, released in early 2009, concerned itself lyrically with thoughts of love and life, how fleeting both are and what it takes to stay the course. The music on the album was a much more sophisticated version of what Springsteen had done on his first two albums, with a greater emphasis on harmony, especially vocal harmonies characteristic of the later work of the Beach Boys. Springsteen's use of a broader musical palette than he had allowed himself since becoming a star resulted in passages reminiscent of soundtrack composer Ennio Morricone as well as of the elaborate pop of the Beach Boys' Brian Wilson and songwriter-arranger Jimmy Webb. In the lyrics, Springsteen's knack for particular detail served him well. Strangely, on such a relatively elaborate production, his ties to the E Street Band seemed stronger than ever.

On February 1, 2009, Springsteen and the band were the featured entertainment at halftime of Super Bowl XLIII; with an average viewership of 98.7 million, the game was one of the most-watched televised sports events in American history. Many fans and much of the press criticized Springsteen for commercializing himself this way. But in the aftermath, it was generally agreed that he had managed to condense

REPRESENTATIVE WORKS

- ▶ *The Wild, the Innocent and the E Street Shuffle* (1973)
- ▶ *Born to Run* (1975)
- ▶ *Darkness on the Edge of Town* (1978)
- ▶ *The River* (1980)
- ▶ *Born in the U.S.A.* (1984)
- ▶ *Bruce Springsteen and the E Street Band Live 1975–1985* (1986)
- ▶ *The Ghost of Tom Joad* (1995)

the structure, message, humour, and athleticism of his live show into the 12 minutes allotted. On the largest popular culture platform available, Springsteen established that some rock artists remained determined to sustain their vitality and creative ambitions all the way to the end. Later in 2009 he was honoured by the Kennedy Center, whose chairman, Stephen A. Schwarzman, observed that "Springsteen has always had his finger on the pulse of America."

In June 2010, Springsteen lost his most important collaborator when Clarence Clemons died of a stroke at age 68. It unmistakably dealt a heavy blow to Springsteen, who referred to "The Big Man" as "my sax man, my inspiration, my partner, my life-long friend." Some speculated that the absence of Clemons meant the end of the E Street Band or even of Springsteen's musical career. Springsteen's eulogy for Clemons, delivered at the funeral, then widely published a week later, rejected this idea explicitly: "Clarence doesn't leave the E Street Band when he dies. He leaves when we die."

Wrecking Ball, Springsteen's 17th studio album, released in March 2012, represented a sharp turn in his social vision and attitude toward the political moment. The album and the tour that followed its release also attempted to reshape the E Street project. On the album, the majestic saxophone that bespoke Clemons appeared on only one track, but there were abundant other horns, including a mariachi set, as well as strings, Celtic pipes and fiddles, synthesizers and samples, a gospel choir, even a brief rap interlude. Old songs—including "Land of Hope and Dreams" from 1999—clashed against tunes that felt newer than anything Springsteen had done since "Streets of Philadelphia." It was the biggest soundscape Springsteen had ever created and it took on the biggest topics in the most direct language he'd ever used. Springsteen's previous social statements, although various ideological messages were read into them, really weren't nearly so much political as moral. He did his best not to take sides, which is one reason his work with Democratic presidential candidates Kerry in 2004 and Barack Obama in 2008 surprised (and alienated) so many of his politically conservative fans. Springsteen generally eschewed naming names even in onstage commentary, and his lyrics concerned an ethos—the horrors of war, poverty, racism, and loss of self-respect—that had little to do with electoral politics. On *Wrecking Ball*, he went further. The album's closing track, "We Are Alive," was typical of the whole. The song was a call for action, evoked by a dream

about the souls of a victimized 19th-century striker, a child martyr of the civil rights movement, and a present-day Central American peasant expired in the Southwestern desert. In addition to its overt advocacy for change, the song's declaration that "it's only our bodies that betray us in the end," offered a way of reading the lyrics as a tribute to Federici and Clemons.

FLEETWOOD MAC

The British blues band Fleetwood Mac evolved into a hugely popular Anglo-American pop-rock group whose 1977 album *Rumours* was one of the biggest-selling albums of all time. The original members were Mick Fleetwood (born June 24, 1947, Redruth, Cornwall, England), John McVie (born November 26, 1945, London), Peter Green (born Peter Greenbaum, October 29, 1946, London), and Jeremy Spencer (born July 4, 1948, West Hartlepool, Durham). Later members included Danny Kirwan (born May 13, 1950, London), Christine McVie (born Christine Perfect, July 12, 1943, Birmingham, West Midlands), Bob Welch (born July 31, 1946, Los Angeles, California, U.S.), Stevie Nicks (born May 26, 1948, Phoenix, Arizona), and Lindsey Buckingham (born October 3, 1947, Palo Alto, California).

Begun in 1967 by ex-members of John Mayall's Bluesbreakers—guitarist Green, drummer Fleetwood, bassist John McVie—and slide guitarist Spencer, Fleetwood Mac found instant success during the British blues boom with its debut album and the hit single "Albatross" (1968). Thereafter the band experienced more moderate success while undergoing multiple personnel changes (including Green's departure and the addition of McVie's wife, keyboardist-vocalist-songwriter Christine). A move to the United States in 1974 and the addition of singer-songwriters Nicks and Buckingham (the latter an accomplished guitarist) infused the group with a pop sensibility that resulted in the multimillion-selling *Fleetwood Mac* (1975) and *Rumours*. Evocatively reflecting the simultaneous breakups of the McVies' marriage and Buckingham and Nicks's relationship, *Rumours* epitomized the band's accomplished songwriting, arresting vocal chemistry, and rock-solid rhythm section.

Following the idiosyncratic *Tusk* (1979), group members began pursuing solo careers. Nicks hit number one with *Bella Donna* (1981), an album that featured singles such as "Edge of Seventeen" and the Tom Petty duet "Stop Draggin' My Heart Around," and Buckingham broke into the Billboard Top Ten with his single "Trouble." The band produced the noteworthy *Mirage* (1982) and *Tango*

in the Night (1987) before the departure of Buckingham. Further lineup changes followed, but Fleetwood, John McVie, Christine McVie, Buckingham, and Nicks reunited to perform at the inauguration of U.S. Pres. Bill Clinton in 1993 (Clinton had used "Don't Stop" from *Rumours* as his campaign theme song). In 1997 the core members gathered again for *The Dance*, a live album that debuted a smattering of new material and fueled a U.S. tour, and the following year Fleetwood Mac was inducted into the Rock and Roll Hall of Fame. The band's 2003 release, *Say You Will*, brought together Fleetwood, John McVie, Buckingham, and Nicks for their first studio album in 16 years, but the absence of Christine McVie highlighted her importance as a mediating influence within the band.

SIR PAUL MCCARTNEY

Paul McCartney (born June 18, 1942, Liverpool, England) helped lift popular music from its origins in the entertainment business and transform it into a creative, highly commercial art form. In addition to his work with the Beatles in the 1960s, he is also one of the most popular solo performers of all time in terms of both sales of his recordings and attendance at his concerts.

McCartney's father, James, worked in the Liverpool Cotton Exchange, and

Paul McCartney (far left) poses with fellow Beatles (from left to right) Ringo Starr, John Lennon, and George Harrison in Manchester, England, November 1963. Hulton Archive/Getty Images

his mother, Mary, was a midwife, out at all hours on her bicycle to deliver babies. Her death from breast cancer in October 1956, when McCartney was age 14, had a profound effect on his life and was the inspiration for his ballad "Let It Be" (1970). His younger brother, Michael, later changed his name to Mike McGear and had a number of hits in the satirical rock group Scaffold. Like fellow Beatles George Harrison and Ringo Starr (Richard Starkey), McCartney grew up in a traditional north of England working-class society, with an extended family frequently visiting the house at 20 Forthlin Road in the Allerton area of Liverpool (the house is now owned by the National Trust). His father had been the leader of Jim Mac's Jazz Band, and in the evenings the family often gathered around the piano, an experience McCartney drew upon for such sing-along songs as "When I'm 64" (1967).

On July 6, 1957, he met John Lennon at Woolton Village Fete and joined his skiffle group, the Quarrymen, which, after several name changes, became the Beatles. When Lennon's mother was killed by a speeding police car in 1958, McCartney, with his own mother's death still fresh in his memory, was able to empathize with the distraught 17-year-old, creating a bond that became the basis of their close friendship. McCartney and Lennon quickly established themselves as songwriters for the group, and, by the time the Beatles signed with EMI-Parlophone in 1962, they were writing most of their own material. By their third album the group stopped recording covers. Lennon and McCartney's songwriting partnership was very important to them, both financially and creatively; even in 1969, when they were estranged over business matters and supposedly not on speaking terms, Lennon brought McCartney his song "The Ballad of John and Yoko," and they worked together on the "middle eight" (the stand-alone section that often comes midway in a song). Their music transcended personal differences.

Though usually associated with ballads and love songs, McCartney also was responsible for many of the Beatles' harder rock songs, such as "Lady Madonna," "Back in the USSR," and "Helter Skelter" (all 1968), but above all he has an extraordinary gift for melodies and sometimes tags an entirely new one on to the end of a song, as he did with "Hey Jude" (1968). This facility extends to his bass playing, which is famously melodic though often overlooked. A multi-instrumentalist, McCartney also played drums on some Beatles tracks and played all the instruments on some of his solo albums, as well as lead guitar at concerts.

The Beatles ceased playing live shows in 1966. After their breakup in 1970, McCartney recorded two solo albums, *McCartney* (1970) and *Ram* (1971), before forming the band Wings with his wife Linda (formerly Linda Eastman), an American photographer and musician whom he had married in 1969. He wanted her with him at all times, and having her onstage solved many of the problems that befall marriages in the world of popular music. Wings toured the world and became the best-selling pop act of the 1970s, with an astonishing 27 U.S. Top 40 hits (beating Elton John's 25) and five consecutive number one albums, including the highly acclaimed *Band on the Run* (1973) and *Wings at the Speed of Sound* (1976).

Inspired by a meeting with Willem de Kooning in the late 1970s, McCartney began painting, and by the late 1980s he was devoting much of his time to it. His work was first shown publicly in May 1999 at a retrospective held in Siegen, Germany. McCartney branched out in other areas too: his semiautobiographical classical composition *Liverpool Oratorio*, written in collaboration with American composer Carl Davis, was first performed in 1991 by the Royal Liverpool Philharmonic Orchestra at Liverpool's Anglican cathedral, where McCartney once failed his audition as a choirboy. He subsequently oversaw the recording of his other classical compositions, including *Standing Stone* (1997), *Working Classical* (1999), and in 2006, *Ecce Cor Meum* (Latin for Behold My Heart). In 2001 a volume of his poetry, *Blackbird Singing*, which also included some song lyrics, was published. McCartney celebrated his 62nd birthday in Russia in 2004, playing his 3,000th concert to an audience of 60,000 in St. Petersburg.

With some 60 gold records and sales of more than 100 million singles in the course of his career, McCartney is arguably the most commercially successful performer and composer in popular music. The 1965 Beatles track "Yesterday" (wholly written by McCartney and performed alone with a string quartet) has been played some six million times on U.S. radio and television, far outstripping its nearest competitor. Moreover, with over 3,000 cover versions, it is also the most-recorded song ever. In 2010 McCartney received the U.S. Library of Congress Gershwin Prize for Popular Song, and later that year he was named a Kennedy Center honoree.

McCartney is a strong advocate of vegetarianism and animal rights and is engaged in active campaigns to relieve the indebtedness of less-developed countries, to eliminate land mines, and to prevent seal culling. More than a rock musician, McCartney is now regarded as a British institution; an icon like warm

POWER POP PIONEERS: BIG STAR

During its brief existence in the early 1970s the American band Big Star helped define power pop, a style in which bright melodies and boyish vocal harmonies are propelled by urgent rhythms. The original members were Alex Chilton (born December 28, 1950, Memphis, Tennessee, U.S.—died March 17, 2010, New Orleans, Louisiana), Chris Bell (born January 12, 1951, Memphis—died December 27, 1978, Memphis), Andy Hummel (born January 26, 1951, Memphis—died July 19, 2010, Weatherford, Texas), and Jody Stephens (born October 4, 1952, Memphis).

Founded in Memphis, Big Star was the proverbial "band ahead of its time." Its records sold poorly but were championed by subsequent generations of rockers, including the Replacements, R.E.M., the Bangles, the Posies, and Teenage Fanclub. Chilton had tasted pop success as the teenage lead singer of the Box Tops, a blue-eyed soul group also from Memphis. Despite scoring seven hit singles with the Box Tops, the singer chafed against the limited opportunities for him as a songwriter, and the group broke up in 1970. He joined with Bell, and they briefly forged a Paul McCartney–John Lennon style songwriting partnership in Big Star, while Hummel and Stephens anchored a formidable rhythm section. Bell and Chilton were fans of both British Invasion rock and Southern soul, and they brought an unusual depth to the three-minute pop song on Big Star's 1972 debut album, *#1 Record*. Although the record was subsequently hailed as a masterpiece, it initially sold so poorly that a discouraged Bell left the group. The follow-up, *Radio City* (1974), included a few Bell songs but was largely driven by Chilton, who pursued a slightly tougher-sounding but equally brilliant direction. Among the album's riches was the cult hit "September Gurls." But again the band was disappointed by negligible sales and began drifting apart.

Recording sessions for a third album were begun with producer Jim Dickinson in the mid-1970s. By this time the band consisted of only Chilton and Stephens, and the record took on a dark, disturbing tone that reflected the group's disintegration. By the time *Third* (also known as *Sister Lovers*) was released in 1978, Chilton had begun a solo career that would cement his reputation as one of rock's most mercurial talents. Chilton's early solo albums (particularly the 1979 release *Like Flies on Sherbert*) and production work for the Cramps and for Tav Falco and Panther Burns won him new recognition with the punk generation. Bell, who was killed in a car accident in 1978, had a similar mystique; his post-Big Star solo recordings finally surfaced in 1992 to critical acclaim.

Chilton recorded with less frequency in subsequent decades, but he was persuaded to reunite with Stephens to play a Big Star show in 1993. The band's lineup was fleshed out by Big Star acolytes Jon Auer and Ken Stringfellow of the Posies. The quartet continued to tour sporadically as Big Star and even recorded a solid but unremarkable studio album, *In Space* (2005). A box set of Big Star's early work was released in 2009, and the band was to be featured at the South by Southwest Music Conference in Austin, Texas, in 2010. But Chilton died on the second day of the conference, and the final Big Star show instead became a tribute concert, with guest vocalists such as Evan Dando, M. Ward, and R.E.M.'s Mike Mills taking turns singing Chilton's songs.

beer and cricket, he has become part of British identity.

BOB SEGER

American singer, songwriter, and guitarist Bob Seger (born May 6, 1945, Dearborn, Michigan, U.S.) became one of the Midwest's most successful rock performers in the 1970s and '80s. Seger was musically influenced by soul and rhythm and blues that were created in his native Detroit (Dearborn is adjacent to Detroit), while his lyrics were largely inspired by the ups and downs in the lives of the working class in the American Heartland. After playing with several bands as a teenager, Seger began releasing records under his own name in 1966, but for a number of years he failed to make an impression beyond the Detroit area. In 1974 he assembled the Silver Bullet Band, which would be his backing group for decades to come. On tour they quickly built a national following, which was soon reflected in Seger's record sales, with *Live Bullet* (1976) staying on the *Billboard* charts for more than three years and commencing a string of seven consecutive Top Ten albums, including *Night Moves* (1976), *Against the Wind* (1980), and *Like a Rock* (1986).

In the 1980s the membership of the Silver Bullet Band began shifting, and Seger reduced his touring and recording profile, releasing only two albums in the 1990s. In 2004 he was inducted into the Rock and Roll Hall of Fame and followed with a new album, *Face the Promise*, in 2006. Even after his public activity had decreased, his music continued to be strongly associated with Midwestern working-class values, leading automobile maker General Motors to feature Seger's "Like a Rock" in a prominent and long-running advertising campaign for Chevrolet.

STEELY DAN

Essentially a studio-based duo, American rock band Steely Dan drew from the gamut of American musical styles to create some of the most intelligent and complex pop music of the 1970s. Named after a prosthetic phallus in William S. Burroughs's novel *Naked Lunch*, Steely Dan was the creation of guitarist Walter Becker (born February 20, 1950, New York, New York, U.S.) and singer-keyboardist Donald Fagen (born January 10, 1948, Passaic, New Jersey), who met at Bard College in Annandale-on-Hudson, New York, in 1967. They moved to New York City in 1969, where they worked on a movie sound track and toured as backing musicians for an "oldies" act, coming to roost in Los Angeles late in 1971 as staff songwriters for ABC Records. Working with ABC producer Gary Katz, they secretly assembled a band with other young musicians, notably guitarists Jeff "Skunk" Baxter and Denny Dias, emerging in 1972 with *Can't Buy a Thrill*. To everyone's surprise, Steely Dan's debut album spawned the hits "Do It Again" and "Reelin' in the Years." By the time Fagen and Becker finished their second album, *Countdown to Ecstasy* (1973), they had sacked vocalist David Palmer, leaving Fagen as sole lead singer. Gradually the duo dropped the pretense of being an actual band and ceased touring, preferring to nurture their eccentric ideas with a regular crew of studio musicians that included guitarists

Larry Carlton, Elliot Randall, and Hugh McCracken, vocalist-keyboardist Michael McDonald, and drummer Jeff Porcaro. The absence of a formal group liberated Fagen and Becker, who did not have to devote energy to dominating other musicians.

Steely Dan reached its peak with *Pretzel Logic* (1974) and *Katy Lied* (1975). Dragging pop music into its high modernist phase, Becker and Fagen took musical ideas from the entire American spectrum, especially jazz, and compressed them into immediately accessible three-minute vignettes. Their songs described lost friendships, abandoned hopes, and joyless perversity, underscoring the paradox of thrilling music about the decay of pleasure. No longer sounding like an electronically enhanced Bob Dylan, Fagen became a distinctive singer who could put across some of the toughest lyrics in pop music with his pungent voice.

The duo's popularity skyrocketed as their music lost its acute edge on *The Royal Scam* (1976) and *Aja* (1977). Difficulties in completing *Gaucho* (1980) persuaded Becker and Fagen to give the group a rest, and they pursued separate careers for many years. Fagen's first solo album, *The Nightfly* (1982), recaptured many of Steely Dan's strengths; Becker produced albums for various artists. In the early 1990s they each put out new solo albums, occasionally performed together onstage, and ultimately toured as Steely Dan, releasing a live album in 1995. By 1998 they were back in the studio working on *Two Against Nature* (2000). The well-crafted album, with its familiar but updated sound, silenced any doubts about the duo's comeback. In 2001 Steely Dan was inducted into the Rock and Roll Hall of Fame.

BOSTON

The American rock group Boston was as well known for the lengthy periods between its albums as for its unique heavy metal–pop sound. The original members were Tom Scholz (born March 10, 1947, Toledo, Ohio, U.S.), Brad Delp (born June 12, 1951, Boston, Massachusetts—found dead March 9, 2007, Atkinson, New Hampshire), Fran Sheehan (born March 26, 1949, Boston), Barry Goudreau (born November 29, 1951, Boston), and John ("Sib") Hashian (born August 17, 1949, Boston).

Boston burst onto the pop music scene in 1976 with the meticulously crafted single "More Than a Feeling," which combined elements of progressive rock and 1960s pop. Generating three American Top 40 hits, the group's eponymous first album became the biggest-selling debut in rock history. Guitarist Scholz, who had earned a master's degree in mechanical engineering at the Massachusetts Institute of Technology (and who later invented the popular Rockman compact amplifier), laboured for seven years in his home recording studio to craft the majestic guitar sound that, along with Delp's distinctive high-register vocals, became the band's trademark. Able to soften their sound on the occasional ballad, Boston appealed to a wide range of music fans. The group's second album, *Don't Look Back* (1978), was criticized for its resemblance to *Boston* but sold well. It took the group eight years to release *Third Stage*, the result of Scholz's perfectionism and a legal battle that ended with the group switching record labels. By this time, only Scholz and Delp remained from the original members, but the band's success formula remained intact, as both the album and the single "Amanda" topped the charts. Boston was not heard from again until the 1994 release of the less successful *Walk On*. *Corporate America* appeared in 2002.

TOM PETTY

American singer and songwriter Tom Petty (born October 20, 1953, Gainesville, Florida, U.S.) crafted a unique guitar rock sound that incorporated elements of American roots music as well as influences from the new-wave movement of the late 1970s.

Petty dropped out of high school in Florida to tour with his band Mudcrutch in the early 1970s. After arriving in Los Angeles, the band quickly disintegrated, but in 1975 Petty and two former members, Mike Campbell and Benmont Tench, joined Ron Blair and Stan Lynch to form Tom Petty and the Heartbreakers. Released in 1976, the band's eponymous debut album initially caused little stir in the United States; but the single "Breakdown" was a smash in Britain, and when it was re-released in the United States the song made the Top 40 in 1978. *Damn the Torpedoes* (1979), featuring the hits "Don't Do Me Like That" and "Refugee," shot to number two, and, though the group's success in the 1980s leveled off, there were several hits, including Petty's duet with Stevie Nicks, "Stop Draggin' My Heart Around" (1981), and the Heartbreakers' "Don't Come Around Here No More" (1985). The band also gained notice for its music videos.

In 1984 Petty shattered his hand after punching a studio wall in frustration, but, to the surprise of doctors, he recovered to play guitar again. The Heartbreakers backed Bob Dylan on tour in 1986, and later Petty joined Dylan in the supergroup the Traveling Wilburys, with whom Petty garnered his first Grammy Award in 1989. That year fellow Wilbury Jeff Lynne (formerly of the Electric Light

Orchestra) produced Petty's first solo album, *Full Moon Fever*, putting Petty back on the charts with the hit single "Free Fallin'." This renewed popularity continued into the 21st century with more group and solo albums.

THE ALLMAN BROTHERS BAND

The bluesy, jam-oriented sound of the Allman Brothers Band helped spark the Southern rock movement of the 1970s and set the stage for several generations of roots-oriented improvisational rock bands. The members were Duane Allman (born November 20, 1946, Nashville, Tennessee, U.S.—died October 29, 1971, Macon, Georgia), Gregg Allman (born December 8, 1947, Nashville), Berry Oakley (born April 4, 1948, Chicago, Illinois—died November, 1972, Macon), Dickey Betts (born December 12, 1943, West Palm Beach, Florida), Jaimoe (born John Lee Johnson, July 8, 1944, Ocean Springs, Mississippi), and Butch Trucks (born Claude Hudson Trucks, Jr., May 11, 1947, Jacksonville, Florida).

From 1960 siblings guitarist Duane and keyboardist Gregg Allman worked together in a number of Florida-based bands. In 1968 Duane began working as a session guitarist at Fame Studios in the Muscle Shoals, Alabama, area, where he contributed to recordings by Wilson Pickett and Aretha Franklin. At the urging of Capricorn Records chief Phil Walden, Duane formed the Allman Brothers Band.

Although their eponymous debut album (1969) had little success outside the South, the group attracted wider attention when Eric Clapton asked Duane to record with Derek and the Dominos in 1970. The jam-oriented *At Fillmore East* (1971) established the Allman Brothers as master improvisers, working within the blues-rock vocabulary but augmenting it with elements of jazz, country, and Latin music. Because of the band's strong Southern roots, its success inspired a host of regional rockers, which in turn led to the notion of a Southern rock boom. Before the band could capitalize on its growing fame, however, Duane was killed in a motorcycle accident in 1971.

Although guitarist Betts assumed leadership of the band, friction with Gregg led to its dissolution in 1976. The band reunited in 1978, but the event took on the air of a soap opera in light of Gregg's marriage to the singer and actress Cher. The Allmans splintered again in 1981. Reuniting yet again in 1989, the Allmans placed an even greater emphasis on blues-based improvisation, a sound that in part served as the template for such 1990s jam bands as the Black Crowes and Blues Traveler. The Allman Brothers

SOUTHERN ROCK

By combining blues jams and boogie licks with lyrics declaring fierce regional pride, Southern rock's aggressive, unpretentious sound helped revitalize American rock in the 1970s. Rock and roll had been an expression of popular culture in the American South since the days of Elvis Presley, but it was not until the rise of Phil Walden's Capricorn Records in the early 1970s that Southernness itself was celebrated as a rock-and-roll virtue. Walden, who got his start managing Otis Redding, signed the Allman Brothers Band in 1969. Once the Allmans caught on, Walden capitalized on the notion of Southern rock by signing the Marshall Tucker Band, the Elvin Bishop Group, and others. Soon, as groups such as Lynyrd Skynyrd, the Charlie Daniels Band, the Outlaws, and Wet Willie joined the fray, fans began to rally around anthems such as Daniels's "The South's Gonna Do It."

Despite their shared geography and cultural pride, Southern rockers had relatively little in common musically. Extended jamming was a hallmark of the Allman Brothers, whose attention to groove gave their instrumental extrapolations a coherence sorely lacking in the equally improvisatory psychedelic rock of the era. Moreover, the Allmans' disciplined twin-guitar leads and double-drummer rhythm section added impact to the playing. By contrast, Lynyrd Skynyrd—which boasted a triple-lead guitar lineup—went for a gritty, blues-based sound that was closer in spirit to that of the Rolling Stones, while other guitar-heavy bands, such as .38 Special, Molly Hatchet, and the Outlaws, amplified and fetishized the boogie-guitar approach of bluesmen Elmore James and John Lee Hooker. The Marshall Tucker Band drew from western swing, Wet Willie borrowed from soul, and the Atlanta Rhythm Section leaned toward country. A few acts, such as Sea Level and the Dixie Dregs, even flirted with jazz-rock.

Although many of the bands continued on, the Southern rock movement ran out of steam by the early 1980s. Later in the decade, as alternative rock bands such as R.E.M. sprang out of college towns in Georgia and the Carolinas, an attempt was made to label them New Southern rockers, but, because the groups lacked any audible regionalism, the label never stuck.

Band was inducted into the Rock and Roll Hall of Fame in 1995.

LYNYRD SKYNYRD

Lynyrd Skynyrd rose to prominence during the Southern rock boom of the 1970s on the strength of its triple-guitar attack and gritty, working-class attitude. The principal members were Ronnie Van Zant (born January 15, 1949, Jacksonville, Florida, U.S.—died October 20, 1977, Gillsburg, Mississippi), Gary Rossington (born December 4, 1951, Jacksonville), Allen Collins (born July 19, 1952—died January 23, 1990, Jacksonville), Steve Gaines (born September 14, 1949, Seneca, Missouri—died October 20, 1977, Gillsburg, Mississippi), Billy Powell (born June 3, 1952, Jacksonville—died January 28, 2009, Orange Park, Florida), Leon Wilkeson (born April 2, 1952—died July 27, 2001, Ponte Vedra Beach, Florida), and Artimus Pyle (born July 15, 1948, Spartanburg, South Carolina).

After playing under various names in Jacksonville, the group settled on Lynyrd Skynyrd (a backhanded compliment to a high-school gym teacher named Leonard Skinner who had disciplined a number of the band members for having long hair); in 1973 they released their first album, *Pronounced Leh-Nerd Skin-Nerd*. "Free Bird," a posthumous tribute to Duane Allman, was an immediate sensation, thanks to the interplay of its three lead guitars, while "Sweet Home Alabama," a response to Neil Young's derisive "Southern Man," opened *Second Helping* (1974) and established the group as Southern rock stalwarts. In 1977, as Skynyrd's success was increasing, a plane carrying the band crashed in Gillsburg, killing singer Van Zant and guitarist Gaines. The group disbanded.

Surviving members reunited in 1987, with Van Zant's younger brother, Johnny, singing lead. The new Skynyrd was embraced by a number of country singers, especially Travis Tritt. In 2006 Lynyrd Skynyrd was inducted into the Rock and Roll Hall of Fame.

ZZ TOP

ZZ Top achieved success with rugged blues-driven guitar work that exalted the group's Texas roots. The trio was formed in the Houston area in 1969 when singer-guitarist Billy Gibbons (born December 16, 1949, Houston, Texas, U.S.), formerly of blues-rock band Moving Sidewalks, united with bass player Dusty Hill (born Joe Michael Hill, May 19, 1949, Dallas, Texas) and drummer Frank Beard (born June 11, 1949, Frankston, Texas), who had previously performed together in the band American Blues.

Taking its sonic cues from such blues artists as John Lee Hooker and Muddy Waters, the band built a following with *ZZ Top's First Album* (1970) and *Rio Grande Mud* (1971). The band's breakthrough came in 1973 when the single "La Grange," from *Tres Hombres*, became a radio hit. Two years later "Tush," off the hit album *Fandango*, cracked the top 40. The band's 1976 Worldwide Texas

Tour—during which they performed on a Texas-shaped stage littered with props that included cacti, snakes, and longhorn cattle—was one of the most successful concert tours of the 1970s.

Throughout the late 1970s and early '80s, ZZ Top's albums enjoyed consistent commercial success, and 1983's *Eliminator* turned them into international superstars. Incorporating electronic synthesizers and disco-influenced rhythms into their signature blues sound, the band projected a cartoonish public image in music videos in which Gibbons and Hill sported scraggly beards and flamboyant suits and which were punctuated by the threesome's comic hand gestures. Buoyed by hits such as "Gimme All Your Lovin'," "Sharp Dressed Man," and "Legs," *Eliminator* went on to sell more than 10 million copies. *Afterburner* (1985) yielded the additional hits "Rough Boy" and "Sleeping Bag."

With 1990's *Recycler*, ZZ Top scaled back the electronics. Though the massive following of the band's 1980s commercial peak had dissipated, subsequent albums such as *Antenna* (1994) and *Mescalero* (2003) still commanded a substantial audience, and the group celebrated its longevity with 1999's *XXX*, marking 30 years of playing together. They remained a popular live act, notably performing at the inauguration of Pres. George W. Bush in 2001. ZZ Top

ZZ Top (from left to right): Frank Beard, Billy Gibbons, and Dusty Hill, 2003.
PRNewsFoto/RCA Records/AP Images

was inducted into the Rock and Roll Hall of Fame in 2004 and released the live album and DVD *Live from Texas* in 2008.

CHAPTER 3

Heavy Metal Thunder

The heavy metal genre of rock music includes a group of related styles that are intense, virtuosic, and powerful. Driven by the aggressive sounds of the distorted electric guitar, heavy metal is arguably the most commercially successful genre of rock music.

Although the origin of the term *heavy metal* is widely attributed to novelist William Burroughs, its use actually dates well back into the 19th century, when it referred to cannon or to power more generally. It has also been used to classify certain elements or compounds, as in the phrase *heavy metal poisoning*. *Heavy metal* appeared in the lyrics of Steppenwolf's "Born to be Wild" (1968), and by the early 1970s rock critics were using it to refer to a specific style of music.

Mid-1960s British bands such as Cream, the Yardbirds, and the Jeff Beck Group, along with Jimi Hendrix, are generally credited with developing the heavier drums, bass, and distorted guitar sounds that differentiate heavy metal from other blues-based rock. The new sound was codified in the 1970s by Led Zeppelin, Deep Purple, and Black Sabbath with the release of *Led Zeppelin II*, *Deep Purple in Rock*, and *Paranoid*, respectively, which featured heavy riffs, distorted "power chords," mystical lyrics, guitar and drum solos, and vocal styles that ranged from the wails of Zeppelin's Robert Plant to the whines of Sabbath's Ozzy Osbourne. By developing increasingly elaborate stage shows and touring incessantly

JEFF BECK

English rock guitarist Jeff Beck (born June 24, 1944, Wallington, Surrey, England) influenced the development of the heavy metal and jazz-rock genres with his fast, intricate playing. A supporting stint with rock-and-roll eccentric Screaming Lord Sutch brought young guitarist Beck to the attention of blues-rock group the Yardbirds, whose lead guitarist he became in 1965, replacing Eric Clapton. The following year, having left the Yardbirds, Beck founded his own combo, the Jeff Beck Group, featuring vocalist Rod Stewart and bassist Ron Wood. On *Truth* (1968) and *Beck-Ola* (1969), the band pioneered a fierce, overdriven approach to the blues that lay the groundwork for early heavy metal.

Stewart and Wood left in 1970 to join the Small Faces (later the Faces), and Beck was injured in a car accident later that year, forcing him to put his career on hiatus. In 1971 he resurfaced with a new Jeff Beck Group that included Bobby Tench on lead vocals and Cozy Powell on the drums. They released two rhythm-and-blues–influenced albums, *Rough and Ready* (1971) and *Jeff Beck Group* (1972). With former Vanilla Fudge members Carmine Appice and Tim Bogert, Beck released *Beck, Bogert & Appice* in 1973. After its negative reception the trio disbanded, and Beck embarked on a solo career. The critically acclaimed *Blow by Blow* (1975), produced by Beatles collaborator George Martin, featured an all-instrumental, jazz fusion approach in which Beck's guitar playing essentially took the place of a lead vocalist. He would record largely without vocals for the rest of his career.

Flash (1985), produced by Nile Rodgers, was Beck's most commercial release. It contained the Grammy Award-winning track "Escape," as well as a cover of the Impressions' "People Get Ready," which featured Stewart on vocals and became Beck's first hit single. In later years Beck maintained a relatively low profile, touring occasionally and recording, including contributions to such albums as Mick Jagger's *Primitive Cool* (1987) and Roger Waters's *Amused to Death* (1992). In 1989 Jeff Beck's *Guitar Shop* won a Grammy Award for best rock instrumental performance, and he was inducted into the Rock and Roll Hall of Fame as a member of the Yardbirds in 1992.

throughout the 1970s to make up for their lack of radio airplay, bands such as KISS, AC/DC, Aerosmith, Judas Priest, and Alice Cooper established an international fan base.

Heavy metal's popularity slumped during the disco years at the end of the 1970s, but it became more successful than ever in the 1980s as Def Leppard, Iron Maiden, and Saxon headed the "new wave of British heavy metal" that, along with the impact of Eddie Van Halen's astonishing guitar virtuosity, revived the genre. A wave of "glam" metal, featuring gender-bending bands such as Mötley Crüe and Ratt, emanated from Los Angeles beginning about 1983; Poison, Guns N' Roses, and hundreds of other bands then moved to Los Angeles in hopes of getting record deals. But heavy metal had become a worldwide phenomenon in both fandom and production with the success of Germany's Scorpions and other

bands from Japan to Scandinavia. The most important musical influence of the decade was the adaptation of chord progressions, figuration, and ideals of virtuosity from Baroque models, especially Bach and Vivaldi, to heavy metal. Like Van Halen, guitarists such as Ritchie Blackmore (of Deep Purple), Randy Rhoads (with Osbourne), and Yngwie Malmsteen demonstrated new levels and styles of rock guitar technique, exploding popular stereotypes of heavy metal as monolithic and musically simple.

Heavy metal fragmented into subgenres (such as lite metal, death metal, and even Christian metal) in the 1980s. A smaller underground scene of harder styles developed in opposition to the more pop-oriented metal of Bon Jovi, Whitesnake, and the glam bands. Metallica, Megadeth, Anthrax, and Slayer pioneered thrash metal, distinguished by its fast tempos, harsh vocal and guitar timbres,

REPRESENTATIVE WORKS

- ▶ Led Zeppelin, *Led Zeppelin II* (1969)
- ▶ Deep Purple, *Deep Purple in Rock* (1970)
- ▶ Black Sabbath, *Paranoid* (1971)
- ▶ KISS, *Alive!* (1975)
- ▶ Van Halen, *Van Halen* (1978)
- ▶ AC/DC, *Back in Black* (1980)
- ▶ Judas Priest, *British Steel* (1980)
- ▶ Ozzy Osbourne, *Blizzard of Ozz* (1981)
- ▶ Def Leppard, *Pyromania* (1983)
- ▶ Iron Maiden, *Powerslave* (1984)
- ▶ Bon Jovi, *Slippery When Wet* (1986)
- ▶ Metallica, *Master of Puppets* (1986)
- ▶ Slayer, *Reign in Blood* (1986)
- ▶ Guns N' Roses, *Appetite for Destruction* (1987)
- ▶ Queensrÿche, *Operation: Mindcrime* (1988)
- ▶ Megadeth, *Rust in Peace* (1990)
- ▶ Pantera, *Vulgar Display of Power* (1992)
- ▶ Soundgarden, *Superunknown* (1994)
- ▶ Emperor, *Anthems to the Welkin at Dusk* (1997)
- ▶ Machine Head, *The Blackening* (2007)
- ▶ Mastodon, *Crack the Skye* (2009)
- ▶ High on Fire, *Snakes for the Divine* (2010)

aggressiveness, and critical or sarcastic lyrics. The more broadly popular styles of heavy metal virtually took over the mainstream of popular music in the late 1980s, but the coherence of the genre collapsed around the turn of the decade; bands such as Guns N' Roses and Nirvana pulled fans in different directions, and many fans also defected to rap music.

Despite (or, perhaps, because of) heavy metal's widespread popularity throughout the 1980s, it became the target of severe criticism. Political and academic groups sprang up to blame the genre and its fans for causing everything from crime and violence to despondency and suicide. But defenders of the music pointed out that there was no evidence that heavy metal's exploration of madness and horror caused, rather than articulated, these social ills. The genre's lyrics and imagery have long addressed a wide range of topics, and its music has always been more varied and virtuosic than critics like to admit.

As metal entered the 21st century, many stars of previous decades, such as Van Halen, Metallica, and Osbourne, experienced continued success alongside newer groups such as Soundgarden, Pantera, and Mastodon, but the name *heavy metal* was less often used to market these groups or to define their fan community. Indeed, as the fragmentation begun in the previous decade became more pronounced, both fans and critics alike were more likely to identify artists by subgenre and country of origin, e.g., "Norwegian troll metal" or "Mexican death metal." Such classifications spoke to the diversity and global reach of the latest generation of metal performers.

BLACK SABBATH

The British band Black Sabbath defined the term *heavy metal* in the 1970s with a bludgeoning brand of guitar-driven rock. The principal members were Ozzy Osbourne (born John Osbourne, December 3, 1948, Birmingham, Warwickshire, England), Terry ("Geezer") Butler (born July 17, 1949, Birmingham), Tony Iommi (born February 19, 1948, Birmingham), and Bill Ward (born May 5, 1948, Birmingham).

Osbourne, Butler, Iommi, and Ward, schoolmates in Birmingham in the late 1960s, formed the blues bands Polka Tulk and Earth. These evolved into Black Sabbath, which was named after a Butler song inspired by a Boris Karloff movie. The band cultivated a dark and foreboding image with ominous guitar riffs, slow-churn tempos, and Osbourne's sullen vocals. Black Sabbath's lyrics, soaked in occult imagery, coupled with the group's coarse musicianship were reviled by critics and shunned by radio programmers, but constant touring turned them into stars, and songs such as "Paranoid," "Iron Man," and "War Pigs" became metal classics. By the end of the 1970s they had sold millions of records and had become the standard by which virtually every heavy metal band had to measure itself. Osbourne left the

OZZY OSBOURNE

Raised in a working-class family, Ozzy Osbourne dropped out of school at age 15 and held several low-paying jobs. He also engaged in petty crime and at 17 was imprisoned for two months for burglary. After his release, he sang in a number of local rock groups, eventually forming the rock band Earth with guitarist Tony Iommi. To avoid confusion with another band of the same name, the group changed its name to Black Sabbath. The group developed a grinding, ominous sound, based on the blues but intensely amplified, and drew attention with its tendency to reference the occult in its lyrics. In February 1970 Black Sabbath released its eponymous first album and quickly developed a following in both Britain and the United States.

The band released albums each year through the mid-1970s, except 1974. After the tour for *Never Say Die* (1978), Osbourne left the band. A period of despair and drug abuse led to Osbourne's divorce from his first wife, Thelma Mayfair. He then met and married Sharon Arden, who encouraged him to start a career as a solo artist. His first effort, achieved with the primary help of guitarist Randy Rhoads, was *Blizzard of Ozz* (1980). A multiplatinum success thanks in part to the standout single "Crazy Train," it was followed by the equally popular *Diary of a Madman* (1981), which sold more than five million copies. A defining moment in Osbourne's career came on the tour for the album, when, thinking that someone in the audience had thrown him a rubber toy, Osbourne bit off the head of a live bat.

Osbourne found his first solo Top 40 hit with "Mama, I'm Coming Home" from the album *No More Tears* (1991), and in 1993 he won a Grammy Award for best metal performance for the song "I Don't Want to Change the World." Despite announcing his retirement in 1992, he continued recording through the decade. Ozzfest, an

(From left) *Ozzy Osbourne with his wife, Sharon; daughter Kelly; and son, Jack.*
PRNewsFoto/Buena Vista Home Entertainment/AP Images

annual summer music festival featuring heavy metal acts organized
by Osbourne and his wife, began in 1996 and toured throughout
the United States and, in some years, parts of Europe. By the end
of the 1990s, Osbourne had reunited the original members of Black
Sabbath for a new album and tour, and in 1999 the band won a
Grammy for best metal performance for the song "Iron Man."

In 2002 the reality television show *The Osbournes*, which
focused on the life of Osbourne and his family, premiered on MTV,
and within two months it had become the third-highest-rated offering on cable television. The hugely popular show ran until 2005.
In 2007 Osbourne released his first solo studio album in six years,
Black Rain (2007), and followed with *Scream* (2010).

band in the late 1970s, and Ward and Butler later followed him out. Iommi kept the Black Sabbath name alive throughout the 1980s with a variety of musicians, and Osbourne forged a solo career marked by outrageous drug-fueled antics, best-selling albums, and the hugely popular MTV reality show *The Osbournes* (2002–05), which followed Osbourne and his family. In the 1990s the band's original lineup reunited on several occasions. Black Sabbath was inducted into the Rock and Roll Hall of Fame in 2006.

AC/DC

Australian heavy metal band AC/DC became one of the most popular stadium performers of the 1980s thanks to the group's theatrical, high-energy shows. The principal members were Angus Young (born March 31, 1955, Glasgow, Scotland), Malcolm Young (born January 6, 1953, Glasgow), Bon Scott (born Ronald Belford Scott, July 9, 1946, Kirriemuir, Angus, Scotland—died February 21, 1980, London, England), Brian Johnson (born October 5, 1947, Newcastle upon Tyne, Tyne and Wear, England), Phil Rudd (born Phillip Rudzevecuis, May 19, 1954, Melbourne, Victoria, Australia), and Cliff Williams (born December 14, 1949, Romford, Essex, England).

The Young brothers formed AC/DC in Sydney, Australia, in 1973 with Angus (famous for his schoolboy short-trousers outfit) on lead guitar and Malcolm on rhythm guitar. The rest of the band's lineup changed when the Youngs moved to Melbourne, and AC/DC's blues-based records and live appearances made them favourites in Australia by the mid-1970s. After relocating to London in 1976 and solidifying their lineup (with Scott as vocalist, Rudd on drums, Williams on bass, and the Youngs), AC/DC found success in Britain with *Let There Be Rock* (1977) and internationally with *Highway to Hell* (1979). AC/DC's rise was hampered by Scott's alcohol-related death in February 1980, but replacement Johnson's falsetto fit in well with the group's tight, clean metal punch and their raucous bad-boy image. The band's next album, *Back in Black* (1980), sold more than 10 million copies in the United States alone, and *For Those About to Rock* (1981) was also a million-seller. The early to mid-1980s was the band's peak period as a live group; a number of personnel changes occurred after that time.

By the 1990s AC/DC found itself comfortably ensconced among the elder statesmen of heavy metal. *The Razor's Edge* (1990) featured the hit singles "Thunderstruck" and "Moneytalks," the latter of which reached number 23 on the *Billboard* chart, making it the group's sole Top 40 single. The band settled into a pattern of roughly two studio releases per decade, following *The Razor's Edge* with *Ballbreaker* (1995), produced by Rick Rubin, and *Stiff Upper Lip* (2000), an album that attempted to capture the stadium-filling sound of the *Back in Black* era. The group was inducted into the Rock and Roll Hall of Fame in 2003, and, after more than 30 years of producing some of the roughest and loudest head-banging anthems in heavy metal history, AC/DC scored its first *Billboard* number one album with *Black Ice* (2008). The band reached another milestone in 2010 when it collected its first Grammy Award (in the category of best hard rock performance) for the single "War Machine."

ALICE COOPER

In addition to producing a string of hits in the 1970s, Alice Cooper—an American hard rock band that shared its name with its leader—was among the first rock groups to infuse their performances with theatrics. The members were Alice Cooper (born Vincent Furnier, February 4, 1948, Detroit, Michigan, U.S.), Michael Bruce (born March 16, 1948), Glen Buxton (born November 10, 1947, Akron, Ohio—died October 19, 1997, Mason City, Iowa), Dennis Dunaway (born December 9, 1946, Cottage Grove, Oregon), and Neal Smith (born September 23, 1947, Akron).

The son of a preacher, Furnier formed a band with four schoolmates in Phoenix, Arizona. After moving to California in 1968, he and the band took the name Alice Cooper. Their hyperamplified club shows, influenced by British glam rock, earned them recognition as "the worst band in Los Angeles" and a contract with Frank Zappa's Straight Records, for

Alice Cooper. PRNewsFoto/VH1/AP Images

which they released two unsuccessful albums before relocating to Detroit. With producer Bob Ezrin (who later worked with KISS, a band much influenced by Alice Cooper's music and presentation, as were the New York Dolls), they crafted a clear, powerful, guitar-heavy sound on such youth anthems as "I'm Eighteen" and "School's Out." Makeup-wearing vocalist Cooper, whose identity soon eclipsed the band's, formed a new group in 1974, adding *Welcome to My Nightmare* (1975) to a list of significant albums that included *Killer* (1971) and *Billion Dollar Babies* (1973), all explorations of decadence, perversion, and psychosis. Best remembered for its shocking stage show, Alice Cooper blended the gore and grotesquerie of horror films with the camp of 1930s Berlin cabaret. The group was inducted into the Rock and Roll Hall of Fame in 2011.

AEROSMITH

One of the biggest arena-rock attractions of the late 1970s, Aerosmith became even more popular with its career revival in the mid-1980s. Principal members were lead singer Steven Tyler (born Steven Tallarico, March 26, 1948, New York, New York, U.S.), lead guitarist Joe Perry (born September 10, 1950, Boston, Massachusetts), guitarist Brad Whitford (born February 23, 1952, Winchester, Massachusetts), bassist Tom Hamilton (born December 31, 1951, Colorado Springs, Colorado), and drummer Joey Kramer (born June 21, 1950, New York).

Formed in 1970, the Boston-based band played bluesy, swaggering rock most reminiscent of the Rolling Stones. (Indeed, vocalist Tyler—the band's driving force, along with guitarist Perry—resembled Mick Jagger.) Their later work also incorporated country music influences. *Toys in the Attic* (1975) and *Rocks* (1976) were multimillion sellers, but substance abuse and a dearth of creativity led to a period of inactivity for the band in the early 1980s. In 1986, two years after the return of Perry (who had left the band in 1979), Aerosmith returned to the limelight when Run-D.M.C. made a rap version of the band's 1975 hit "Walk This Way." Converted to sobriety, Aerosmith produced the multiplatinum-selling albums *Permanent Vacation* (1987) and *Pump* (1989). The latter featured the Grammy-winning "Janie's Got a Gun," and it marked a return to the hard rock success of *Toys in the Attic*. The band followed with *Get a Grip* (1993), an album that generated a pair of Grammys for the singles "Livin' on the Edge" and "Crazy." During this time, Aerosmith was a constant presence on MTV, and the group won numerous music video awards. The band's next release, *Nine*

Lives (1997), reached the top of the Billboard 200 chart, and the single "Pink" garnered a Grammy. In 2001 Aerosmith was inducted into the Rock and Roll Hall of Fame.

Later albums include *Just Push Play* (2001) and the blues tribute *Honkin' on Bobo* (2004). In 2008 the band starred in the console video game *Guitar Hero Aerosmith*, in which players could perform some of the group's greatest hits in a variety of virtual settings. A public feud between Tyler and Perry in 2009 fueled rumours of a possible breakup, with Perry suggesting that Aerosmith would find a replacement lead singer. Tyler underwent drug rehabilitation, returning to front the band for a summer 2010 tour, and in 2011 he became a judge on the reality television show *American Idol*, a position he held for two seasons, announcing his departure in July 2012.

VAN HALEN

American heavy metal band Van Halen was distinguished by the innovative playing of lead guitarist Eddie Van Halen and the onstage antics of a pair of charismatic front men. The original members were guitarist Eddie Van Halen (born January 26, 1957, Nijmegen, Netherlands), drummer Alex Van Halen (born May 8, 1955, Nijmegen), bassist Michael Anthony (born June 20, 1955, Chicago, Illinois,

U.S.), and lead singer David Lee Roth (born October 10, 1955, Bloomington, Indiana). Later members were Sammy Hagar (born October 13, 1947, Monterey, California), Gary Cherone (born July 26, 1961, Malden, Massachusetts), and Wolfgang Van Halen (born March 16, 1991, Santa Monica, California).

Exposed to music early by their father, a jazz musician, and classically trained, Eddie and Alex Van Halen turned to rock music soon after their family emigrated from the Netherlands to southern California in the 1960s. In time Eddie, a drummer, and Alex, a guitarist, switched instruments. A demo financed by Gene Simmons of KISS led to their band's critically acclaimed debut album, *Van Halen* (1978), which sold more than six million copies. Featuring the hits "Jump" and "Panama," *1984* (1984) made megastars of the Los Angeles-based band. Soon after, flamboyant lead singer Roth left Van Halen to pursue a solo career. With his replacement, Hagar, the band produced three chart-topping albums between 1986 and 1991. Hagar departed in 1996, and Roth returned briefly but was replaced by former Extreme lead singer Gary Cherone.

Cherone was greeted with dismal album sales and lukewarm fan response, and he left the group in 1999. The band drifted without a singer for three years, and rumours circulated about possible replacements. Meanwhile, Roth and Hagar shared headlining duties on a 2002 tour that featured each singer's solo material, as well as selections from both Van Halen eras. Quick to capitalize on the interest generated by the unlikely pairing of the two former frontmen, Van Halen released the greatest hits collection *The Best of Both Worlds* (2004) and recruited Hagar for a North American tour. In 2006 Anthony left the band and was replaced on bass by Eddie's teenage son Wolfgang. The following year, Van Halen was inducted into the Rock and Roll Hall of Fame, and, with Roth once again filling in as lead singer, the group embarked on its most successful tour to date. Throughout the band's frequent lineup changes what endured was Eddie's virtuoso technique—notably his masterful use of the "whammy" (vibrato) bar and string bending and his adaptation of baroque music stylings—which influenced countless heavy metal guitarists in the 1980s.

DEF LEPPARD

The British rock band Def Leppard was one of the prime movers of the new wave of British heavy metal. The original members were Pete Willis (born February 16, 1960, Sheffield, South Yorkshire, England), Rick Savage (born December 2, 1960, Sheffield), Joe Elliott (born August 1, 1959, Sheffield), and Tony Kenning. Later members included Steve Clark (born April 23, 1960, Sheffield—died January 8, 1991, London, England), Phil Collen (born December 8, 1957, London), Rick Allen (born November 1, 1963, Dronfield, Derbyshire), and Vivian Campbell (born August 25, 1962, Belfast, Northern Ireland).

Formed in Sheffield by teenagers Willis, Savage, and Elliott in 1977, at the height of punk rock, Def Leppard forged an accessible melodic version of heavy metal that was slower to catch on at home than in the United States, where a new British Invasion of pop-oriented heavy metal bands revived the fading genre. After releasing an extended-play record on their own label, the band reached the British charts with their first album, *On Through the Night* (1980). Wide exposure for music videos that capitalized on the band's good looks pushed *High 'n' Dry* (1981), Def Leppard's second album (and their first with producer-cowriter Robert ["Mutt"] Lange), to sales of two million copies; however it was the metal classic *Pyromania* (1983), with hits such as "Photograph" and sales of more than 10 million copies, that assured the group's place in rock history. *Hysteria* (1987) followed, selling more than 14 million copies and generating hit singles for two years, as the band survived Willis's firing and drummer Allen's loss of an arm in an automobile accident. In 1991 guitarist Clark died of a drug overdose, and, though the band continued to produce hits in the 1990s, it never regained its exalted status.

GUNS N' ROSES

Guns N' Roses invigorated the late 1980s heavy metal scene with its raw energy. The principal members were Axl Rose (born William Bailey, February 6, 1962, Lafayette, Indiana, U.S.), Slash (born Saul Hudson, July 23, 1965, Stoke-on-Trent, Staffordshire, England), Duff McKagan (born Michael McKagan, February 5, 1964, Seattle, Washington), Izzy Stradlin (born Jeff Isbell, April 8, 1962, Lafayette), Steve Adler (born January 22, 1965, Cleveland, Ohio), Matt Sorum (born November 19, 1960, Long Beach, California), Dizzy Reed (born Darren Reed, June 18, 1963, Hinsdale, Illinois), and Gilby Clarke (born August 17, 1962, Cleveland, Ohio).

Guns N' Roses was formed in Los Angeles in 1985 by Rose and Stradlin. After changes in personnel, the band's lineup stabilized with Rose as the vocalist, McKagan on bass, Adler on drums, and Slash and Stradlin on guitar. Signing with Geffen Records, they released the extended-play recording *Live ?!*@ Like a Suicide* in 1986, followed by the landmark album *Appetite for Destruction* in 1987. The music's sizzling fury, with Rose's wildcat howls matched by Slash's guitar pyrotechnics, made the album a smash hit, with sales of more than 17 million.

After that high point the band was dogged by a changing lineup, violence at their concerts, substance abuse, and allegations of racism and homophobia stemming from the lyrics to their song "One in a Million." The band's two 1991 albums, *Use Your Illusion I* and *II*, sold well but were generally regarded as less compelling than their previous work. The 1993 album *The Spaghetti Incident?* generated further controversy by including a song written by mass murderer Charles Manson.

Despite the departures of Adler, Stradlin, McKagan, and Slash and the absence of new product, Rose carried on with the band into the early 21st century. The "new" Guns N' Roses played a handful of live shows in 2000 and 2001, with Rose leading a lineup that included former members of Primus and Nine Inch Nails. Meanwhile, Slash, McKagan, and Matt Sorum (who had replaced Adler on drums prior to the *Use Your Illusion* recording sessions) recruited former Stone Temple Pilots lead singer Scott Weiland to form Velvet Revolver. Velvet Revolver's debut album, *Contraband* (2004), topped the Billboard charts and received solid marks from both fans and critics. Rose returned to the studio to continue working on the

Axl Rose performing with Guns N' Roses, 2006. PRNewsFoto/Sanctuary Entertainment; Major League Baseball—George Chin/AP Images

next Guns N' Roses full-length album, a process that began in 1994 with a completely different set of musicians. As the production entered its second decade, comparisons were made to the Beach Boys' Brian Wilson's lost-and-found masterpiece *Smile*, and many expressed doubts that the album would ever be released.

In August 2008, nine tracks from the album, tentatively titled *Chinese Democracy*, were leaked to the Internet. After some 14 years, an estimated $13 million in production costs, and an exclusive distribution deal with electronics retailer Best Buy, *Chinese Democracy* hit store shelves in November 2008. It was greeted with generally positive reviews, but it was ultimately the band's worst-selling studio album by a wide margin. Rose was quick to blame his record label for *Chinese Democracy*'s poor performance, but the changing music industry climate was likely a significant factor. Albums simply no longer sold in the quantities that they did in the early 1990s, when the band was at the height of its popularity. In 2012 Guns N' Roses was inducted into the Rock and Roll Hall of Fame.

METALLICA

The American heavy metal band Metallica was influential in the development of the speed metal subgenre in the early and mid-1980s. The principal members were lead singer and rhythm guitarist James Hetfield (born August 3, 1963, Downey, California, U.S.), drummer Lars Ulrich (born December 26, 1963, Gentofte, Denmark), lead guitarist Kirk Hammett (born November 18, 1962, San Francisco, California), and bassist Cliff Burton (born February 10, 1962, San Francisco—died September 27, 1986, near Stockholm, Sweden). Jason Newsted (born March 4, 1963, Battle Creek, Michigan) took over on bass after Burton was killed in a tour bus accident in 1986.

Formed by guitarist Hetfield and drummer Ulrich in 1981, Metallica drew upon punk and early 1980s British metal styles for their first album, *Kill 'Em All* (1983). The band followed with *Ride the Lightning* (1984), an album that shattered notions of what defined heavy metal. With social and political themes that seemed more suited to art rock, *Ride the Lightning* demonstrated that the band was willing to stretch the boundaries of heavy metal—perhaps most notably with the album's closing track, the nine-minute instrumental "The Call of Ktulu."

Heralded as a masterpiece by critics, Metallica's third album, *Master of Puppets* (1986), sold more than three million copies with very little support from broadcast radio. The album's title track opened with what would become one of heavy metal's most recognizable guitar riffs, and songs such as "Battery" and "Damage, Inc." defined thrash metal for an entire generation of fans. Metallica was touring in support of *Master of Puppets* when the band's bus rolled over on a patch of icy road outside of Stockholm. Burton was thrown through a window and was killed instantly. The band returned home to San Francisco and hired Flotsam and Jetsam bassist Jason Newsted to replace Burton.

The new lineup debuted on ... *And Justice for All* (1988), an album that included "One," the group's first Top 40 single. Metallica produced its first music video for "One," and the antiwar anthem received heavy rotation on MTV. The band followed with *Metallica* (also known as the *Black Album*; 1991), which sold more than 15 million copies on the strength of singles such as "Enter Sandman," "The Unforgiven," and "Sad but True." Metallica explored a Southern rock sound on *Load* (1996) and its follow-up *Reload* (1997). The two albums were seen as more commercially accessible than previous releases, and "The Memory Remains," a song featuring haunting backing vocals by Marianne Faithfull, demonstrated that Hetfield retained his knack for aggressive and intelligent lyrics. However, the driving thrash metal sound of *Master of Puppets* had clearly become part of the band's past.

It was perhaps an attempt to recapture the revolutionary sound of their early years that inspired Metallica to enlist the San Francisco Symphony Orchestra in the group's next project, *S&M* (1999). The album collected material from a pair of concerts that explored the entire Metallica back catalog, reworked for accompaniment by the full orchestra. Metallica spent much of the next year on tour, but band members, most notably Ulrich, were becoming increasingly visible as crusaders against illegal Internet file sharing services such as Napster. While this stance ultimately doomed Napster (which was reborn as a legal pay-for-play music service similar to Apple's iTunes), it generated backlash against the band.

In January 2001 Newsted left the group, leaving Metallica without a bassist once again. Work on a new album was delayed while the band sought a replacement for Newsted, and Hetfield entered treatment for alcoholism. Bob Rock, who had produced the band since 1991's *Black Album*, filled in on bass as Metallica entered the studio to record *St. Anger* (2003). True to its title, the album was a rage-fueled exploration of Hetfield's psyche that confirmed to listeners that sobriety had not dulled the singer's edge. Metallica added Robert Trujillo, former bassist for Ozzy Osbourne and skate-punk band Suicidal Tendencies, to the band's lineup prior to embarking on the *St. Anger tour*. The period from Newsted's departure to his replacement by Trujillo was captured in the documentary *Metallica: Some Kind of Monster* (2004). The film showed a band at cross purposes with itself, trying to reconcile family and adult responsibilities with the creative and personal conflicts borne of two decades as one of the biggest names in heavy metal.

Metallica enlisted producer Rick Rubin for their ninth studio album, *Death Magnetic* (2008), and the single "My Apocalypse" earned the band a Grammy Award for best metal performance. In 2009 the band was inducted into the Rock and Roll Hall of Fame. The group then teamed with Lou Reed for the audacious but critically reviled *Lulu* (2011), a two-disc collection inspired by the plays of German dramatist Frank Wedekind.

CHAPTER 4

The Sounds of So-Cal: Country Rock

Country rock incorporated musical elements and song-writing idioms from traditional country music into late 1960s and '70s rock. Usually pursued in Los Angeles, the style achieved its commercial zenith with the hits of the Eagles, Linda Ronstadt, and many other less consistent performers. Country rock arose from the conviction that the wellspring of rock and roll was the work of 1950s and '60s regionalists such as Hank Williams, Johnny Cash, and George Jones, as well as, to some extent, that of the Carter Family and Lester Flatt and Earl Scruggs and other artists who had blossomed in local folk and bluegrass scenes before the establishment of the Nashville recording industry.

This evolutionary link seemed so essential to groups such as the Byrds and Buffalo Springfield that (perhaps influenced by Bob Dylan's similarly inclined 1967 album, *John Wesley Harding*) they sought to import country's vocabulary and instrumentation into their countercultural pursuit of psychological and formal adventure. Under the sway of Gram Parsons, the Byrds created country rock's pivotal album, *Sweetheart of the Rodeo* (1968), the country-purist goals of which seemed somewhat avant-garde in a rock world that had come to disdain all things conceivably old-fashioned. To hear the Byrds perform the Louvin Brothers' country standard "The Christian Life" was to enter a distanced, highly artistic realm where 1960s counterculture assumptions about the preeminence of loud volume and the obsolescence of tradition were called into question. Because the movement's very instrumentation—pedal steel guitars, fiddles, mandolins, Dobro guitars, unobtrusive percussion—promoted milder, generally acoustic sonic auras, country rock's overall effect seemed drastically different.

Significantly, however, the style occurred not in a city alive with the values of contemporary art but in Los Angeles, which during the previous decades had attracted many rural Southerners. Moreover, country rock's rise to prominence paralleled the rise of the big-budget Hollywood recording studio ethic, the desire to compete with London in the effort to make pop recordings of the most highly advanced sonic clarity and detail then imaginable. Country rock had begun by insisting that the sources—and not the means—of popular music were of signal importance. Yet in the end the movement succeeded by adopting the same exacting production techniques pioneered by the Beatles and their producer George Martin.

It was only a short, exhaustively well-rehearsed and well-recorded step away to the Eagles and Ronstadt (and Asylum Records). Their careers proved central to those of surrounding singer-songwriters such as Jackson Browne, Karla Bonoff, and Warren Zevon, whose simultaneous countryesque confessions creatively fed both the band and the singer. For Ronstadt, country rock progressively gave way to a wide variety of other styles, always approached from the point of view of her American sources, always mounted with the painstaking studio finesse exemplified by producer Peter Asher. For the Eagles, working first with the English producer Glyn Johns and later with Bill Szymczyk, the style became so full-blown that the band's multimillion-selling album *Hotel California* (1976) both dramatized the Los Angeles milieu that underpinned the country-Hollywood connection and reflected the growing significance of the symbolism of country rock. Surrounding these careers were a number of other key figures. In addition to founding the influential Flying Burrito Brothers, Parsons introduced former folksinger Emmylou Harris to the music of George Jones, spawning her pursuit of a vernacular vocal art of operatic seriousness and intensity. Neil Young, formerly of Buffalo Springfield, began the traditionalist part of a gnarled, varied body of music that grew into a stylistic cosmos of genius unto itself. Like the Dillards, who came to country rock from a bluegrass background,

REPRESENTATIVE WORKS

- ▶ Buffalo Springfield, *Buffalo Springfield Again* (1967)
- ▶ The Byrds, *Sweetheart of the Rodeo* (1968)
- ▶ Bob Dylan, *Nashville Skyline* (1969)
- ▶ The Flying Burrito Brothers, *The Gilded Palace of Sin* (1969)
- ▶ Neil Young, *Harvest* (1972)
- ▶ The Eagles, *Desperado* (1973)
- ▶ Gram Parsons, *Grievous Angel* (1974)
- ▶ Linda Ronstadt, *Heart Like a Wheel* (1974)
- ▶ Emmylou Harris, *Pieces of the Sky* (1975)
- ▶ Jason and the Scorchers, *Fervor* (1983)

all three chose not to work as commercially as the Eagles, Ronstadt, or Poco, whose driving force, Richie Furay, was another former member of Buffalo Springfield. Instead they preferred to have their music felt over time in ways less direct and less oriented to mass culture.

By the end of the 1970s, punk and new wave pushed country rock out of the pop charts and the media limelight. The 1980s saw a resurgence of the genre, more geared to rockabilly force than folk and country balladry. Christened "roots rock," it yielded underground champions such as Nashville's Jason and the Scorchers,

ultimately manifesting itself in the mainstream work of Bruce Springsteen, John Mellencamp, and others. Also by the end of that decade, country music in Nashville had begun to adapt some of the riskier guitar tones and rhythms for its less traditional artists. Elsewhere a new wave of young country rockers, notably Son Volt and Wilco, lumped together under the banner "alternative country" in the 1990s, tried to resurrect the less glitzy side of the movement. But country rock in the most popular sense became a period style, left to evoke the 1970s, a time when artists dressed up deep aesthetic and personal concerns in music that only sounded soft.

THE FLYING BURRITO BROTHERS

The Flying Burrito Brothers were one of the chief influences on the development of country rock in the late 1960s and '70s. The original members were Chris Hillman (born December 4, 1942, Los Angeles, California, U.S.), "Sneaky" Pete Kleinow (born August 20, 1934, South Bend, Indiana—died January 6, 2007, Petaluma, California), Gram Parsons (born Ingram Cecil Connor III, November 5, 1946, Winter Haven, Florida—died September 19, 1973, Yucca Valley, California), and Chris Ethridge (born 1947, Meridian, Mississippi—died April 23, 2012, Meridian). Later members included Michael Clarke (born June 3, 1944, New York City, New York—died December 19, 1993, Treasure Island, Florida), Bernie Leadon (born July 19, 1947, Minneapolis, Minnesota), and Rick Roberts (born August 31, 1949, Clearwater, Florida).

Parsons, having tasted success earlier in the year as the driving force behind Sweetheart of the Rodeo, and Hillman, another former member of the Byrds, founded the Flying Burrito Brothers in Los Angeles in 1968. They appropriated the name from a group of local musicians who gathered for jam sessions. The Burritos' first album, *The Gilded Palace of Sin* (1969), also displayed Parsons's guiding hand: he contributed most of the songs and shaped its combination of classic country and western—punctuated by Kleinow's pedal-steel guitar—and hard-driving southern California rock. Even after Parsons left the Burritos in 1970 (replaced by Roberts), his songs continued to appear on the group's albums, including the live *Last of the Red Hot Burritos* (1972), which also prominently featured bluegrass musicians. Numerous other personnel changes—including the arrival and departure of Leadon, who helped found the Eagles—and the group's limited commercial appeal outside a small, devoted following contributed to its dissolution by 1973. Kleinow and Ethridge re-formed the band in 1975, and there were other short-lived incarnations into the 1990s.

Parsons is often called the originator of country rock. Although he disdained that moniker, his work provided the link from straight-ahead country performers such as Merle Haggard to the Eagles, who epitomized 1970s country rock. Numerous performers have cited Parsons as a major influence, notably Emmylou Harris, Elvis Costello, and alternative rocker Evan Dando.

THE DILLARDS

The Dillards took Ozark Mountain style to California and helped lay the groundwork for country rock as well as for a "progressive" style of bluegrass music. The original members were Douglas Dillard (born March 6, 1937, East St. Louis, Illinois, U.S.—died May 16, 2012, Nashville, Tennessee), Rodney Dillard (born May 18, 1942, East St. Louis), Mitchell Jayne (born May 7, 1930, Hammond, Indiana—died August 2, 2010, Columbia, Missouri), and Roy Dean Webb (born March 28, 1937, Independence, Missouri). Significant later members were Paul York (born June 4, 1941, Berkeley, California), Byron Berline (born July 6, 1944, Caldwell, Kansas), and Herb Pederson (born April 27, 1944, Berkeley).

Banjoist Doug Dillard and guitarist Rodney Dillard found early success as performers in south-central Missouri before moving to California. There, against the backdrop of the folk music revival of the early 1960s, they issued three well-received albums that demonstrated their mastery of the rock idiom as well as their deep roots in traditional mountain music. Doug left the Dillards to pursue this country-rock fusion, eventually teaming with Gene Clark, formerly of the Byrds, to form the pioneering country-rock band the Dillard and Clark Expedition. Meanwhile, Rodney took the Dillards in the direction of "progressive bluegrass," adding drums, pedal steel guitar, and amplified instruments and featuring cover versions of material by contemporary songwriters such as Tim Hardin, Bob Dylan, and the Beatles. The Dillard brothers continued to be a presence in bluegrass and country rock into the 1980s.

THE EAGLES

The Eagles cultivated country rock as the reigning style and sensibility of white youth in the United States during the 1970s. The original members were Don Henley (born July 22, 1947, Gilmer, Texas, U.S.),

The Eagles, c. *1970* (from left to right)*: Bernie Leadon, Don Henley, Glenn Frey, Don Felder, and Randy Meisner.* GAB Archive/Redferns/Getty Images

Glenn Frey (born November 6, 1948, Detroit, Michigan), Bernie Leadon (born July 19, 1947, Minneapolis, Minnesota), and Randy Meisner (born March 8, 1946, Scottsbluff, Nebraska). Later members included Don Felder (born September 21, 1947, Topanga, California), Joe Walsh (born November 20, 1947, Wichita, Kansas), and Timothy B. Schmit (born October 30, 1947, Sacramento, California).

Los Angeles-based professional pop musicians, the Eagles recorded with Linda Ronstadt before the 1972 release of their eponymous debut album. Clearly, from the band's earliest laid-back grooves on hits such as "Take It Easy" to the title song of their 1973 *Desperado* album— the "Ave Maria" of 1970s rock—to the later studio intricacies of *One of These Nights* (1975), Henley's band felt a mission to portray emotional ups and downs in personal ways. However, the Eagles were content to do so within the boundaries of certain musical forms and music industry conventions, pushing and expanding them gently or aggressively at different junctures along the way. This willingness to play by the rules may have been as responsible for the success of their resolutely formal, exceptionally dramatic songs as was the Eagles' hankering for the fiddles and dusty ambiences of the country rock movement they polished for popular consumption.

Before the Eagles recorded, country rock was a local alternative in late 1960s Los Angeles. After they recorded, it became the sound track for the lives of millions of 1970s rock kids who, keen on the present yet suspicious of glam rock and disco, donned suede jackets and faded jeans to flirt with the California dream restyled as traditional Americana.

The band's *Hotel California* (1976) was, in this respect, their masterpiece. With the craft of songwriting as central to their approach as it is to that of any country singer, the Eagles' music had begun as well-detailed melodies delivered by Henley and Frey with some nasality. The arrangements, with percussion far more forward than anything Nashville producers would have brooked, started out in a starkly rock mode with rustic accents. By the time they began work on *Hotel California*, they were joined by ex-James Gang guitarist Walsh, who combined technical expertise with native rambunctiousness.

His contribution, mixed with an increasingly assured blend of country directness and Hollywood studio calculation, made for an unmatched country rock–pop fusion that started with *One of These Nights* and reached its apex with *The Long Run* (1979). *Hotel California*, coming at the midpoint of the band's later period, captured the style at its most relaxed and forceful. Afterward, as punk and new wave repeated country rock's journey from underground to mainstream, the Eagles' music subsided.

Beginning in the 1980s, Henley enjoyed a solo career as an increasingly subtle singer-songwriter. As the Eagles had done in the 1970s, he engaged stylistically with his times, staring down electropop on 1984's moving "Boys of Summer" smash. The Eagles' music, although never exactly replicated, became the envy of mainstream Nashville artists who longed for some sort of mainstream edge. In 1993 *Common Thread: The Songs of the Eagles*, a tribute album performed by country artists such as Vince Gill and Travis Tritt, became a blockbuster in that field. The group's nostalgia-tinged yet still musically vibrant reunion tour and album in 1994 featured four new songs and proved even more successful. In 1998 the Eagles were inducted into the Rock and Roll Hall of Fame.

The band reunited again for *Long Road Out of Eden* (2007), a double

CHECK OUT ANY TIME YOU LIKE: L.A. IN THE 1970S

Los Angeles had been an important music-business city since the 1930s. The city's movie industry, the favourable climate, the influx of European émigrés and Southern blacks during World War II, and the founding of Capitol Records in 1942 all contributed to the city's growth as a music centre. But it was only in the 1970s that Los Angeles took New York City's place as pop music's capital. While New York City was troubled by economic collapse and rising crime, encumbered by obsolete studio work practices, and uncomfortable with the studied informality of post-hippie America, Los Angeles crested on California's new fashionability and economic buoyancy—based in part on the Cold War strength of the aerospace industry. A willingness to abandon the past, an easygoing outlook, the early rumblings of the personal development movement, and a new wave of young entrepreneurs all combined to foster the development of new musical styles.

Taking their cue from the new approach to recording developed by the Beatles while making *Sgt. Pepper's Lonely Hearts Club Band*, Los Angeles-based musicians reveled in the freedom of creating their music in the studio. This was the heyday of singer-songwriters (many of whom gravitated to Asylum Records), of country rock artists, and of disco (particularly that produced by Casablanca Records). What nearly all of them shared was the belief in the power of positive hedonism, which would dissipate in the early 1980s in response to AIDS and economic recession.

album that represented the Eagles' first collection of completely new material in almost three decades. It was a hit with both critics and fans, and the album also signaled the group's departure from the traditional industry model of production and distribution. Released on the band's own Eagles Recording Company label, the North American version of the album was available only through the Eagles' official Web site and at Wal-Mart stores. In 2009 "I Dreamed There Was No War," a track from *Long Road Out of Eden*, won the Grammy Award for best pop instrumental performance.

LINDA RONSTADT

American singer Linda Ronstadt (born July 15, 1946, Tucson, Arizona, U.S.) brought a pure, expressive soprano voice and eclectic artistic tastes to the 1970s music scene. Her performances called attention to a number of new songwriters and helped establish country rock music.

After winning attention with a folk-oriented trio, the Stone Poneys, in California in the mid-1960s, Ronstadt embarked upon a solo career in 1968, introducing material by songwriters such as Neil Young and Jackson Browne and collaborating with top country-oriented rock musicians (including future members of the Eagles). Produced by Briton Peter Asher, Ronstadt's album *Heart Like a Wheel* (1974) sold more than a million copies. It also established the formula she would follow on several successful albums, mixing traditional folk songs, covers of rock-and-roll standards, and new material

Linda Ronstadt, 1979. © AP Images

by contemporary songwriters (e.g., Anna McGarrigle, Warren Zevon, and Elvis Costello).

In the 1980s and '90s, with mixed success, Ronstadt branched out. She starred in the Broadway version of the Gilbert and Sullivan musical *The Pirates of Penzance* (1981–82) as well as the film (1983). Working with big-band arranger Nelson Riddle, she released three albums of popular standards, *What's New* (1983), *Lush Life* (1984), and *For Sentimental Reasons* (1986). Her two collections of Spanish-language songs, *Canciones de mi padre* (1987) and *Mas canciones* (1991), won Grammy Awards, as did her Latin album *Frenesí* (1992). A long-awaited collaboration with country singers Dolly Parton and Emmylou Harris resulted in *Trio* (1987), followed by *Trio II* (1999), which included the Grammy Award-winning single "After the Gold Rush." Her album of children's songs, *Dedicated to the One I Love*, also won a Grammy in 1996.

POCO

Poco continued the synthesis of country and southern California rock pioneered by such groups as the Byrds and Buffalo Springfield. The original members were Richie Furay (born May 9, 1944, Yellow Springs, Ohio, U.S.), George Grantham (born November 20, 1947, Cordell, Oklahoma), Randy Meisner (born March 8, 1946, Scottsbluff, Nebraska), Jim Messina (born December 5, 1947, Maywood, California), and Rusty Young (born February 23, 1946, Long Beach, California). Later members included Timothy B. Schmit (born October 30, 1947, Sacramento, California) and Paul Cotton (born February 26, 1943, Los Angeles, California).

The group formed in Los Angeles in mid-1968 around Buffalo Springfield veterans Furay and Messina and originally called itself Pogo; objections from Walt Kelly, creator of the *Pogo* comic strip, prompted the name change to Poco. Furay, already established as a writer of tender, clear-voiced ballads, added to these a series of exuberant, fast-paced songs that became Poco signature pieces. Messina, an accomplished record producer, contributed his skill for writing catchy, well-crafted songs and his sharp, insightful guitar playing. The addition of Young's virtuoso work on the pedal steel guitar and Meisner's clean, high voice were the final elements of the snappy instrumental work and tight multipart vocal harmonies that were showcased on the group's debut album, *Pickin' Up the Pieces* (1969).

A string of critically acclaimed albums followed, notably *A Good Feelin' to Know* (1972) and *Crazy Eyes* (1973). The group maintained considerable stylistic consistency despite numerous personnel changes, including the departures of Meisner (replaced by Schmit), who played with Rick Nelson before helping to found the Eagles, and Messina (replaced by Cotton), who left in 1970 to team with Kenny Loggins for the highly successful duo Loggins and Messina. In 1973 Furay joined in a short-lived collaboration with Chris Hillman and songwriter J.D. Souther, and in 1977 Schmit replaced Meisner in the Eagles. Poco had only modest commercial success throughout its career; *Legend* (1978) was its top-selling album. A reunion of the original quintet in 1989 yielded the highly regarded *Legacy*.

CHAPTER 5

The Song-Poets: Singer-Songwriters

In the wake of the communal fervour of 1960s rock, professional troubadours performing autobiographical songs ascended to the forefront of commercial pop. For the baby boom generation that had chosen rock as a medium for political and social discourse, the new preeminence of the singer-songwriters, which lasted until the late 1970s, was a natural development. As countercultural heroes such as Bob Dylan, John Lennon, and Paul Simon reached age 30, they experienced their first intimations of mortality and faced uncertain commercial futures in a youth-oriented music market.

Dylan, who had almost single-handedly dragged folk music from the political into the personal realm in the mid-1960s, had made it safe for untrained, idiosyncratic voices to sing their original "song-poetry." In 1970, after leaving the Beatles, Lennon released his confessional "primal scream" album, *John Lennon/Plastic Ono Band*, in which he repudiated the group's deified mystique. Simon, following his breakup with Art Garfunkel, released a wistful solo debut, *Paul Simon* (1972), with several songs that addressed physical deterioration and death.

In the early 1970s a white, mostly middle-class pantheon of soloists coalesced—Joni Mitchell, Van Morrison, Neil Young, Randy Newman, James Taylor, Carly Simon, Cat Stevens, Carole King, Laura Nyro, Leonard Cohen, Jackson Browne, and Loudon Wainwright III, all of whom owed much to Dylan for having broken down conventional song form and undermining traditional vocal decorum.

Mitchell, extremely gifted and influential, smoothed out Dylan's narrative line in songs of unprecedented candour and poetic refinement about her restless search for love in a hedonistic, sexually liberated age, and in the mid-1970s she opened up the genre to jazz influences. Young, in his raw acoustic ballads, epitomized a hippie visionary painfully shaking off his dreamy idealism. Morrison created cryptic dreamscapes tinged with Celtic mysticism, sung with artfully slurred diction. Newman, who came from a family of Hollywood composers, wrote ironic dramatic monologues that juxtaposed the musical worlds of Gustav Mahler, Stephen Foster, and Fats Domino. Taylor, who grew up in North Carolina, fused Appalachian mountain music with sophisticated, often enigmatic personal confessions of emotional disorder.

Carly Simon, who was married to Taylor in the 1970s, personified white, East Coast, upper middle-class longing in her blunt folk-pop songs. Stevens, an English hippie mystic, wrote impenetrably fanciful but pretty folk-pop meditations. King, a professional New York songwriter, embodied an optimistic, commonsense earth mother in her plain, keyboard-based songs with gospel chords. Nyro, vastly influential but only marginally successful, invented an intensely passionate and private, keyboard-based style that borrowed from gospel, folk, jazz, and Broadway. Cohen, a Canadian poet-turned-songwriter, mixed biblical and erotic imagery in elevated folk-pop songs that had a droning Middle Eastern flavour. Browne's morally searching generational anthems borrowed the harmonic vocabulary of Protestant hymns. Wainwright, a brilliant comic buffoon, punctured his own and his peers' self-seriousness in needling, clownish light verse. The genre reached its commercial peak in the mid-1970s with the formal country-pop ballads of John Denver that substituted official good cheer for intimate personal revelation.

Other pioneering singer-songwriters of artistic note included John Prine, a homespun comic fabulist and storyteller from Illinois; Tom Waits, a Californian who acted the role of raspy-voiced hipster and latter-day beatnik saint; and Waits's female counterpart, Rickie Lee Jones, whose pop-jazz suites echoed Nyro's effusions. In England, Richard Thompson wrote scathingly despairing social realist ballads, while the hugely prolific Elvis Costello, whose first album was released in 1977, brought the anger and skepticism of punk rock

REPRESENTATIVE WORKS

- ▶ Leonard Cohen, *The Songs of Leonard Cohen* (1968)
- ▶ Laura Nyro, *Eli and the Thirteenth Confession* (1968)
- ▶ James Taylor, *Sweet Baby James* (1970)
- ▶ Carole King, *Tapestry* (1971)
- ▶ John Prine, *John Prine* (1971)
- ▶ Carly Simon, *Carly Simon* (1971)
- ▶ Randy Newman, *Sail Away* (1972)
- ▶ Loudon Wainwright III, *Album III* (1973)
- ▶ Tom Waits, *Closing Time* (1973)
- ▶ Jackson Browne, *Late for the Sky* (1974)
- ▶ Richard and Linda Thompson, *I Want to See the Bright Lights Tonight* (1974)
- ▶ Rickie Lee Jones, *Rickie Lee Jones* (1979)

into his trickily rhymed circumlocutory songs that often explored situations from multiple perspectives.

Although the reign of the singer-songwriters ended with the twin upsurge of punk and disco in the late 1970s, the genre has remained relatively stable, and the market for personal, idiosyncratic, overwhelmingly female voices with lofty, often unrealized, artistic goals has proved extremely remunerative for a select few.

JOHN LENNON

John Lennon (born October 9, 1940, Liverpool, England—died December 8, 1980, New York City, New York, U.S.) was the quick, gifted, sensitive son of fun-loving working-class parents who married briefly and late and declined to raise him. Separated traumatically from each of them by age five, he was raised strictly (in Woolton, a Liverpool suburb) by his maternal aunt, Mimi Smith, whose husband died during Lennon's adolescence, as did his biological mother, who had taught him to play the banjo. Such circumstances were not uncommon in the wake of World War II, but in Lennon they generated anger that he sublimated with brilliance and difficulty and an intense need for human connection. At age 21 he married the supportive, traditional Cynthia Powell, whom he divorced in 1968. At age 28 he married the independent, unconventional Yoko Ono. And much earlier, at age 16, he founded a skiffle band that evolved into the Beatles, the most important musical group of the second half of the 20th century.

The Beatles were essentially a joint venture between practical pop adept Paul McCartney and alienated rock-and-roll rebel Lennon, but, as a disruptive cultural force, they always bore Lennon's stamp. Musically, just two of countless examples are the forthright candour his vocal added to Smokey Robinson's vulnerable "You've Really Got a Hold on Me" in 1964 and the "I used to be cruel to my woman" bridge he added to McCartney's positive-thinking "Getting Better" in 1967. Culturally too, Lennon assumed the role of the candid provocateur. All four Beatles were witty, all four irreverent. But only Lennon would have observed "We're more popular than Jesus now" or boiled the story of youth culture down to "America had teenagers and everywhere else just had people."

Lennon's genius encompassed writing and the visual arts, the only field in which he received formal training. His natural gifts in both were considerable, but in the end he proved a minor humorist and a casual if indelible cartoonist. In music, he had less inborn facility, though his paternal grandfather worked for years as a blackface minstrel. But music was where he put his substance. Lennon was one of the great rock rhythm guitarists, his signature a nervous rest-one-two-and-rest that complicated his foursquare attack, and his strong, nasal singing overshadowed McCartney's more physically capable rocking and crooning. Declarative where the rockabilly singers he admired were frantic, almost a blues shouter in spirit if not in timbre, Lennon often undercut the masculinity of this approach with a canny, playful high voice deployed to humorous and even campy effect.

Such layered, contradictory meanings typified the Beatles, part of whose power lay in the multiplicity and collectivity they projected. But as Lennon began to withdraw from the Beatles, a process accelerated as of 1968 by his relationship with Ono, his declarative side took over. This dovetailed with the artistic ideas of Ono, a well-born Japanese avant-gardist seven years his senior. Lennon was

John Lennon and Yoko Ono in Cannes, France, 1971. Keystone/Hulton Archive/Getty Images

first fascinated and then influenced by her terse, sometimes paradoxical directives, such as: "Count all the words in the book instead of reading them" (*Number Piece 1*, from the book *Grapefruit* [1964]). Much of the music Lennon recorded after 1968—from "Yer Blues" and "I'm So Tired" on *The Beatles* (1968) through the solo debut *Plastic Ono Band* (1970) through his half of *Double Fantasy* (1980)—reflects Ono's belief in art without artifice. Whether or not they actually eschewed artifice, that was one impression they strove to create.

Until *Double Fantasy*, most of the films and recordings Lennon created with Ono were of limited public usefulness. But the stark *Plastic Ono Band* is generally considered a masterpiece, and the more conventional Lennon album that followed, *Imagine* (1971), is a major work keynoted by its beloved title track, a hymn of hope whose concept he attributed to Ono. Like the earlier "Give Peace a Chance," "Imagine" is living proof of the political orientation that dominated Lennon's public life with Ono, which came to a head in 1972 with the failed agitprop album *Some Time in New York City* and the defeat of Democratic presidential candidate George McGovern by incumbent Pres. Richard Nixon, whose administration was attempting to deport Lennon, a vocal and adamant opponent of the Vietnam War.

Lennon's most enduring political commitment was to feminism. When he and Ono separated in the fall of 1973, he spent a "lost weekend" of more than a year drinking and making highly uneven music in Los Angeles. When the couple reunited, they soon conceived a son, Sean, born on Lennon's birthday in 1975. Lennon retreated from music and became a reclusive househusband, leaving his business affairs to Ono. The details of this very private period are unclear, although it is unlikely that the couple's domestic arrangements were as idyllic as they pretended. Nevertheless, as a piece of art, their marriage projected as powerful an image as their activism had. It ended as fact when Lennon was shot to death by a deranged fan, Mark David Chapman, in front of Lennon's Manhattan apartment building on December 8, 1980. But it continues as part of his legend, which remains undiminished.

GEORGE HARRISON

As the lead guitarist of the Beatles, George Harrison (born February 25, 1943, Liverpool, England—died November 29, 2001, Los Angeles, California) infused rock and roll with new depth and sophistication. In addition to his role as a member of one of the most important and influential bands in the history of rock music, he later achieved singular success as a songwriter and performer.

Harrison was the youngest of the "Fab Four" and was known as the "quiet Beatle," and though he had wanted to be successful, he never became comfortable with fame. He met Paul McCartney when the two were grammar-school students at the Liverpool Institute. McCartney and John Lennon had formed a rock band, the Quarrymen—which changed its name to Johnny and the Moondogs and then the Silver Beatles before it became the Beatles—and eventually invited Harrison and later Ringo Starr to join. Although Lennon and McCartney wrote most of the songs the Beatles performed, Harrison contributed some of their finest ones, including "While My Guitar Gently Weeps," "Here Comes the Sun," and "Something"—the latter eventually recorded by some 150 other artists, second only to "Yesterday" among Beatles tunes covered.

In 1965 Harrison, having become intrigued with the sound of the sitar, studied with Ravi Shankar so that sitar music could be used in Beatles songs. After it was heard in "Norwegian Wood" (1965), musicians in other groups also began featuring it. Harrison was also becoming increasingly interested in Eastern religions and culture, and in 1968 he and the Beatles, as well as a number of other celebrities, explored transcendental meditation with the Maharishi Mahesh Yogi in India. This trip helped bring Eastern religion to the attention of the West and influenced dozens of subsequent Beatles songs, but Harrison was the only Beatle to actually make these religious principles part of his life.

Following the breakup of the Beatles in 1970, Harrison released the first of his many post-Beatles recordings, the highly successful triple album *All Things Must Pass* (1970); in 1971 he staged two concerts to raise money to fight starvation in Bangladesh—the prototype for later star-studded fund-raising events; and in 1979 he ventured into a new field, film production, as a founder of Handmade Films. Among the company's efforts were the Monty Python film *Life of Brian* (1979), *Time Bandits* (1981), and *Mona Lisa* (1986). In 1987 Harrison scored one of his biggest solo successes with the album *Cloud Nine*. Some of his most memorable songs as a solo artist included "My Sweet Lord," "Give Me Love (Give Me Peace on Earth)," and "I Got My Mind Set on You." Although Harrison spent much of his time in near seclusion with his family following the murder of Lennon in 1980, in the late 1980s he recorded and performed with the Traveling Wilburys, which also included Bob Dylan, Roy Orbison, Tom Petty, and Jeff Lynne, and in the mid-1990s he took part in the Beatles anthology project. The last years of Harrison's life were difficult. In 1997 he was treated for throat cancer, and in late 1999 he was attacked in his home by a deranged intruder and suffered multiple stab wounds. The cancer recurred in mid-2001, and treatments were unsuccessful.

PAUL SIMON

Originally half of the renowned folk duo Simon and Garfunkel, U.S. singer, songwriter, and guitarist Paul Simon (born Paul Frederic Simon, October 13, 1941, Newark, New Jersey) went on to become a successful solo pop entertainer. With a career spanning more than three decades, Simon distinguished himself from other folk-based artists with a musical style as unique and expressive as his lyrics. Experimenting with a variety of musical styles—including rock, jazz, reggae, salsa, blues, gospel, New Orleans, South African, and Brazilian—Simon created his own blend of pop, showcasing world music a decade before the term became a common musical category.

Simon grew up in Queens, New York. His father was a jazz bassist who later became a college professor. As a young boy, Paul accompanied him to music stores where he was exposed to a variety of musical styles. Paul met Art Garfunkel in grade school in the early 1950s, and by high school they had formed a duet called Tom and Jerry. Their first hit single, "Hey Schoolgirl," was recorded while they were still in high school.

During the early 1960s Simon recorded a number of solo singles under the name Jerry Landis while continuing to work with Garfunkel. He attended Queens College in Brooklyn and entered Brooklyn Law School, dropping out after a year to devote himself to music full time. He earned money making demo tapes with other performers, including Carole King. Meanwhile, he and Garfunkel had begun performing in local New York clubs and honing their sound; eventually the duo starting to call themselves Simon and Garfunkel. Their first album, *Wednesday Morning, 3 AM* (1964), which included their classic "The Sounds of Silence," was not a commercial success. The album was rereleased two years later as *The Sounds of Silence* (1966), and the title track became a hit. They followed up with a string of hits (and numerous Grammy awards) including "The Boxer"; "Mrs. Robinson," from the film *The Graduate* (1968); "The 59th Street Bridge Song (Feelin' Groovy)"; "Scarborough Fair/Canticle"; and "Bridge over Troubled Water."

In 1971 Simon and Garfunkel split, though they continued to perform and record together on occasion throughout their individual solo careers. The duo was inducted into the Rock and Roll Hall of Fame in 1990. Throughout the 1970s Simon had one hit after another with "Me and Julio Down by the Schoolyard," "Loves Me Like a Rock," "Slip Slidin' Away," and "Fifty Ways to Leave Your Lover." The album *Still Crazy After All These Years* (1975) earned him a Grammy award. Simon played a small, nonsinging role in Woody Allen's film *Annie Hall* (1977), and he later wrote the screenplay and sound track and starred in a much less successful film, *One-Trick Pony* (1980).

During the 1980s Simon saw his career rise and fall. After the critical and commercial failure of *Hearts and Bones* (1983), Simon traveled to South Africa, where he jammed with local black South African bands. His next album, *Graceland* (1985), which featured the whimsical single "You Can Call Me Al," was unlike any of his previous work. *Graceland* eventually sold more than 10 million copies, earning Simon another Grammy award. His *The Rhythm of the Saints* (1990) combined Brazilian, zydeco, and West African music.

Following the failure of his Broadway play *The Capeman* in 1998, Simon began work on the album *You're the One*, which was nominated for a Grammy in 2001. Simon was inducted into the Rock and Roll Hall of Fame as a solo performer in 2001. In 2007 he became the first recipient of the Library of Congress Gershwin Prize for Popular Song.

NEIL YOUNG

Canadian guitarist, singer, and songwriter Neil Young (born November 12, 1945, Toronto, Ontario, Canada) is best known for his eclectic sweep, from solo folkie to grungy guitar-rocker. Young grew up in Winnipeg, Manitoba, with his mother after her divorce from his father, a well-known Canadian sportswriter. Having performed in bands since his teens and later as a soloist in Toronto coffeehouses, Young was both folkie and rocker, so when he arrived in Los Angeles in 1966 he was ready for Buffalo Springfield, the versatile and pioneering group he joined. His material defied categorization and tested unusual forms and sounds. Fuzztone guitar duels with Stephen Stills offset Young's high-pitched, nasal vocals; his lyrics veered from skewed romanticism to metaphoric social commentary, but his voice's naked, quavering vulnerability remained the constant in Young's turbulent, shape-shifting explorations.

His 1969 solo debut, *Neil Young*, sold poorly but staked out ambitious musical territory. Its follow-up, *Everybody Knows This Is Nowhere* (1969), teamed Young with the garage band Crazy Horse. When nascent FM radio played "Cinnamon Girl," whose one-note guitar solo encapsulated Young's sly sarcasm about established forms, and "Down by the River," a long, raw-edged guitar blitzkrieg around lyrics about murder, the album made Young an icon.

Soon he joined Crosby, Stills and Nash, who had already released their first hit album. Young added heft, but Crosby, Stills, Nash and Young was an ongoing clash of egos. Following the release of the quartet's first album, *Déjà Vu* (1970), Young penned and sang "Ohio," an anthem that rallied campus activists after National Guardsmen killed four anti-war demonstrators at Kent (Ohio) State University in May 1970.

Young's next characteristic zigzag led him back to acoustic music—a move forecast by *Déjà Vu*'s "Helpless," which depicted him as totally vulnerable, trying to bare his emotional world musically. His confessional singer-songwriter mode became a key part of his multifaceted persona. On his next solo album, *After the Gold Rush* (1970), Young underlined his stance as a rock-and-roll shaman, a visionary who projected his psyche onto the world and thereby exorcised his own demons and those of his audience. *Harvest* (1972) continued the confessional vein, and its rare stylistic continuity made it one of Young's best-selling but, in the minds of some, least-satisfying discs. Its simplistic attitudes apparently

set off an internal reexamination; at least it started a decade's artistic wanderings. The experimentation cost Young both artistically and commercially. Nevertheless, in 1979 *Rust Never Sleeps* reasserted his mastery—ironically, in response to the punk revolt. Young made the Sex Pistols' singer, Johnny Rotten, the main character in "Hey Hey, My My." Thus, Young's reenergized reaction to punk sharply contrasted with that of his aging peers, who generally felt dismissed or threatened. It also demonstrated how resistant he was to nostalgia—a by-product of his creative restlessness.

Young's resurgence culminated in *Live Rust* (1979), a live recording with Crazy Horse. He continued to be an artistic chameleon, releasing in quick succession the acoustic *Hawks and Doves* (1980), the punkish *Re-ac-tor* (1981), the proto-techno *Trans* (1982), which led his new record company to sue him for producing an "unrepresentative" album, and the rockabilly-flavoured *Everybody's Rockin'* (1983). On 1989's *Freedom*, he resurrected the social engagement and musical conviction of earlier triumphs such as "Ohio." This disc marked yet another creative resurgence for Young and brought him a younger audience; soon he would tap emerging bands such as Social Distortion and Sonic Youth as opening acts. The peak of this particular

Neil Young, 2008. PRNewsFoto/Live Nation/AP Images

artistic rebirth came in 1990 with *Ragged Glory*, with its thick clouds of sound, riddled with feedback and distortion, and gritty, psychologically searing lyrics. Examining time's passage and human relationships, Young never succumbed to easy, rose-coloured allure. Typically, he followed this critical and commercial success with defiantly howling collages, *Arc* and *Weld* (both 1991).

In 1992 Young again reversed direction, releasing *Harvest Moon*, a plaintive, mostly acoustic sequel to *Harvest* that reached number 16 on the album charts. His next significant album, *Sleeps with Angels* (1994), was a meditation on death that mixed ballads with more-typical Crazy Horse-backed rockers. In 1995 Young was inducted into the Rock and Roll Hall of Fame and added to his grunge bona fides with *Mirror Ball*, a collaboration with Pearl Jam. His long-standing interest in film manifested itself in two projects with director Jim Jarmusch, who chronicled Crazy Horse's 1996 tour in the documentary *Year of the Horse* (1997) and for whose film *Dead Man* (1996) Young provided the guitar score.

In 2001 Young responded to the September 11 attacks with "Let's Roll," a song honouring passengers' efforts to foil the hijacking of one of the planes (Flight 93) used in the attack. Young's politics continued to be as mercurial as his music. In the mid-1980s he had expressed admiration for conservative U.S. Pres. Ronald Reagan. In 2006 Young's angry opposition to the Iraq War and conservative Pres. George W. Bush's handling of it was expressed in the album *Living with War*, which was performed on a tour with Crosby, Stills and Nash that was captured in the film *Déjà Vu* (2008; directed by Young under his filmmaking pseudonym, Bernard Shakey). Earlier, in 2003, Young had written and directed another film, *Greendale*, a family saga and an exercise in environmentalist agitprop based on his album of the same name.

The documentary *Heart of Gold* (2005), directed by Jonathan Demme, captured a pair of emotional performances by Young in Nashville that came in the wake of his brush with death caused by a brain aneurysm and that drew on Young's reflective, deeply autobiographical album *Prairie Wind* (2005). Young, who frequently voiced his contempt for industry accolades, collected his first Grammy Award in 2010, in the unlikely category of best art direction for a boxed set, for his 2009 rarities collection *Neil Young Archives Vol. 1 (1963–1972)*. The following year he won his first Grammy for music, when he was awarded best rock song for "Angry World," a track from his 2010 album *Le Noise*.

ASYLUM RECORDS

The driving force behind Asylum Records, the musical embodiment of the "Me Decade" (writer Tom Wolfe's characterization of the 1970s), was New York City-born David Geffen, who nurtured most of the major figures in the wave of singer-songwriters who followed Bob Dylan's lead. Having learned the ropes with the William Morris Agency, Geffen and Elliot Roberts left that company to form a management partnership whose roster included Joni Mitchell, Neil Young, Jackson Browne, Linda Ronstadt, and Crosby, Stills and Nash. Although few of these stars were native Californians, let alone Angelenos, they became Los Angeles archetypes: white, long-haired, and self-interested, they made acoustic-based music that was as drenched in the California sun as the paintings of British expatriate David Hockney.

Geffen founded Asylum in 1970, sold out roughly two years later to Warner Brothers, and became president of the new Elektra-Asylum merger in 1973. By the time temporary ill health forced him into early retirement, the spirit of Asylum was typified by the Eagles. At one time Ronstadt's backing group, they started out as a country rock outfit but mutated into the definitive guitar-based soft rock group whose songs mostly celebrated "takin' it easy" but occasionally dug deeper—*Hotel California* (1976) was an unexpectedly sardonic take on the hedonistic lifestyle of Los Angeles in the 1970s. Those lampooned by the album's title song were sometimes its most ardent admirers, unaware of the irony that it was recorded on the opposite coast in Miami's Criteria Studios.

Having fathered two sons with cerebral palsy, Young helped establish and support the Bridge School in San Francisco to help meet the needs of those challenged by the disease. A self-taught electrical engineer who invented an innovative switching system for model trains, Young also dedicated himself in the early 21st century to developing an automobile that would not be dependent on fossil fuels.

JONI MITCHELL

Canadian experimental singer-songwriter Joni Mitchell (born Roberta Joan Anderson, November 7, 1943, Fort McLeod, Alberta, Canada) achieved her greatest popularity in the 1970s. Once described as the "Yang to Bob Dylan's Yin, equaling him in richness and profusion of imagery," Mitchell, like her 1960s contemporary, turned pop music into an art form.

Mitchell studied commercial art in her native Alberta before moving to Toronto in 1964 and performing at local folk clubs and coffeehouses. After a brief marriage to folksinger Chuck Mitchell, she relocated to New York City, where in 1967 she made her eponymous debut album (also known as *Songs to a Seagull*). Produced by David Crosby, this concept album was acclaimed for the maturity of its lyrics.

With each successive release, Mitchell gained a larger following, from *Clouds* (which in 1969 won a Grammy Award for best folk performance) to the mischievous euphoria of *Ladies of the Canyon* (1970) to *Blue* (1971), which was her first million-selling album. By the early 1970s Mitchell had branched out from her acoustic base to experiment with rock and jazz, with *The Hissing of Summer Lawns* (1975) marking her transition to a more complex, layered sound. Whereas earlier albums were more confessional in their subject matter, *The Hissing of Summer Lawns*, on which she satirized the role of the 1970s housewife, showed Mitchell's movement toward social observation. Although she had a number of pop hits, especially in 1970 with "Big Yellow Taxi" and "Woodstock" (this song about the famous festival spawned three hit cover versions by other artists), Mitchell's impact was as a long-term "album artist." With its carefully precise yet improvisational feel, her music is at times difficult to listen to. She does not opt for straight melody or satisfying conclusions. "My music is not designed to grab instantly. It's designed to wear for a lifetime, to hold up like a fine cloth," she once said.

With *Hejira* (1976) and *Don Juan's Reckless Daughter* (1977), she continued to disregard commercial considerations, while *Mingus* (1979) was considered by many as beyond the pale. An album that began as a collaboration with the jazz bassist Charles Mingus ended up as a treatment of his themes after his death. Mitchell moved ever further beyond her own experience, delving not only deeper into jazz but also into black history; the album was as much a

NICK DRAKE

English singer, songwriter, and guitarist Nick Drake (born June 19, 1948, Rangoon [now Yangon], Myanmar [Burma]—died November 25, 1974, Tanworth-in-Arden, England) was known for emotive vocals, sombre lyrics, and rich melodies. He never achieved widespread recognition in his lifetime but inspired a cult following in the decades following his death.

Drake was raised principally in the English village of Tanworth-in-Arden and played the saxophone and clarinet in school. He took up the guitar at age 16 and began writing songs two years later. In 1968 he was discovered at a London performance by Ashley Hutchings of the folk rock group Fairport Convention and shortly thereafter signed a contract with Island Records. Drake's debut album, *Five Leaves Left* (1969), which was shepherded by Fairport Convention's renowned producer, Joe Boyd, juxtaposed gentle melodies and subtle melancholy lyrics. Featuring members of Fairport Convention and again produced by Boyd, Drake's next album, *Bryter Later* (1970), revealed a more lush and buoyant sound.

Always averse to performing live, Drake, by 1970, had given it up entirely. He sank into prolonged periods of depression and grew increasingly reclusive, recording his final album, *Pink Moon* (1972), entirely alone and checking himself into a psychiatric institution for several weeks shortly after its completion. After recording a few more songs, in late 1974 he died at his parents' home from an overdose of antidepressant medication. The coroner considered him a likely suicide, though some friends and family disagreed with the assessment.

Although none of his albums sold well while he was alive, Drake's music continued to be discovered by new fans and performed by other singers. In the early 21st century his songs began appearing in films and television commercials, bringing a new level of awareness to his music.

voice for the dispossessed as it was a biography of Mingus. Though fans were confused, *Mingus* remains a brave homage that does not fit neatly into either the rock or jazz genre.

Having proved that she could make commercially successful albums and win critical acclaim, Mitchell became a prestige artist. Moreover, because her songs had become hits for others, she was a source of considerable publishing revenue for her record companies. As a result, they went along with her musical experiments. After *Mingus*, however, Mitchell stood back a little from the pop world. From the beginning of her career she had illustrated her own album covers, so it was not surprising that in the 1980s she began to develop her visual art, undecided about whether to concentrate more on painting or music.

Although not as prolific as in the 1960s and '70s, Mitchell continued to create penetrating, imaginative music, from the Thomas Dolby-produced *Dog Eat Dog* (1985) to the more reflective *Night Ride Home* (1991) and the Grammy Award-winning *Turbulent Indigo* (1994). Having dealt with international political and social issues such as Ethiopian famine on *Dog Eat Dog*, she returned, by the early 1990s, to more personal subject matter—singing about true love, for instance, on *Turbulent Indigo*. One of the first women in modern rock to achieve enviable longevity and critical recognition, Mitchell has been a major inspiration to everyone from Dylan and Prince to a later generation of female artists such as Suzanne Vega and Alanis Morissette. Although she regularly collaborated with producers, musicians, and arrangers—such as Jaco Pastorius, Mike Gibbs, and Larry Klein—Mitchell maintained coproducer credit and always had control over her material. Her songs have been covered by a range of stars, including Dylan, Fairport Convention, Judy Collins, Johnny Cash, and Crosby, Stills and Nash. Though unworried about pop chart trends, in 1997 she enjoyed major success with a new, young audience when Janet Jackson sampled from Mitchell's "Big Yellow Taxi" for the massive hit "Got 'Til It's Gone." In 1997 she published a new collection of her work, entitled *Joni Mitchell: The Complete Poems and Lyrics*. That year she was also inducted into the Rock and Roll Hall of Fame.

CARLY SIMON

Known chiefly for her romantic ballads sung in a melancholy alto voice, American singer and songwriter Carly Simon (born June 25, 1945, New York, New York) had her greatest success in the early 1970s with a series of soft-rock singles and albums with emotional, highly personal themes. Although her recording career slowed in the 1980s, she maintained her visibility within the music industry largely by writing music for motion pictures. She also ventured into children's book publishing.

The daughter of Richard Simon, cofounder of the publishing company Simon & Schuster, Inc., she dropped out of Sarah Lawrence College in Bronxville, New York, to pursue a folksinging career with her sister Lucy. In 1966 she began work on a solo album that was eventually abandoned. Several years later, however, Simon became a regular on the top-ten rock charts, beginning with the hit single "You're So Vain" (1971), with backing vocals by Mick Jagger of the Rolling Stones. Her early albums included *Anticipation* (1971), which featured the hit single by the same title; *No Secrets* (1972), with the hit "The Right Thing to Do"; and *Hotcakes* (1974), including "Haven't Got Time for the Pain." Among her later albums were *Hello Big Man* (1983), *Have You Seen Me Lately?* (1990), *Letters Never Sent* (1994), and *The Bedroom Tapes* (2000).

Simon began writing music for motion pictures with the sound track to *Love Child* (1982). In 1989 she won an Academy award and a Grammy award for her song "Let the River Run" from the movie *Working Girl* (1988). Among the other films to which she contributed music were *Heartburn* (1986), *Postcards from the Edge* (1990), *Marvin's Room* (1996), *Primary Colors* (1998), and *Madeline* (1998).

In 1989 Simon published *Amy the Dancing Bear*, the first of several books she wrote for children. Her other titles include *The Boy of the Bells* (1990) and *Mother Goose's Basket Full of Rhymes* (2000).

JAMES TAYLOR

American singer, songwriter, and guitarist James Taylor (born March 12, 1948, Boston, Massachusetts, U.S.) virtually defined the singer-songwriter movement of the 1970s. Bob Dylan brought confessional poetry to folk rock, but Taylor became the epitome of the troubadour whose life was the subject of his songs.

Among the experiences that shaped Taylor, who grew up in an upper-middle-class North Carolina family, were voluntary stays in mental institutions—once as a teenager and later to overcome heroin addiction. Having played in bands with his brother Alex and friend Danny Kortchmar, Taylor traveled to England, where he released his largely unnoticed debut album in 1968 on the Beatles' Apple label. His next album, *Sweet Baby James* (1970), and its melancholy hit "Fire and Rain" began Taylor's reign as a chronicler of the life passages of middle-class baby boomers (for instance, later, his failed marriage to singer-songwriter Carly Simon). Conveyed by his gentle tenor, his contemplative songs—rooted in complex chord changes and influenced by Appalachian folk music, Hank Williams, and early soul vocalists—were set against his deft accompaniment on acoustic guitar and the rock-oriented backing of a regular group of studio musicians that included Kortchmar. Ironically, among his biggest hits were cover versions of rhythm-and-blues songs such as Otis Blackwell's "Handy Man." With a plethora of albums of varying commercial success to his credit, Taylor remained a prolific writer and performer at the beginning of the 21st century. He was inducted into the Rock and Roll Hall of Fame in 2000.

EMMYLOU HARRIS

American singer and songwriter Emmylou Harris (born April 12, 1947, Birmingham, Alabama, U.S.) ranged effortlessly among folk, pop, rock, and country-and-western styles. She added old-time sensibilities to popular music and sophistication to country music, and established herself as "the queen of country rock."

After being discovered while singing folk songs in a club, Harris added her satin-smooth, country-inflected soprano to Gram Parsons's two solo albums (1973–74), landmarks in country rock. After Parsons's death, Harris carried his vision forward, first in *Pieces of the Sky* (1975), which included her tribute to Parsons ("From Boulder to Birmingham"). Following this major-label debut album, she issued a remarkable string of critically acclaimed and commercially successful recordings produced by her husband, Brian Ahern.

Harris's collaborations with other prominent artists or covers of their songs were legion and included Simon and Garfunkel, Linda Ronstadt, Hank Williams, the Band, Jule Styne, and Bruce Springsteen. Her 1995 release, *Wrecking Ball*, on which she performed songs written by Neil Young, Bob Dylan, and Jimi Hendrix, among others, was especially notable. Harris joined a host of folk and country artists on the Grammy Award-winning sound track for the Coen brothers' film *O Brother, Where Art Thou?* (2000), and she later released the solo efforts *Stumble into Grace* (2003) and *All I Intended to Be* (2008). In 2008 the Country Music Association inducted Harris into the Country Music Hall of Fame.

LAURA NYRO

American singer-songwriter Laura Nyro (born Laura Nigro, October 18, 1947, New York City, New York, U.S.—died April 8, 1997, Danbury,

Connecticut) welded urban folk blues to the gospel resonance of the girl group sound. She is remembered both as a unique vocal stylist and as the composer of songs that were major hits for other recording artists.

The daughter of a jazz trumpeter, Nyro began playing the piano at an early age and attended New York City's High School of Music and Art. She also began writing songs while young, and, though her own recording career started slowly, others had success with songs she had written, notably the Fifth Dimension ("Wedding Bell Blues" and "Stoned Soul Picnic"), Barbra Streisand ("Stoney End"), Three Dog Night ("Eli's Coming"), and Blood, Sweat and Tears ("And When I Die"). A wayward yet reclusive artist, Nyro resisted pressure to streamline her songs for mass consumption. She was shaken after being booed off the stage by Janis Joplin fans at the 1967 Monterey (California) Pop Festival, but, under the guidance of agent and later music mogul David Geffen, she grew more popular with the release of the cult-classic albums *Eli and the Thirteenth Confession* (1968) and *New York Tendaberry* (1969). Nyro incorporated a diversity of influences in her writing and performing, drawing on rhythm and blues, soul, gospel, folk, jazz, and Brill Building- and Tin Pan Alley-style pop. Despite "retiring" from the music scene twice in

the 1970s, Nyro continued to record and perform periodically until her death from cancer at age 49. In 2012 she was inducted into the Rock and Roll Hall of Fame.

ISAAC HAYES

American singer-songwriter and musician Isaac Hayes (born Isaac Lee Hayes, Jr., August 20, 1942, Covington, Tennessee, U.S—died August 10, 2008, East Memphis, Tennessee) helped to popularize soul music, and his recordings influenced the development of such musical genres as disco, rap, and urban-contemporary. He was perhaps best known for his sound track for the 1971 film *Shaft*; the title song, "Theme from Shaft," became a chart-topping hit and earned Hayes an Academy award for best original song.

While he was an infant, Hayes's mother died, and he was raised by his grandparents. Hayes taught himself to play piano and saxophone and in 1964 found work as a studio musician at Memphis-based Stax Records, which produced such notable recording artists as Sam and Dave, Wilson Pickett, and Otis Redding. While at Stax, Hayes teamed with lyricist David Porter to write a series of soul hits, including Sam and Dave's "Soul Man" and "Hold On, I'm Comin'."

Hayes recorded his first solo album, *Presenting Isaac Hayes*, in

1967, but he did not gain wide attention until the release of *Hot Buttered Soul* in 1969. The idiosyncratic album featured just four songs, one of which was an 18-minute-long version of "By the Time I Get to Phoenix." The songs included long spoken sections that Hayes described as "rapping." Hayes became known for his baritone voice and laid-back delivery, as well as for his trademark shaved head and dark sunglasses. Among his other notable albums were *Black Moses* (1971), *Joy* (1973), *Live at the Sahara Tahoe* (1973), and *Chocolate Chip* (1975).

By the late 1970s, Hayes had moved into disco music and scored a few hits, such as "Juicy Fruit." He also acted in several films, including *Escape from New York* (1981) and *I'm Gonna Git You Sucka* (1988), a parody of the "blaxploitation" film genre of the 1970s, of which Shaft was a popular example. Hayes earned new fans with his work on the animated television series *South Park*, for which he provided (1997–2006) the voice of the character Chef. Hayes, a Scientologist, left the show after expressing unhappiness with an episode's depiction of Scientology.

HARRY CHAPIN

American singer-guitarist Harry Chapin (born December 7, 1942, New York, New York, U.S.—died July 16, 1981, Jericho, New York) became as well known for his humanitarian efforts—particularly his antihunger crusade—as for his music. Born into a musical family from the Brooklyn Heights section of New York City, Chapin played in bands with his brothers and made documentary films before debuting as a recording artist when he was nearly 30 years old. Success came quickly; his first album, *Heads and Tales* (1972), stayed in the Top 100 for more than six months, buoyed by the success of the hit single "Taxi." Two other albums, *Short Stories* (1973) and *Verities and Balderdash* (1974), also produced hits—"W.O.L.D." and the chart-topping "Cat's in the Cradle," respectively. Critics, however, charged that his narrative lyrics—as well as his grainy vocals and folkish arrangements—were masks for the sentimentality of musical theatre, a judgment some would say was borne out when Chapin produced a Broadway revue called *The Night That Made America Famous* (1975).

But if Chapin wore his heart on his sleeve, he also was a man of action. Asked to organize a benefit concert to fight world hunger, he embraced the cause, cofounding World Hunger Year in 1975 and making numerous trips to Capitol Hill and other forums. His tireless efforts garnered high praise from politicians and the press. Chapin's music funded his activism in the second half of the decade, with every other concert a benefit. When he died in an auto accident in 1981, eulogies poured forth from all over the country, and Chapin's widow accepted a Special Congressional Gold Medal on his behalf at a Carnegie Hall tribute concert in 1987. An album documenting the event, *Harry Chapin Tribute*, was released in 1990.

LOU REED

The place of singer-songwriter Lou Reed (born Lewis Alan Reed, March 2, 1942, Brooklyn, New York, U.S.) in the rock pantheon is secured primarily by his role in the Velvet Underground. From 1965 to 1970 he guided the New York City-based quartet through a period that produced four poor-selling but enormously influential studio albums. Reed's post-Velvets career, though erratic, saw him emerge as a star performer in his own right, albeit an unconventional one, as the chronicler of the misbegotten who trolled New York's City sleazy after-hours bars, alleys, and drug dens. Reed's best songs did not judge or exploit his misfit characters; instead, he infused them with a rare dignity, and his lyrics pulsed with literary ambition.

After quitting the Velvets, Reed reemerged as a solo performer in England, where he was adopted by admirers such as glam rock pioneer David Bowie, who produced and performed on his breakthrough hit, "Walk on the Wild Side" (1973), and Mott the Hoople, who covered Reed's Velvets' classic "Sweet Jane." Later Patti Smith and Television's Tom Verlaine would cite him as an inspiration for the mid-1970s New York City punk scene. Yet, all the while, Reed flirted with self-parody and self-destruction, through drug and alcohol abuse and a string of wildly erratic recordings and concerts. His albums embraced everything from rote pop to heavy metal and included an orchestrated song cycle about a sadomasochistic love affair, *Berlin* (1973), and a double album of guitar drones, *Metal Machine Music* (1975), that are among his most notorious works. Onstage, his image and appearance changed yearly, from a leather-bondage-wearing ghoul feigning heroin injections to a deadpan guitar-strumming troubadour.

At the onset of the 1980s, Reed recruited his finest post-Velvets band, including guitarist Robert Quine and bassist Fernando Saunders, and reimmersed himself in raw guitar rock on *The Blue Mask* (1982), addressing his fears, ghosts, and joys with riveting frankness. No longer bedeviled by his addictions, Reed adopted a more serious if less daring tone on his recordings, peaking with three releases that were less concept albums than song cycles: *New York* (1989), about the spiritual death of his hometown; *Songs for Drella* (1990), an elegy for his 1960s mentor, Pop art conceptualist Andy Warhol, done in collaboration with former Velvets bandmate John Cale; and *Magic and Loss* (1991), inspired by the deaths of two friends. He was inducted, along with the other Velvets, into the Rock and Roll Hall of Fame in 1996. A romantic relationship with American performance artist and musician Laurie Anderson rejuvenated him again in the mid-1990s, resulting in the playful *Set the Twilight Reeling* (1997) and the harder-hitting *Ecstasy* (2000).

In 2000–01 Reed collaborated with director Robert Wilson to bring to the stage *POEtry*, a deconstruction of the work of Edgar Allen Poe. The songs from the show also were packaged on *The Raven* (2003), with spoken-word interludes—an ambitious if critically panned experiment. It was followed by *Animal Serenade* (2004), an excellent live recording that echoed Reed's landmark 1974 concert album *Rock'n' Roll* Animal. In 2006 Reed celebrated New York City in a book, *Lou Reed's New York*, which collected his photography. He teamed with heavy metal icons Metallica on the two-disc collection *Lulu* (2011). The album, inspired by the plays of German dramatist Frank Wedekind, was derided by critics, but it demonstrated that Reed's experimental tendencies remained as audacious as ever.

JACKSON BROWNE

German-born American singer, songwriter, pianist, and guitarist Jackson Browne (born October 9, 1948, Heidelberg, Germany) helped define the singer-songwriter movement of the 1970s. Born to a musical family with deep roots in southern California, Browne grew up in Los Angeles and Orange county. His interest in music led to his membership in the fledgling Nitty Gritty Dirt Band and to late-1960s stints in New York City as a backing musician for Nico of the Velvet Underground and for Tim Buckley. He was first noticed as a songwriter, and his compositions were recorded by performers such as Tom Rush, the Byrds, and Linda Ronstadt before he recorded his eponymous debut album in 1972 (featuring the Top Ten hit "Doctor My Eyes"). Part of a coterie of musicians that established Los Angeles as the home of country rock, Browne cowrote several songs for the Eagles (most notably "Take It Easy").

Profoundly influenced by Bob Dylan and in the tradition of Jack Kerouac and Thomas Wolfe, Browne created a protagonist whose quest for love, understanding, and justice was a mythic extension of his

WARREN ZEVON

American singer-songwriter Warren Zevon (born January 24, 1947, Chicago, Illinois—died September 7, 2003, Los Angeles, California) was critically acclaimed and much admired by other songwriters despite having had only one major hit, "Werewolves of London," from the album *Excitable Boy* (1978). He studied classical piano, was music director for the Everly Brothers, and wrote songs recorded by Linda Ronstadt and the Turtles before employing his rough-hewn baritone on albums such as *Warren Zevon* (1976) and *Sentimental Hygiene* (1987), featuring poetic songs that were by turns hard-boiled, humorous, tough, and tender. He survived inoperable lung cancer long enough to complete a final, touching album, *The Wind* (2003).

own experience. After winning a cult following with his first three albums—the last two, including the highly regarded *Late for the Sky*, featured instrumentalist David Lindley—Browne had million-selling hits with *The Pretender* (1976) and the live album *Running on Empty* (1978). His musical style ranged from romantic folk-rock ballads to up-tempo rock and reggae.

In the 1980s his music took a political turn that mirrored his activism, especially on *Lives in the Balance* (1986), which evidenced his vehement opposition to U.S. policy in Central America. His albums in the 1990s and 2000s largely reflected a return to more personal concerns, though political activism and political songs remained central to his identity.

In 2004 Browne was inducted into the Rock and Roll Hall of Fame. He returned to his coffeehouse folk roots on *Solo Acoustic Vol. 1* (2005) and *Solo Acoustic Vol. 2* (2008), a pair of recordings of live performances of many of his signature songs. In 2008 he also released a collection of new songs, *Time the Conqueror*. *Love Is Strange*, another live recording that documented Browne's acoustic tour of Spain with Lindley in 2006, was released in 2010.

RANDY NEWMAN

American composer, songwriter, singer, and pianist Randy Newman (born November 28, 1943, Los Angeles, California, U.S.) crafted character-driven, ironic, and often humorous compositions that won him a cult audience and praise from critics but were atypical of the singer-songwriter movement of the 1970s that gave him his start as a performer. Born in Los Angeles but taken to New Orleans as an infant, Newman was still a young boy when his family returned to Los Angeles, where his uncle Emil Newman was a conductor and his uncles Lionel and Alfred Newman composed scores for motion pictures. He studied musical composition at the University of California at Los Angeles and worked as a staff songwriter for a publishing company.

His first releases as a performer, in the late 1960s and early 1970s, sold poorly but prompted cover versions by artists such as Three Dog Night (who topped the charts with "Mama Told Me Not to Come") and Harry Nilsson. Bringing his love for the New Orleans piano-oriented rhythm and blues of Fats Domino and Professor Longhair to the pop music tradition of George Gershwin, Newman released *Sail Away* (1972) and *Good Old Boys* (1974), with sardonic songs whose underlying humaneness and sense of social justice were often misinterpreted by listeners but much praised by critics. The tongue-in-cheek quality of Newman's biggest hits, "Short People" from *Little Criminals* (1977) and "I Love L.A." from *Trouble in Paradise* (1983), was lost on many listeners. *Land of Dreams* (1988) was Newman's most personal album; in 1995 he released *Faust*, a concept album based on Johann Wolfgang von Goethe's *Faust*. The boxed-set *Guilty: 30 Years of Randy Newman* appeared in 1998 and was followed by *Bad Love* (1999), his first album of new songs in 11 years. It would be nearly another decade before he released *Harps and Angels* (2008).

Newman had a successful parallel career as the composer of scores and songs for motion pictures, most notably for *Ragtime* (1981) and *The Natural* (1984); he earned his first Grammy Award for his sound track for the latter film. In 1995 he began a fruitful collaboration with Pixar Animation Studios, and he received two Academy Award nominations for his work on *Toy Story* (1995). He received three more Grammys for the Pixar films *A Bug's Life* (1998), *Toy Story 2* (1999), and *Monsters, Inc.* (2001) before his Academy Award drought came to an end. After 16 nominations, he won his first Oscar in 2002 for "If I Didn't Have You" from *Monsters, Inc.* Newman's Pixar sound tracks continued to bear fruit, as he won a Grammy for the song "Our Town" from *Cars* (2006) and for the instrumental score for *Toy Story 3* (2010). The latter film also earned him a second Oscar, for the song "We Belong Together."

STEVE EARLE

American singer, songwriter, and guitarist Steve Earle (born January 17, 1955, Fort Monroe, Virginia, U.S.) bridged the genres of rock and country music. As a child growing up in Texas, Earle acquired his first guitar at age 11 and was playing proficiently two years later. Although he showed musical promise, Earle was often in trouble with the law and was disliked by local country music fans because of his long hair and precocious anti-Vietnam War stance. He left home as a teenager to live with an uncle in Houston and dropped out of high school. Making his way to Nashville, Tennessee, Earle sought to establish himself as a songwriter. In the process he forged friendships with a pair of his musical idols, Guy Clark and Townes Van Zandt, country music "outlaws" of long standing. Earle's debut album as a performer, *Guitar Town* (1986), won praise from critics and was a commercial success, with both its title track and "Goodbye's All We Got Left" reaching the Top Ten on the country music chart.

Much influenced by Van Zandt, Earle's music contains elements of country and rock yet fits wholly into neither genre. Of Earle's more than 15 albums, *Copperhead Road* (1988) was particularly popular. His career sometimes was sidetracked by drug and alcohol addictions, as well as by several divorces, and he served nearly a year in prison and rehab following his conviction for narcotics possession. The turmoil of Earle's personal life is particularly evident in his album *The Hard Way* (1990).

Earle's political fervour (especially in his opposition to the death penalty) was often evident. His leftist leanings came through clearly on *Jerusalem* (2002), an agitprop-filled album that features the controversial "John Walker's Blues," an empathetic consideration of John Walker Lindh, the "American Taliban." The similarly political *The Revolution Starts...Now* (2004) won a Grammy Award (best contemporary folk album) in 2005, and *Washington Square Serenade* (2007), Earle's romantic confessional collaboration with his sixth

TOWNES VAN ZANDT

American country and folk musician Townes Van Zandt (born March 7, 1944—died January 1, 1997) inspired a new generation of songwriters including Nanci Griffith, who recorded a well-known version of Van Zandt's "Tecumseh Valley." His public obscurity was countered by the high esteem with which he was held by the musicians who transformed his haunting ballads into such hits as "Pancho and Lefty" (Willie Nelson and Merle Haggard) and "If I Needed You" (Emmylou Harris and Don Williams).

wife, singer Allison Moorer, won a Grammy (best contemporary folk/Americana album) in 2008. His 2009 tribute to Van Zandt, titled *Townes*, earned him another Grammy Award for best contemporary folk album. Earle followed with *I'll Never Get out of This World Alive* (2011), which took its title from the last single released by Hank Williams before he died. The album explores notions of mortality, and T Bone Burnett's stripped-down production evoked the bygone era that Williams inhabited.

Earle authored a collection of short stories, *Doghouse Roses* (2001), and was the subject of a film documentary, *Steve Earle: Just an American Boy* (2003). He also appeared in bit roles in the television dramas *The Wire* and *Treme* (both produced by David Simon) and in the comedy-thriller film *Leaves of Grass* (2009). Earle's debut novel, *I'll Never Get out of This World Alive* (2011), was published shortly after the release of the album of the same name.

NEIL DIAMOND

American singer-songwriter Neil Diamond (born January 24, 1941, Brooklyn, New York, U.S.) began his career writing pop songs for other musicians and then launched a solo recording career that spanned more than four decades. Diamond's interest in music began at age 16, when he

Neil Diamond, 2006. TM and © QVC, Inc., all rights reserved/PRNewsFoto/ AP Images

obtained his first guitar. After graduating from high school, Diamond attended New York University with the intention of entering medical school. However, he left college during his final year to take a job as a staff songwriter for the Sunbeam Music Company. His tenure at Sunbeam was short, and he became one of a stable of songwriters who worked out of New York's famed Brill Building.

In 1965 Diamond signed a recording contract with Bang Records, and one year later his debut album, *The Feel of Neil*, was released. Shortly thereafter he wrote the song "I'm a Believer" (1966), recorded and made famous by the Monkees. In 1967 Diamond signed a new recording contract with Uni Records, with whom he recorded such hits as "Brother Love's Traveling Salvation Show" (1969), "Sweet Caroline" (1969), "Cracklin' Rosie" (1970), "I Am...I Said" (1971), and "Song Sung Blue" (1972).

After leaving Uni for Columbia Records, Diamond recorded the sound track for the film *Jonathan Livingston Seagull* (1973), which earned him a Grammy Award. He went on to release a string of successful albums during the 1970s, including *Serenade* (1974), *Beautiful Noise* (1976), *Love at the Greek* (1977), *You Don't Bring Me Flowers* (1978; a duet with Barbra Streisand), and *September Morn* (1979).

In 1980 Diamond made his motion picture debut: he starred in a remake of the film *The Jazz Singer*, for which he also wrote and performed the sound track. Notable later albums include *Heartlight* (1982), *Live in America* (1994), *In My Lifetime* (1996), and *The Neil Diamond Collection* (1999). In the early 21st century Diamond released, among other albums, *The Essential Neil Diamond* (2001), *Stages* (2003), and *12 Songs* (2005). He also made a cameo appearance as himself in the film *Saving Silverman* (2001).

Diamond was honoured twice by the Songwriters' Hall of Fame—first upon his induction in 1984 and later in 2000, when he was presented with the Sammy Cahn Lifetime Achievement award. He was inducted into the Rock and Roll Hall of Fame in 2011. That year Diamond also received a Kennedy Center Honor.

TOM WAITS

American singer-songwriter Tom Waits (born December 7, 1949, Pomona, California, U.S.) won a loyal if limited following and the admiration of critics for his gritty, sometimes romantic depictions of the lives of the urban underclass.

Born into a middle-class California family but enamoured of the bohemian lifestyle depicted in

Tom Waits, 2006. Market Wire/AP Images

Beat literature, Waits lived in his car and in seedy Los Angeles hotels as he embarked on his career. His raspy vocals, delivered in his signature growl, evoked the late-night atmosphere of the smoky clubs in which he first performed in the late 1960s. Drawing on jazz, blues, pop, and avant-garde rock music, he combined offbeat orchestrations with his own piano and guitar playing and stream-of-consciousness lyrics that reflected the influence of writers Jack Kerouac and Charles Bukowski. Although Waits's albums found considerable commercial success in Britain beginning in the mid-1980s, even his best-selling albums—*Small Change*

(1976) and *Heartattack and Vine* (1980)—failed to crack the American Top 40. His songs, however, have been recorded by the Eagles ("Ol' 55"), Bruce Springsteen ("Jersey Girl"), and Rod Stewart ("Downtown Train"). He also scored films, cowrote the stage musical *Frank's Wild Years* (which premiered in 1986), and collaborated with writer William S. Burroughs and theatre director Robert Wilson on another musical, *The Black Rider* (1990). Waits's 1992 release *Bone Machine*, typical of his increasingly experimental musical efforts in the 1990s, won a Grammy Award for best alternative music album. His 1999 album, *Mule Variations*, was also much praised. Later albums include *Blood Money* (2002), *Alice* (2002), *Real Gone* (2004), and *Orphans: Brawlers, Bawlers, and Bastards* (2006), a sprawling collection of 56 songs. In 2009 Waits released *Glitter and Doom*, a series of live recordings from his 2008 concert tour. Waits's first studio release since 2004, *Bad as Me* (2011), a collection of blues-tinged, whiskey-soaked love songs, was greeted with wide critical acclaim. He was inducted into the Rock and Roll Hall of Fame in 2011.

The theatrical posturing of Waits's live performances led in the 1980s to an alternate career as a film actor, notably in *Down by Law* (1986). He made further appearances in *Dracula* (1992), *Mystery Men* (1999), *Coffee and Cigarettes* (2003), and *Domino* (2005). His saturnine features and gravelly voice perfectly suited him to Mephistophelian roles, and he deployed these attributes to memorable effect as one of the "people in charge" of purgatory in *Wristcutters: A Love Story* (2006) and as the Devil himself in *The Imaginarium of Doctor Parnassus* (2009).

JOAN ARMATRADING

Joan Armatrading (born December 9, 1950, Basseterre, St. Kitts) was among the first female British singer-songwriters to make an impact performing her own compositions. First touted by the critics in the 1970s, she maintained a devoted audience into the 21st century, especially in the United Kingdom.

As a child, Armatrading emigrated with her family from the West Indies to Birmingham, England. After studying piano and guitar as a youth, she won a role in a touring production of *Hair*, through which she met Pam Nestor, another West Indian immigrant, with whom she began composing songs. After collaborating on a first album with Nestor in 1972, Armatrading began working solo, winning critical acclaim with *Joan Armatrading* (1976), which cracked the U.K. Top 20 and featured the Top 10 single "Love and Affection." Armatrading's romantic, bittersweet lyrics conveyed in her rounded, expressive voice dominated a series of best-selling albums, notably *Show Some Emotion* (1977), *To the Limit* (1978), *Me Myself I* (1980), and *Walk Under Ladders* (1981). Her music blends folk, reggae, and jazz with rock, which dominated *The Key* (1983). Thereafter, though Armatrading's sales dipped somewhat, she remained a critic's darling, an unwavering favourite with her dedicated listeners in both the United Kingdom and the United States, and an important influence on later singer-songwriters. She was made a Member of the Order of the British Empire in 2001.

MICHAEL MCDONALD

As front man for the 1970s band the Doobie Brothers, Michael McDonald (born February 12, 1952, St. Louis, Missouri) became a fixture on rock radio with his soulful vocals and keyboards. He followed up his successful stint with the Doobies with a durable solo career, producing hits as a solo artist, in duets, and on film sound tracks.

McDonald grew up listening to rhythm and blues and rock and roll. He formed his first band, Mike and the Majestics, while in high school and later developed his singing and keyboard skills while working in St. Louis nightclubs. In the early 1970s he relocated to Los Angeles, where he recorded several unsuccessful singles before joining the rock group Steely Dan as a backup vocalist and keyboardist.

In 1975 he replaced vocalist Tom Johnston in the Doobie Brothers, a northern California rock band. McDonald's rich baritone and gospel-inflected keyboard style transformed the Doobies' raucous rock and roll into smoother rhythm and blues. As the Doobies' lead vocalist, McDonald wrote and performed such hit singles as "Takin' It to the Streets" (1976), "It Keeps You Runnin" (1976), the Grammy-winning "What a Fool Believes" (1979), "Minute by Minute" (1979), and "Real Love" (1980).

Over the years McDonald collaborated with other popular vocalists. He recorded "Let Me Go, Love" (1978) with Nicolette Larsen and "Ride Like the Wind" (1979) with Christopher Cross. He appeared on numerous albums by performers that included Carly Simon, Bonnie Raitt, Elton John, Rickie Lee Jones, Kenny Loggins (with whom he cowrote "What A Fool Believes"), Aretha Franklin, Joni Mitchell, and the Pointer Sisters, among others.

The Doobies disbanded in 1982, in large part because of McDonald's increasing focus on his solo career. His debut album, *If That's What It Takes* (1982), featured the jazzy hit single "I Keep Forgettin' (Every

Time You're Near)." His second solo effort, *That Was Then* (1982), was a collection of early material from McDonald's days at Bell Records. His next release, *No Lookin' Back* (1985), had a harder rock sound and spawned a minor hit with the title track. While developing his solo career McDonald continued collaborating with other artists. His duets with James Ingram on "Yah Mo B There" (1984) and with Patti LaBelle on "On My Own" (1986) became hits. His solo recording of "Sweet Freedom," the theme song from the feature film "Running Scared" (1986), made it to the top ten.

McDonald combined rock and soul on *Take It to Heart* (1990). In 1992 he reunited with former Steely Dan band mates Donald Fagen and Walter Becker to record and tour with the New York Rock and Soul Review, a musical collective that also included Phoebe Snow and Boz Skaggs. For *Blink of an Eye* (1993), which featured a soulful remake of the 1963 Freddie Scott hit "Hey, Girl," McDonald enlisted a variety of performers, including rock musicians Tom Petty and Peter Gabriel, country singer Vince Gill, and bluegrass singer Allison Kraus.

BILLY BRAGG

British singer, songwriter, and guitarist Billy Bragg (born December 20, 1957, Barking, Essex, England) became a critic's darling and a champion of populist activism in the mid-1980s as he fused the personal and the political in songs of love and conscience. Born into a working-class family in eastern Greater London, Bragg played briefly in a punk band (Riff Raff), then bought his way out of the British army before becoming a modern-day troubadour. Inspired by the Clash, part punk and part folksinger, he banged out songs on his electric guitar on any stage open to him. His debut album, *Life's a Riot with Spy vs. Spy*, brought critical acclaim, reached the British Top 30, and yielded the hit "A New England" in 1984. A committed socialist, Bragg played a number of benefit performances during the British miners' strike of 1984–85. (He later helped form Red Wedge, an organization and tour that supported the Labour Party.)

Adding to the spare instrumentation of his first albums, Bragg began releasing increasingly polished work, including *Talking with the Taxman About Poetry* (1986), featuring the Motown-inspired "Levi Stubbs' Tears," and *Workers Playtime* (1988). After the more dogmatic *The Internationale* (1990), his songwriting resumed its characteristic blend of simple, poetic lyrics and evocative melodies, conveyed by Bragg's limited but emotive Cockney-inflected voice, on *Don't Try This at Home*

(1991) and *William Bloke* (1996). More popular in Britain (where he reached number one with a cover version of the Beatles' "She's Leaving Home" in 1988) than in the United States, Bragg nevertheless collaborated with American alternative-rock band Wilco on *Mermaid Avenue* (1998), an album built on lyrics by folk music legend Woody Guthrie; *Mermaid Avenue Vol. II* was released in 2000. Subsequent albums included *England, Half English* (2002) and *Mr. Love & Justice* (2008), which borrowed its title from a novel by Colin MacInnes, chronicler of British youth culture in the 1950s and '60s. As British cultural and political life both devolved to the United Kingdom's component nations and became increasingly multicultural, Bragg became interested in the notion of English identity, one of the subjects at the centre of his book *The Progressive Patriot: A Search for Belonging* (2006).

SONGWRITING GOES POP

By adapting the singer-songwriter formula to the classic pop ballad, a trio of piano-playing showmen became some of the top-selling solo artists of the 1970s. Each drew on a diverse range of influences, from glam to soul and disco, and each adopted a wildly different stage persona.

SIR ELTON JOHN

British singer, composer, and pianist Elton John (born Reginald Kenneth Dwight, March 25, 1947, Pinner, Middlesex, England) was one of the most popular entertainers of the late 20th century. He fused as many strands of popular music and stylistic showmanship as Elvis Presley in a concert and recording career that included the sale of hundreds of millions of records. A child prodigy on the piano, John was awarded a scholarship to the Royal Academy of Music at 11. Gravitating toward pop after discovering rhythm and blues, he joined Bluesology, later John Baldry's backing band, in the mid-1960s. He met his major songwriting collaborator, Bernie Taupin (born May 22, 1950, Sleaford, Lincolnshire), after both responded to an advertisement in a trade magazine, and his first British recording success was with "Lady Samantha" in 1968. His first American album, *Elton John*, was released in 1970 and immediately established him as a major international star.

Throughout his career John demonstrated a supreme talent for assimilating and blending diverse pop and rock styles into a propulsive, streamlined sound that was extroverted, energetic, and somewhat impersonal. His recordings were among the first to homogenize electric guitar and acoustic piano with synthesized instrumentation. His vocal style, with its Southern accent and gospel inflections, was strongly American-influenced, as was his pianism, an ornate, gospel-flavoured elaboration of the stylings of Little Richard and Jerry Lee Lewis. His first American hit, "Your Song," in 1970, was a love ballad that combined the introspective mood of the era's singer-songwriters with a more traditional pop craftsmanship. John's early 1970s recordings paid homage to country rock and folk rock models such as the Band and Crosby, Stills and Nash.

By 1973 John was one of the world's best-selling pop performers. His typical compositions, written with Taupin, were affectionate parodies and pastiches of everything from the Rolling Stones ("The Bitch Is Back" [1974]) to Frank Sinatra ballads ("Blue Eyes" [1982]) to 1950s rock and roll ("Crocodile Rock" [1972]) to Philadelphia soul ("Philadelphia Freedom" [1975]). He also demonstrated deeper musical ambitions in longer works such as "Burn Down the Mission" on *Tumbleweed Connection* (1971) and "Funeral for a Friend/ Love Lies Bleeding" on *Goodbye Yellow Brick Road* (1973).

Beginning in 1976 with the album *Blue Moves*, his rock influences became less pronounced, and a more churchlike English pop style emerged in ballads like "Sorry Seems to Be the Hardest Word" (1976), which typified the staid declamatory aura of his mature ballads. In the late 1970s and '80s, as he experimented with other collaborators, his music lost some of its freshness and his popularity dipped a bit, but he remained an extremely popular mainstream entertainer who brought into the pop arena an old-fashioned gaudily costumed flamboyance reminiscent of the Las Vegas piano legend Liberace. In the 1990s John was the first male pop star to declare his homosexuality, suffering no noticeable career damage. With lyricist Tim Rice he also wrote songs for the film *The Lion King* (1994), which was adapted into a Broadway musical in 1997. The same year, a new version of his 1973 song "Candle in the Wind," revised by Taupin to mourn the death of Diana, princess of Wales, became the most successful pop single in history, selling more than 30 million copies.

In 1998 John reteamed with Rice to write the stage musical *Elaborate Lives: The Legend of Aida* (revised in 1999 as *Aida*), a loose adaptation of the Giuseppe Verdi opera. He and Taupin cowrote the musical *Lestat* (2005), based on a series of novels by Anne Rice, and he also composed the score for *Billy Elliot*, a stage adaptation of

Elton John performing at Caesars Palace in Las Vegas, 2005. PRNewsFoto/ Caesars Palace/AP Images

the popular film. The latter musical premiered on London's West End in 2005 and made its Broadway debut in 2008. The following year it won 10 Tony Awards, including best musical. From 2003 to 2009 John had an open engagement at Caesars Palace in Las Vegas. The show, titled *Elton John and the Red Piano*, was a multimedia retrospective of his career, with visuals provided by photographer David LaChapelle.

John continued to release solo recordings in the 21st century, and he contributed sound tracks to the animated movies *The Road to El Dorado* (2000) and *Gnomeo & Juliet* (2011). He was inducted into the Rock and Roll Hall of Fame in 1994, and in 1998 he was knighted by Queen Elizabeth II.

BILLY JOEL

American singer, pianist, and songwriter Billy Joel (born May 9, 1949, Bronx, New York, U.S.) achieved his greatest popularity in the 1970s

Billy Joel performing at a USO concert at Zeppelin Field in Nürnberg, Ger., June 12, 1994. SRA Andrew J. Rice—U.S. Department of Defense

and '80s with a string of hits in the pop ballad tradition. The son of a German-Jewish Holocaust survivor but raised as a Roman Catholic in Hicksville, a middle-class suburb on Long Island, New York, Joel was steered toward classical music by his parents and began piano lessons at age 4. At age 14, enamoured of the British Invasion and soul music, he began playing in bands. With the Hassels, he recorded two albums in the late 1960s, and a stint in the heavy metal duo Attila followed.

In 1971, recast as a singer-songwriter, Joel recorded the poorly produced *Cold Spring Harbor* for Family Productions, which locked him into an exploitative long-term contract. Seeking refuge in Los Angeles, he performed under a pseudonym in a local piano bar. Meanwhile, a live recording of Joel's song "Captain Jack" caught the attention of Columbia Records executives, who extricated him from his contract. His first album for Columbia, *Piano Man* (1973), featured a hit single of the same name; based on his piano bar experience, it became his signature song. Mixtures of soul, pop, and rock, *Piano Man* and Joel's subsequent albums—*Streetlife Serenade* (1974) and *Turnstiles* (1976)—earned praise from critics and set the stage for *The Stranger* (1977). Featuring four U.S. hit singles (one of which, "Just the Way You Are," won Grammy Awards for song of the year and record of the year), it sold five million copies, surpassing Simon and Garfunkel's *Bridge Over Troubled Water* to become Columbia's best-selling album to date.

Joel's string of hit-producing, award-winning platinum albums continued with *52nd Street* (1979), *Glass Houses* (1980), and *The Nylon Curtain* (1982). On the last, Joel, whose lyrics had previously dealt primarily with romance and slices of life, introduced his first socially conscious songs, "Allentown" and "Goodnight Saigon" (about unemployed steel workers and Vietnam War veterans, respectively). In the early 1980s Joel was among the first established rock performers to make music videos. During this period he married supermodel Christie Brinkley (the second of his three marriages). From *An Innocent Man* (1983), his tribute to his doo-wop and vocal group influences, through *Storm Front* (1989) and *River of Dreams* (1993), Joel continued to produce well-received

albums. In 1999 he was inducted into the Rock and Roll Hall of Fame. *Fantasies and Delusions*, featuring classical compositions by Joel, was released in 2001. *Movin' Out*, a dance-focused musical based on two dozen songs by Joel and conceived, choreographed, and directed by Twyla Tharp, premiered in 2002. In 2006, having earlier undergone treatment for alcohol abuse, Joel released *12 Gardens Live*, a concert album.

BARRY MANILOW

American pop singer and songwriter Barry Manilow (born Barry Alan Pincus, June 17, 1943, Brooklyn, New York, U.S.) specialized in elaborately orchestrated romantic ballads, which first won him a wide audience in the 1970s. Barry Pincus grew up in a lower-class neighbourhood in Brooklyn. When he was two years old, his father left the family, and several years later Barry assumed his mother's maiden name, Manilow. In his youth he took up the accordion and the piano, becoming an accomplished musician, and through his stepfather he acquired a taste for jazz and Broadway show tunes. After briefly studying advertising at City College of the City University of New York, Manilow took classes at the New York College of Music (now part of New York University) and later at Juilliard School of Music.

Barry Manilow performing in Chicago, 2006. TM and © QVC, Inc., all rights reserved/PRNewsFoto/Arista Records/AP Images

To support his education, Manilow worked in the mail room at CBS, which eventually led to jobs for the network's local television affiliate, first as a film editor and then, in 1967, as the music director for a talent show. By the early 1970s he had composed and arranged songs for an Off-Broadway theatrical production and had written a number of jingles for nationally broadcast television commercials. While working as a piano accompanist in nightclubs, he met the singer Bette Midler and soon became her music director, accompanying her on tour and coproducing her first two albums.

About the same time, Manilow recorded his own debut album, *Barry Manilow* (1973; later released as *Barry Manilow I*), a stylistically diverse collection of songs that initially sold tepidly. He found greater success with *Barry Manilow II* (1974), mostly owing to "Mandy," a florid ballad that rose to the top of the *Billboard* singles chart. A string of other popular albums soon followed, featuring such hits as "I Write the Songs" (1975), which, ironically, he did not write; the sentimental "Looks Like We Made It" (1976); and the disco-inspired "Copacabana (At the Copa)" (1978), which won a Grammy Award for best male pop vocal performance. A skilled entertainer, Manilow also regularly performed during this time. A concert that he presented on Broadway in 1976–77 earned him a special Tony Award and yielded a live album (1977) that eventually sold more than three million copies. In addition, beginning in the late 1970s Manilow starred in a number of television specials, for which he won two Emmy Awards (1977, 2006).

In 1984 Manilow moved away from mainstream pop with the jazz album *2:00 AM Paradise Cafe* (1984), which featured appearances from Sarah Vaughan and Gerry Mulligan, among others. Subsequent albums—including *Swing Street* (1987), *Showstoppers* (1991), and *Singin' with the Big Bands* (1994)—found Manilow seeking further inspiration from the pre-rock era. As his career progressed, he continued to work on projects beyond the recording studio. In 1985 Manilow starred in *Copacabana*, a television movie that he had also helped create; it was later adapted for the stage. After composing the sound tracks to the animated films *Thumbelina* (1994) and *The Pebble and the Penguin* (1995), Manilow cowrote (with Bruce Sussman) the musical *Harmony*, which was performed in La Jolla, California, in 1997.

Although Manilow's album sales had declined in the 1980s and '90s, his recording career experienced a resurgence in the 21st century. *The Greatest Songs of the Fifties* (2006) was his first number one album in nearly 30 years, and later albums in which Manilow covered songs of the past also proved popular. While his adeptly crafted, heartfelt music attracted legions of fans throughout his career, Manilow was not without his critics, who derided his style as schmaltzy and bombastic. An autobiography, *Sweet Life: Adventures on the Way to Paradise*, was released in 1987.

CHAPTER 6

Classical Influences: Art Rock and Progressive Rock

Art rock is an eclectic branch of rock music that emerged in the late 1960s and flourished in the early to mid-1970s. The term is sometimes used synonymously with progressive rock, but the latter more accurately describes album-oriented rock by such British bands as Genesis, King Crimson, Pink Floyd, and Yes. The term *art rock* is best used to describe either classically influenced rock by such British groups as the Electric Light Orchestra (ELO), Emerson, Lake and Palmer (ELP), Gentle Giant, the Moody Blues, and Procol Harum or the fusion of progressive rock and English folk music created by such groups as Jethro Tull and the Strawbs. In common, all these bands regularly employ complicated and conceptual approaches to their music. Moreover, there has been a relatively fluid movement of musicians between bands that fall under the most general definition of art rock. Among the musicians who contributed to numerous bands are Bill Bruford (Yes, King Crimson, and U.K.), Steve Howe (Yes and Asia), Greg Lake (King Crimson and ELP), and John Wetton (King Crimson, U.K., and Asia). Some of the experimental rock by such American and British artists as Laurie Anderson, David Bowie, Brian Eno, the Velvet Underground, and Frank Zappa is also often categorized as art rock.

In 1965 the Beatles began to explore the compositional use in rock music of multitrack recording, classical-type orchestrations, and avant-garde or experimental influences. The debut album by American experimental rock composer Frank Zappa's Mothers of Invention followed in 1966, and in the next two years Caravan, Jethro Tull, the Moody Blues, the Nice, Pink Floyd, the Pretty Things, Procol Harum, and Soft Machine released art-rock-type albums. Much of this music combined roots in British Invasion manifestations of rhythm and blues or eclectic pop with psychedelic, avant-garde, or classical tendencies. From 1972 to 1974 Genesis, King Crimson, ELP, and Yes (all of whom debuted in 1969–70) turned out ambitious suites that filled album sides. In addition to the standard rock-band lineup (guitar, bass guitar, drums, and vocals), these groups often featured the Mellotron (a tape-loop-based keyboard instrument often used for orchestral sounds), organ, piano, and early synthesizers. Because of the prior experience of many art rock musicians in classical music and the availability of high-tech electronic supplements to traditional instruments, keyboardists such as Keith Emerson (ELP) and Rick Wakeman (Yes) moved from having supporting roles to making featured contributions.

Art rock often featured complicated and frequent rhythm changes, imaginative lyrics (including socio-political or science-fiction themes), and unified, extended compositions (often in the form of "concept albums"). Classical instrumentation (including symphony orchestras) and pseudo-orchestral ensemble playing by rock bands (including reworkings of classical compositions) were also prevalent. Art rock had widespread appeal in its virtuosity and in the complexity of its music and lyrics, and it was intended primarily for listening and contemplation rather than for dancing. The stage shows and album art that went along with this music—especially Roger Dean's elaborate designs for Yes—also appealed to artistically inclined teenagers and young adults. Early 1970s shows by Genesis were especially visually oriented, with lead singer Peter Gabriel dressed in a bewildering array of fanciful costumes and arriving on stage from above, courtesy of opera-style stage machinery.

Notwithstanding the appearance of the influential British art rock bands U.K. and Marillion in the late 1970s and early 1980s, respectively, and the continued presence of Genesis, King Crimson, Yes, Pink Floyd, and ELP in various incarnations, for the most part art rock tendencies were continued beyond the mid-1970s by British and American pop rock and hard rock groups such as Asia, Boston, Foreigner, Journey, Kansas, the Alan Parsons Project, Queen, Steely Dan, Styx, and Supertramp and the Canadian band Rush. "Arty" 1970s and '80s British pop rock artists such as Roxy Music, Peter Gabriel, and Kate Bush and the 1980s and '90s American heavy metal bands Metallica and Dream Theater also explored a number of stylistic features earlier associated with art rock.

The experimental rock of eccentric late 1960s and '70s musicians such as Captain Beefheart, the Velvet Underground, and Frank Zappa also often included progressive rock tendencies, although somewhat more haphazardly than was the case with art rock bands. Ambient composer, rock producer, and former Roxy Music member Brian Eno's late 1970s and early 1980s collaborations with the American rock band Talking Heads and with the eclectic British rock singer David Bowie are also exemplary of the successful infusion of art rock tendencies into other popular music genres. The 1970s, '80s, and '90s music of the American performance artist Laurie Anderson and the 1990s music of the American singer-songwriter-pianist Tori Amos were similarly infused. However, much of Eno and Anderson's work is also related to the minimalism that was so influential in the "art" music of the late

1960s and '70s and to the "pop-minimalism" of 1990s techno music.

THE MOODY BLUES

Art rock pioneers the Moody Blues were formed in Birmingham, West Midlands, England, in 1964. The original members were Mike Pinder (born December 27, 1941, Birmingham, England), Ray Thomas (born December 29, 1941, Stourport-on-Severn, Hereford and Worcester), Graeme Edge (born March 30, 1941, Rochester, Kent), Denny Laine (born Brian Hines, October 29, 1944, near Jersey, Channel Islands), and Clint Warwick (born Clinton Eccles, June 25, 1939, Birmingham). Later members included Justin Hayward (born October 14, 1946, Swindon, Wiltshire), John Lodge (born July 20, 1945, Birmingham), and Patrick Moraz (born June 24, 1948, Morges, Switzerland).

Although best known for their psychedelic-era music and grandiose lyrics, the Moody Blues began as a British Invasion rhythm-and-blues group with the hit single "Go Now" (1964). After a change in band members, including the departure of Laine (who later joined Paul McCartney's Wings) and the addition of Hayward and Lodge, the group released their landmark *Days of Future Passed* (released in Britain in late 1967 and in the United States in early 1968). One of the first successful concept albums, it marked a turning point in the development of classical rock (an assemblage of musicians calling itself the London Festival Orchestra backed the band) and yielded two hits, "Tuesday Afternoon" and the signature "Nights in White Satin." On *In Search of the Lost Chord* (1968) they traded the orchestra for the Mellotron. They continued to use electronic instruments in subsequent albums and had a number of hit singles, though, ironically, by *Long Distance Voyager* (1981) and *The Present* (1983) the originality of their efforts was obscured by their success, which had helped make synthesizers and philosophy part of the rock mainstream. Their rich symphonic sound influenced groups such as Yes, Genesis, the Electric Light Orchestra, and Deep Purple.

YES

The British progressive rock band Yes was known for its extended compositions and virtuoso musicianship. Its principal members were Jon Anderson (born October 25, 1944, Accrington, Lancashire, England), Chris Squire (born March 4, 1948, London), Steve Howe (born April 8, 1947, London), Rick Wakeman (born May 18, 1949, London), and Alan White (born June 14, 1949, Pelton, Durham). Other members

included Bill Bruford (born May 17, 1949, Sevenoaks, Kent), Patrick Moraz (born June 24, 1948, Morges, Switzerland), and Trevor Rabin (born January 13, 1954, Johannesburg, South Africa).

Founded in 1968 by vocalist Anderson and bassist Squire, Yes went through several early personnel changes before stabilizing around Anderson, guitarist Howe, Squire, and keyboardist Wakeman, all of whom played on the group's fourth album, *Fragile* (1972). Featuring the hit "Roundabout," the album established Yes as one of progressive rock's leading bands, rivaled only by Genesis and Emerson, Lake and Palmer. *Fragile* also marked the beginning of Yes's relationship with artist Roger Dean, whose album covers and stage designs defined the group's visual style. Their sound, which featured Anderson's falsetto vocals and Howe's complex guitar supported by Squire's bass and Wakeman's multilayered keyboards, further developed with *Close to the Edge* (1972) and *Tales from Topographic Oceans* (1973).

Wakeman's departure in 1974 marked the beginning of several years' increasing instability, as members dropped out or concentrated on solo projects (only Squire remained with the band from its founding). Despite a changing lineup, Yes released four more albums before

WBCN

While many progressive rock stations died painful, public deaths, one of the first—WBCN in Boston, Massachusetts—carried on. Founded in 1967 by Ray Riepen, club owner (the Boston Tea Party) and later underground newspaper publisher (*The Phoenix*), WBCN quickly grew in popularity and power. Its most famous alumnus was Peter Wolf, a rhythm-and-blues and blues fanatic who not only knew the music but performed it as lead singer and songwriter for the J. Geils Band. Wolf called himself "Woofuh Goofuh" on the air; he left the station in 1969 to tour with the band. His replacement, Charles Laquidara, became one of WBCN's most enduring personalities. Laquidara was at KPPC in Los Angeles when that station became the first underground rock outlet in southern California, and his *Big Mattress* morning show became an institution in New England.

Punk rock arrived at WBCN with Oedipus, who had established his new-wave credentials in local clubs and on college radio (the Massachusetts Institute of Technology's WTBS). By 1981 he was WBCN's program director, gathering numerous industry honours for keeping WBCN on the cutting edge.

dissolving in 1981. It reconvened two years later under the leadership of guitarist Trevor Rabin. This incarnation, which featured Anderson, Squire, and White, enjoyed commercial success with *90125* (1983) and *Big Generator* (1987); the creation of another group by other Yes veterans (including Bruford, Howe, and Wakeman) led to legal wrangling over ownership of the band's name. The dispute, which was settled by 1991, showed that even though (like many progressive-rock bands) it lacked the energy and vision of its youth, Yes had evolved from an avant-garde experiment into a valuable commercial franchise.

GENESIS

The British rock group Genesis experienced a rather dramatic shift in its sound over the course of more than three decades. It began as an atmospheric progressive rock band in the 1970s before transitioning to a straightforward pop ensemble that scored hits with a string of extremely popular albums and singles in the 1980s and '90s. The principal members were Peter Gabriel (born February 13, 1950, Woking, Surrey, England), Tony Banks (born March 27, 1950, East Hoathly, East Sussex), Michael Rutherford (born October 2, 1950, Guildford, Surrey), Phil Collins (born January 31, 1951, London), and Steve Hackett (born February 12, 1950, London).

Founded in 1967 by schoolmates at the Charterhouse public school,

Genesis, c. 1974 (from left to right): Peter Gabriel, Phil Collins, Tony Banks, Mike Rutherford, and Steve Hackett. Dennis Stone/Hulton Archive/ Getty Images

Genesis were first known for their songwriting talents and Gabriel's uniquely theatrical onstage performances. After their lineup stabilized with the addition of drummer Collins and guitarist Hackett in 1970, the group developed a style that featured heavy synthesizers and arrangements emphasizing group performance over the individual pyrotechnics favoured by many progressive rock groups. The band developed a dedicated following in the early 1970s; after the release of their acclaimed *The Lamb Lies Down on Broadway* (1974), Gabriel left to pursue a solo career. With Collins performing lead vocals, the band slowly developed a more mainstream sound marked by the successful albums *Duke* (1980), *Abacab* (1981), and *Invisible Touch* (1986) and scored a host of hit singles. Despite many successful side projects—most notably Rutherford's pop combo Mike + the Mechanics— and the departure of Collins in 1995, the band continued to record with the 1997 release *Calling All Stations*. This proved to be the group's final studio album, however, as a 2007 reunion tour, with Collins back as lead vocalist, did not lead to any new material. Genesis was inducted into the Rock and Roll Hall of Fame in 2010.

PETER GABRIEL

After leaving Genesis in 1975, Peter Gabriel found great success as a solo artist. He became known for the intelligence and depth of his lyrics and for his commitment to various political causes. Gabriel also developed a deep interest in world music rhythms and textures, reflected in four eponymous albums (the last, released in 1982, was titled *Security* for its American release), while songs like "Games Without Frontiers" and "Biko" announced his political convictions. This two-sided involvement in Third World affairs led to his cofounding of the WOMAD (World of Music, Arts, and Dance) Festival in 1982 and Real World Records in 1989. His 1986 album, *So*, was a more personal statement; strengthened by the contributions of Laurie Anderson, Kate Bush, and Senegalese pop star Youssou N'Dour, it brought Gabriel critical acclaim and was a multimillion-seller. His next album, *Passion: Music for "The Last Temptation of Christ"* (1989), featured a number of African and Middle Eastern artists (several of whom released albums with Real World) and won a Grammy Award. Gabriel's work also has been marked by an imaginative visual component. His performances with Genesis were noted for their supreme theatricality, and his music videos set new standards for the nascent medium; the video for "Sledgehammer" was voted best video of all time by *Rolling Stone* magazine in 1993, and two of

Gabriel's other videos, based on his 1992 album *Us*, won Grammy Awards in 1992 and 1993.

In 1994 Gabriel released *Xplora 1*, one of the first multimedia CD-ROMs created by a mainstream artist, and six years later he composed *OVO*, a multimedia presentation for London's Millennium Dome. In 2000 Gabriel showed that he remained ahead of the technological curve when he founded On Demand Distribution, an Internet service that became one of Europe's leading online music providers; he later sold the company for $38 million. New material emerged in a slow trickle from the Real World studios as Gabriel contributed single songs to film sound tracks or appeared as a guest performer on other artists' albums. In 2002 he composed *Long Walk Home*, the score to the film *Rabbit-Proof Fence*, and he followed later that year with *Up*, his first full-length studio release in 10 years. The former recalled his work on *Passion*, while the latter was a dark meditation on loss and longing. In 2008 Gabriel received the Ambassador of Conscience award from Amnesty International for the decades of support he had given that organization. That year also saw the realization of Big Blue Ball, a world music project that had been 17 years in the making, and the resulting album featured performances by Gabriel,

Sinead O'Connor, Joseph Arthur, and a host of international artists. Gabriel once again distinguished himself for his sound track work with Pixar Animation's *WALL-E* (2008). Collaborating with composer Thomas Newman, Gabriel crafted "Down to Earth," an upbeat track that won the Grammy Award for best song written for a motion picture in 2009. He was honoured again later that year when the Royal Swedish Academy of Music conveyed upon him the Polar Music Prize for lifetime achievement, stating that Gabriel had "redefined the very concept" of popular music.

EMERSON, LAKE AND PALMER

Emerson, Lake and Palmer was formed by three veterans of the British art rock scene: keyboardist Keith Emerson (born November 1, 1944, Todmorden, Lancashire, England), who had formerly led the Nice; Greg Lake (born November 10, 1948, Bournemouth, Dorset), who had been bassist and lead singer for King Crimson; and drummer Carl Palmer (born March 20, 1950, Birmingham). ELP made synthesizer keyboards rather than guitars the centrepiece of its sound and developed an eclectic and innovative style blending classical music, jazz, blues, electronic music (then still a novelty), and Tin

KRAFTWERK AND KRAUTROCK

Ralf Hütter (born August 20, 1946, Krefeld, Germany) and Florian Schneider (born April 7, 1947, Düsseldorf), the duo who formed the core of the German experimental group Kraftwerk, are widely regarded as the godfathers of electronic pop music. Hütter and Schneider met while studying classical music at Düsseldorf Conservatory in the late 1960s, and their early work with a five-piece band called the Organisation showed the influence of the German keyboard band Tangerine Dream. Adopting the name Kraftwerk ("power plant"), Hütter, Schneider, and a series of collaborators forged an austere sound and image as part of a small but highly influential cult of German bands that experimented with electronic instruments long before it was fashionable. The movement, dubbed "Krautrock" by British journalists, also included innovative bands such as Can, Faust, and Neu!, but Kraftwerk became the best known.

The foundation for Kraftwerk's music was the sounds of everyday life, a concept first fully realized on the 22-minute title track of the *Autobahn* album (1974). Repetitious, monotonous, lulling and entrancing, "Autobahn" became an unlikely hit in Europe and the United States (where it was played on commercial radio stations in severely edited form). Subsequent albums explored such subjects as radios and trains with a combination of childlike wonder and cold objectivity. The band revolutionized ideas about how a "rock" tour should look and sound by appearing in the United States in the guise of identical mannequins who performed their music exclusively on keyboards. The title of their album *The Man-Machine* (1978) epitomized the concept. Although the band rarely recorded in the 1980s and '90s and virtually stopped touring, its music was a huge influence on New York hip-hop, particularly Afrika Bambaataa's hit "Planet Rock"; Detroit techno dance music; Neil Young's album *Trans* (1983); the collaborations between David

Bowie and Brian Eno; and the synth-pop of Depeche Mode, Soft Cell, and countless others.

The group resumed a limited touring schedule in the early 2000s and released *Tour de France Soundtracks* (2003), their first album of original material in some 17 years. Schneider left Kraftwerk in early 2009, on the eve of the band's scheduled South American tour with Radiohead.

Pan Alley. Their numerous albums (including six live albums, drawn from concerts featuring spectacular lighting and special effects) featured lengthy, elaborate original compositions such as "Tarkus" and "Karn Evil Number 9"; imaginative covers of serious classical compositions, most notably Modest Mussorgsky's "Pictures at an Exhibition," Aaron Copland's "Fanfare for the Common Man," and the hilarious blues version of "Nutcracker Suite"; and occasional ballads or hymns, all played with great technical virtuosity.

ELP disbanded in 1979 but reunited in the early 1990s. However, as was the case with many re-formed 1970s rock groups, the trio's new recordings neither recaptured the passion of their earlier work nor struck out in new musical directions.

ROXY MUSIC

Roxy Music fused glam rock campiness with sophisticated, often experimental musicianship, arch humour, and world-weary romanticism to become one of the most influential art rock bands of the 1970s. The principal members were Bryan Ferry (born September 26, 1945, Washington, Durham, England), Brian Eno (born May 15, 1948, Woodbridge, Suffolk), Andy Mackay (born July 23, 1946, England), Phil Manzanera (born Philip Targett-Adams, January 31, 1951, London), Paul Thompson (born May 13, 1951, Jarrow, Northumberland), and Eddie Jobson (born April 28, 1955, Billingham, Durham).

Formed in 1971, Roxy Music was largely the brainchild of vocalist-songwriter Ferry, who had studied

Roxy Music at the Royal College of Art in London, 1972. (From left to right): Andy Mackay, Paul Thompson, Brian Ferry, Brian Eno, Phil Manzanera, and Rik Kenton. Brian Cooke/Redferns/Getty Images

with Richard Hamilton, a key figure in British pop art. A shifting early lineup stabilized around Ferry, saxophonist Mackay, keyboardist Eno, guitarist Manzanera, and drummer Thompson. The band's eponymous debut album, the nonalbum single "Virginia Plain" (both 1972), and the follow-up album *For Your Pleasure* (1973) were hits in Britain, as Roxy Music's fully textured sound and lush instrumentation set it apart from mainstream rock. When Eno departed to pursue his remarkable career as a solo performer and producer, Ferry became even more the band's focal point, cultivating a suave persona he projected in a solo career that paralleled his work with Roxy Music. Following British success with *Stranded* (1973) and *Country Life* (1974), the band broke through in the United States with *Siren* and its hit single "Love Is the Drug" in 1975. Splitting, re-forming, and splitting again, Roxy Music had commercial success with its albums in the late 1970s and early 1980s but failed to regain its earlier critical acclaim.

KATE BUSH

British singer and songwriter Kate Bush (July 30, 1958, Bexleyheath, Kent, England) created imaginative and inventive art rock—marked by theatrical sensuality, textural experimentation, and allusive subject matter—that made her one of the most successful and influential female musicians in Britain in the late 20th century. Bush was the youngest child of an artistic family. Her father, who was a doctor, played the piano, and her mother, a nurse, had competed as a folk dancer in her native Ireland. As a child, Bush studied violin and piano and frequently joined her parents and older brothers in performing traditional English and Irish tunes at home. By age 14 she had begun writing her own musical compositions, and two years later a family friend introduced her to Pink Floyd guitarist David Gilmour, who helped her win a contract with EMI Records. For the next several years Bush took vocal lessons and studied dance and mime in London while preparing material for her first recording.

In 1978 Bush released her first single, "Wuthering Heights," inspired by characters from Emily Brontë's novel of the same name. Although its high keening vocals, florid instrumentation, and literary affectations were out of step with the punk rock that was then fashionable in Britain, the song became an unexpected number one hit there and elsewhere and boosted sales of Bush's debut album, *The Kick Inside* (1978), which featured similarly ornate and romantic fare. She quickly capitalized on her early success with another album, *Lionheart* (1978), after which she embarked on a European tour. The performance schedule exhausted Bush, however, and she subsequently focused primarily on recording.

Bush returned in 1980 with *Never for Ever*, which produced such hits as "Babooshka" and was praised for its musical sophistication. On *The Dreaming* (1982), the first album she produced entirely on her own, she employed new synthesizer technology to create densely layered arrangements for songs that explored such subjects as the life of Harry Houdini and the plight of Australian Aborigines. The album sold only modestly, however. Bush then reached a critical and commercial apex with the lush *Hounds of Love* (1985). Its moody otherworldly single "Running Up That Hill" even provided a breakthrough for Bush in the United States, although her following there ultimately remained limited. The greatest-hits collection

The Whole Story (1986) and the single "Don't Give Up" (1986), a duet with Peter Gabriel, further increased her popularity.

With *The Sensual World* (1989) and *The Red Shoes* (1993), Bush continued to draw out bold emotions and alluring pop melodies from songs that were elaborately constructed and sometimes inspired by erudite sources. (The title track of the former record, for instance, is a reimagining of Molly Bloom's soliloquy in James Joyce's *Ulysses*, and the latter record is named after the Michael Powell-Emeric Pressburger ballet film.) She also collaborated with a number of guest musicians, including Gilmour, Prince, Eric Clapton, and a Bulgarian vocal trio.

After directing and starring in *The Line, the Cross & the Curve* (1993), a short film featuring songs from *The Red Shoes*, Bush took a 12-year hiatus from music. She resurfaced with the atmospheric *Aerial* (2005), a double record imbued with themes of domesticity and the natural world that earned her some of the most favourable reviews of her career. Bush later released *Director's Cut* (2011)—for which she rerecorded songs from *The Sensual World* and *The Red Shoes*—and *50 Words for Snow* (2011), a contemplative piano-focused set of new material.

CHAPTER 7

Fierce Fusion: Jazz-Rock

Jazz-rock is just one of a long line of fusion styles that have evolved alongside jazz. In it, modern jazz improvisation is accompanied by the bass lines, drumming styles, and instrumentation of rock music, with a strong emphasis on electronic instruments and dance rhythms. Since the recordings of 1920s bands, notably Paul Whiteman's, there have been fusions of jazz and popular music, usually presenting jazz's "hot," swinging, staccato qualities in contrast to "sweet," legato popular music characteristics. With the slow development of a unique identity in rock music, occasional jazz tunes also began including rock rhythms in the 1960s. Beginning in 1969, trumpeter Miles Davis and associates such as drummer Tony Williams, guitarist John McLaughlin, saxophonist Wayne Shorter, and electric keyboardists Joe Zawinul, Herbie Hancock, Larry Young, and Chick Corea broke through to distinctive fusion musics. Jazz and rock elements contrasted, even competed with or enhanced each other, in bands of the early 1970s such as Davis's increasingly African-music-oriented groups, Williams's Lifetime quartet, McLaughlin's fiercely loud and energetic Mahavishnu Orchestra, the light, danceable music of Hancock's Headhunters and Corea's Return to Forever, and the mobile sound and rhythmic colours of Zawinul's and Shorter's Weather Report.

The most important work by these musicians dates from the early 1970s; since then, most have alternated between

JOHN MCLAUGHLIN

English guitar virtuoso and bandleader John McLaughlin (born January 4, 1942, Yorkshire, England) became one of the most popular and influential jazz-rock musicians thanks to his extremely loud, highly energetic, eclectic soloing. McLaughlin began his career playing blues and rock in London in the early 1960s and went on to play free jazz with important British figures before moving to the United States in 1969. There he contributed rock- and blues-derived guitar passages to Miles Davis's early fusion albums *In a Silent Way* and *Bitches Brew* (both 1969) and played in Tony Williams's seminal jazz-rock trio Lifetime.

In 1970 he became a disciple of spiritual guru Sri Chinmoy; he acquired the name Mahavishnu and formed the Mahavishnu Orchestra in 1971. The Orchestra was initially a quintet noted for radically high volume levels, complex textures, and fast modal playing, especially by McLaughlin, in long passages of 16th-note scales and arpeggios, on a guitar with two parallel necks, one with 6 strings, the other with 12. They played concerts in rock, rather than jazz, venues and were among the handful of stars of jazz-rock fusion music; they recorded popular albums such as *The Inner Mounting Flame* (1971). The involvement of electric violinist Jean-Luc Ponty in 1974–75 enhanced the Orchestra's popularity.

In the mid-1970s McLaughlin left Chinmoy, abandoned the name Mahavishnu, and began playing acoustic guitar in his trio Shakti, with Indian violinist L. Shankar and tabla player Zakir Hussain. His new guitar had two fretboards, one with raised strings crossing the other. McLaughlin's improvising—with phrases from blues, rock (especially Jimi Hendrix), flamenco, jazz, and Indian music—fit readily into a variety of fusion music. He went on to play duets and trios with fellow guitar virtuosos Al DiMeola, Paco De Lucia, and Larry Coryell, to team with Indian percussionist Trilok

Gurtu, to play electric guitar in a revived Mahavishnu Orchestra in the mid-1980s, and to perform guitar concerti by Mike Gibbs (1985) and by himself (1990) with symphony orchestras.

periods of playing fusion music and playing mainstream jazz. The jazz-rock idiom gained one of the largest jazz audiences since the swing era ended in the mid-1940s. The style was also known as crossover because sales of the music crossed over from the jazz market to the popular music market. Guitarist Larry Coryell was popular in the early years of jazz-rock fusion; guitarist Pat Metheny, with his pastoral harmonies, has been a star since the late 1970s.

Meanwhile, two other kinds of fusion music were also current. The most popular jazz-rock strain grew out of hard bop: the funky 1960s jazz of musicians such as flutist Herbie Mann, alto saxophonist Hank Crawford, and the Crusaders. Their repertoires included original and standard rock tunes over which they improvised jazz. In the 1970s the CTI record label in particular offered this kind of fusion music on albums by Stanley Turrentine, Freddie Hubbard, and others. Less commercially success-

ful was the free jazz fusion of Ornette Coleman's Prime Time group (beginning in 1973) and his associates, guitarist James Blood Ulmer, bassist Jamaaladeen Tacuma, and drummer Ronald Shannon Jackson, though all led valuable bands in the 1980s. One problem was that the recurring rhythmic-harmonic patterns of rock tended to dominate, reducing jazz improvisation to mere decoration.

A later development of jazz-rock—contemporary jazz, or light jazz—appeared on the radio in the 1980s and '90s. The most popular kind of fusion music, it abandoned jazz elements almost completely and frequently used a minimum of improvisation. Stars of contemporary jazz included saxophonist Kenny G and the group Spyro Gyra. Two jazz-rock fashions of the 1990s were acid jazz, a catchall term for bop and free jazz improvising over funk and hip-hop rhythms; and neo-swing, which revived the shuffle rhythms of small 1940s swing ("jump") bands.

CHICAGO

The America rock band Chicago, initially a jazz-rock unit, thrived as it moved toward a lighter, ballad-oriented rock style. The group ranked among the most popular American recording artists of all time, with sales of more than 100 million records. Its original members were Terry Kath (born January 31, 1946, Chicago, Illinois, U.S.—died January 23, 1978, Los Angeles, California), Peter Cetera (born September 13, 1944, Chicago), Robert Lamm (born October 13, 1944, New York, New York), Walter Parazaider (born March 14, 1945, Chicago), Danny Seraphine (born August 28, 1948, Chicago), James Pankow (born August 20, 1947, Chicago), and Lee Loughnane (born October 21, 1946, Chicago).

Called the Chicago Transit Authority before shortening its name to that of the city in which it was founded in 1967, Chicago distinguished itself from other rock bands of the late 1960s by the inclusion of horns in its lineup. The band's early albums, including its debut, *Chicago Transit Authority* (1969)—made after the group relocated to Los Angeles— were resonant with soul-inflected jazz influences. By the early 1970s principal songwriters Cetera, Lamm, and Pankow and producer-manager James Guercio began to steer Chicago

in a more pop-oriented direction. A series of hit albums over the next decade featured Top Ten songs such as "Does Anybody Really Know What Time It Is?" and "Saturday in the Park." In the late 1970s, following the death of guitarist Kath, Chicago slumped; the band topped the charts again in the '80s with hits such as "Hard to Say I'm Sorry," though it failed to maintain that momentum in the '90s. Vocalist Cetera also experienced some success as a soloist.

EARTH, WIND AND FIRE

Earth, Wind and Fire became one of the best-selling and most influential black groups of the 1970s with their unique blend of pop, soul, and jazz-fusion. The principal members were Maurice White (born December 19, 1941, Chicago, Illinois, U.S.), Philip Bailey (born May 8, 1951, Denver, Colorado), Verdine White (born July 25, 1951, Chicago), Fred White (born January 13, 1956, Chicago), Al McKay (born February 2, 1948, New Orleans, Louisiana), Johnny Graham (born August 3, 1951, Kentucky), Ralph Johnson (born July 4, 1951, Los Angeles, California), Larry Dunn (born Lawrence Dunhill, June 19, 1953, Denver), and Andrew Woolfolk (born October 11, 1950, Texas).

Earth, Wind and Fire was the brainchild of Maurice White, a

Earth, Wind and Fire. GAB Archive/Redferns/Getty Images

drummer raised in Memphis, Tennessee, who returned to his birthplace, Chicago, and became a veteran session player at Chess Records and a member of the Ramsey Lewis Trio. He drew upon a wide variety of influences, including his Memphis church-singing roots, his broad recording duties at Chess, and his stint at the Chicago Conservatory of Music, to create a truly original fusion of styles with his innovative group.

Capitalizing on his reputation as a session player, White was able to establish the group in Los Angeles as a jazz-fusion act in 1970, recording two albums for Warner Brothers. While on tour in Denver in 1971, the group shared a bill with a local act that featured vocalist Bailey, keyboardist Dunn, and saxophonist Woolfolk, all of whom soon after joined a reconstituted Earth, Wind and Fire that developed a broader musical range encompassing funk, soul, and pop. The group switched labels, and their second album for Columbia, *Head to the Sky* (1973), sold a half-million copies, setting the stage for the huge success that followed. *That's the Way of the World* (1975) lifted Earth, Wind and Fire to superstardom, yielding the hit singles "Shining Star" and "Reasons." Their phenomenal string of 11 consecutive gold albums (sales of 500,000 copies), 8 of which also attained platinum status (sales of 1,000,000 copies), included *Gratitude* (1975), *Spirit* (1976), *All 'n' All* (1977), *The Best of Earth, Wind and Fire, Vol. 1* (1978), and *Raise!* (1981).

Part of the band's appeal was its remarkable versatility, as it delivered soulful ballads, spiritual anthems, Afro-Caribbean jazz, driving funk and rock, and upbeat disco dance hits. Earth, Wind and Fire's songs offered uplifting, poetic lyrics with romantic and playful themes of universal brotherhood, spiritual enlightenment, and sentimental romance. The group was known for spectacular concerts that featured gigantic stage props, elaborate costumes, grand illusions, and frenetic musical energy. The multitalented White and falsetto vocalist Bailey led an ensemble that often reached 15 players onstage. White's affection for Egyptology and use of African instruments such as the kalimba (thumb piano) further embellished the group's unique image.

Earth, Wind and Fire spawned a number of imitations during the 1970s, as groups adopted mystical three-part names, imitated their elaborate dress and choreography, or attempted to reproduce the poetry, lush orchestration, and mysticism of Earth, Wind and Fire's albums and concerts. Despite a brief hiatus during the 1980s, White's group remained an international stage attraction into the 21st century. In 2000 Earth, Wind and Fire was inducted into the Rock and Roll Hall of Fame.

HERBIE HANCOCK

From child prodigy to influential jazz-rock performer, Herbie Hancock (born April 12, 1940, Chicago, Illinois, U.S.) spent much of his life in the spotlight. He achieved success as an incisive, harmonically provocative jazz pianist and then went on to gain wide popularity as a leader of electric jazz-rock groups.

At age 11 Hancock played the first movement of a Mozart concerto with the Chicago Symphony Orchestra, and he formed his first band while a high school student. After graduating from Grinnell College in Iowa in 1960, he joined trumpeter Donald Byrd's group and moved (1961) to New York City. There his clever accompaniments and straightforward soloing with bebop groups led to tours with Miles Davis (1963–68). The Davis quintet's mid-1960s investigations of rhythmic and harmonic freedom stimulated some of Hancock's most daring, arrhythmic, harmonically colourful concepts. Meanwhile, he recorded extensively in bebop and modal jazz settings, ranging from funky rhythms to ethereal modal harmonies; as a sideman on Blue Note albums and a leader of combos, he played original themes including "Maiden Voyage," "Cantaloupe Island," and "Watermelon Man," which became a popular hit in Mongo Santamaria's recording.

In the 1970s, after playing in Davis's first jazz-rock experiments, Hancock began leading fusion bands and playing electronic keyboards, from electric pianos to synthesizers. Compelling sound colours and rhythms, in layers of synthesizer lines, characterized jazz-funk hits such as "Chameleon," from his best-selling *Headhunters* album (1973). Later dance hits by Hancock included "You Bet Your Love" (1979) and "Rockit" (1983). Meanwhile, he also composed music, both jazz-rock and straight-ahead jazz, for broadcast commercials, television, and films such as *Blow-Up* (1966), *Death Wish* (1974), and *Round Midnight* (1986); for the last one he won an Academy Award. Since the mid-1970s he has played acoustic piano in jazz projects, played duets with Chick Corea, and performed in combos with former Davis associates and trumpeters such as Freddie Hubbard and Wynton Marsalis.

Interest in Hancock's Blue Note catalog was renewed in 1993 when a sample of "Cantaloupe Island" appeared in Us3's international hit "Cantaloop (Flip Fantasia)." In 1998 he reunited his Headhunters group, and the turn of the millennium saw the launch of a number of collaborative projects. On *Future 2 Future* (2001), Hancock teamed with jazz legend Wayne Shorter and some of the biggest names in techno music to produce a beat-filled fusion of jazz and electronic music. His next project, *Possibilities* (2005), was a venture into pop music with such guest performers as Stevie Wonder, Paul Simon, and Santana. Hancock added to his already extensive Grammy collection with a pair of awards—including album of the year—for his Joni Mitchell tribute *River: The Joni Letters* (2007). In 2011 he won yet another Grammy with *The Imagine Project* (2010), a covers album that featured guest performances by Pink, Jeff Beck, and John Legend, among others.

CHAPTER 8

Tear the Roof Off: Funk

Funk, a rhythm-driven musical genre popular in the 1970s and early 1980s, linked soul to later African-American musical styles. Like many words emanating from the African-American oral tradition, *funk* defies literal definition, for its usage varies with circumstance. As a slang term, *funky* is used to describe one's odour, unpredictable style, or attitude. Musically, *funk* refers to a style of aggressive urban dance music driven by hard syncopated bass lines and drumbeats and accented by any number of instruments involved in rhythmic counterplay, all working toward a "groove."

The development of the terms *funk* and *funky* evolved through the vernacular of jazz improvisation in the 1950s as a reference to a performance style that was a passionate reflection of the black experience. The words signified an association with harsh realities—unpleasant smells, tales of tragedy and violence, erratic relationships, crushed aspirations, racial strife—and flights of imagination that expressed unsettling yet undeniable truths about life.

James Brown's band established the "funk beat" and modern street funk in the late 1960s. The funk beat was a heavily syncopated, aggressive rhythm that put a strong pulse on the first note of the musical measure ("on the one"), whereas traditional rhythm and blues emphasized the backbeat (the second and fourth beats of the measure). Brown and others, such as Sly and the Family Stone, began to use funk rhythms

REPRESENTATIVE WORKS

- ▶ James Brown, *It's a Mother* (1969)
- ▶ Sly and the Family Stone, *Stand!* (1969)
- ▶ Sly and the Family Stone, *There's a Riot Goin' On* (1971)
- ▶ The Temptations, *All Directions* (1972)
- ▶ Herbie Hancock, *Headhunters* (1973)
- ▶ Kool and the Gang, *Wild and Peaceful* (1973)
- ▶ Stevie Wonder, *Innervisions* (1973)
- ▶ James Brown, *The Payback* (1974)
- ▶ The Ohio Players, *Fire* (1974)
- ▶ Funkadelic, *Let's Take It to the Stage* (1975)
- ▶ The Isley Brothers, *The Heat Is On* (1975)
- ▶ Parliament, *Mothership Connection* (1976)
- ▶ Bootsy's Rubber Band, *Ahh…The Name Is Bootsy, Baby!* (1977)
- ▶ Prince, *Dirty Mind* (1980)
- ▶ Rick James, *Street Songs* (1981)

as their musical foundation while their lyrics took on themes of urgent social commentary.

In the early 1970s funk became the musical standard for bands such as the Ohio Players and Kool and the Gang and soul singers such as the Temptations and Stevie Wonder, its driving beat accompanied by lush, melodic arrangements and potent, thoughtful lyrics. Parliament-Funkadelic and other bands sang the praises of funk as a means of self-development and personal liberation, while established jazz artists such as Miles Davis and Herbie Hancock adapted and explored the funk groove. The disco music of the late 1970s evolved from the rhythmic and social foundation of funk.

In the 1980s the sexually expressive aspects of funk were popularized through the works of Rick James and

DISCO, PUNK, NEW WAVE, HEAVY METAL, AND MORE

Prince, while the funk beat became the primary rhythm in black popular music. The influence of funk spread to other styles in the 1980s—mixing with the gritty realism of hard rock and punk and the experimentation of much of the electronic music of the time. With the rise of rap music in the 1980s and its "sampling" of 1970s funk songs, funk grew in stature and significance in hip-hop culture. It became associated with ancient mysteries in the black tradition, providing hip-hop with a historical link to artists and cultural movements of the past. As part of hip-hop's influence on popular culture, funk provided the rhythmic basis for most American dance music of the 1990s.

PARLIAMENT-FUNKADELIC

Parliament-Funkadelic (also known as P-Funk) was a massive group of performers that greatly influenced black music in the 1970s. The original members were George Clinton (born July 22, 1941, Kannapolis, North Carolina, U.S.), Raymond Davis (born March 29, 1940, Sumter, South Carolina), Calvin Simon (born May 22, 1942, Beckley, West Virginia), Fuzzy Haskins (born Clarence Haskins, June 8, 1941, Elkhorn, West Virginia), and Grady Thomas (born January 5, 1941, Newark, New Jersey). Later members included Michael Hampton

(born November 15, 1956, Cleveland, Ohio), Bernie Worrell (born April 19, 1944, Long Beach, New Jersey), Billy Bass Nelson (born January 28, 1951, Plainfield, New Jersey), Eddie Hazel (born April 10, 1950, Brooklyn, New York—died December 23, 1992), Tiki Fulwood (born Ramon Fulwood, May 23, 1944, Philadelphia, Pennsylvania—died October 29, 1979), Bootsy Collins (born William Collins, October 26, 1951, Cincinnati, Ohio), Fred Wesley (born July 4, 1943, Columbus, Georgia), Maceo Parker (born February 14, 1943, Kinston, North Carolina), Jerome Brailey (born August 20, 1950, Richmond, Virginia), Garry Shider (born July 24, 1953, Plainfield—died June 16, 2010, Upper Marlboro, Maryland), Glen Goins (born January 2, 1954, Plainfield—died July 29, 1978, Plainfield), and Gary "Mudbone" Cooper (born November 24, 1953, Washington, D.C.). The group scored 13 Top Ten rhythm-and-blues and pop hits from 1967 to 1983 (including six number one rhythm-and-blues hits) under a variety of names, including the Parliaments, Funkadelic, Bootsy's Rubber Band, and the Brides of Funkenstein, as well as under the name of its founding father, Clinton.

The band combined the hard rock of Jimi Hendrix, the funky rhythms of James Brown, and the showstopping style of Sly and the Family Stone to fashion an outrageous tribal

George Clinton. GAB Archive/Redferns/Getty Images

funk experience. P-Funk emphasized the aesthetics of funk as a means of self-fulfillment; to "give up the funk" meant to achieve transcendence.

Organized and produced by Clinton, the original Parliaments began as a doo-wop quintet based in Plainfield. The group's first charting single, "(I Wanna) Testify," in 1967 led to their first tour, but legal problems that arose with the demise of their record company resulted in the loss of the group's name. Performing throughout the northeastern United States and recording in Detroit, the group began to emphasize its backing band, Funkadelic. Led by bassist Nelson, guitarist Hazel, drummer Fulwood, and classically trained keyboardist Worrell, Funkadelic incorporated the influence of amplified, psychedelic rock into its distinctive sound.

By 1970 Clinton was producing albums for both the renamed Parliament and Funkadelic—essentially the same entity recording for different labels. In the process he recruited key new performers: Collins on bass, Wesley on trombone, and Parker on saxophone (all from James Brown's band the JBs), along with drummer Brailey, vocalist Cooper, lead guitarist Hampton, and vocalist-guitarists Shider and Goins. Success came in 1976 with the release of Parliament's album *Mothership Connection* and the single "Give Up the Funk (Tear the Roof Off the Sucker)," which earned a gold record. Other hit singles followed, including "Flash Light" (1977) by Parliament, "One Nation Under a Groove" (1978) by Funkadelic, and "Atomic Dog" (1982) by Clinton.

P-Funk reached its peak in the late 1970s, sporting a massive stage act (with more than 40 performers) that showcased Clinton's visionary album concepts, Collins's spectacular bass effects, and Worrell's synthesizer innovations. However, by the early 1980s the large overhead and multifaceted legal identity of the group led to a collapse of the enterprise.

P-Funk defined the dance music of its time and influenced a range of styles from hard rock to house music. The P-Funk catalog is among the most sampled by rap music producers. Parliament-Funkadelic was inducted into the Rock and Roll Hall of Fame in 1997.

SLY AND THE FAMILY STONE

As a performer, songwriter, and social satirist, bandleader Sly Stone stands among the giants of rock. His group, Sly and the Family Stone, became widely popular in the late 1960s with a string of anthemlike pop singles, stirring socially relevant albums, and memorable live performances. The members were Sly Stone (born

Sly and the Family Stone (Sly centre, front). GAB Archive/Redferns/Getty Images

Sylvester Stewart, March 15, 1943, Denton, Texas, U.S.), Freddie Stone (born Freddie Stewart, June 5, 1946, Vallejo, California), Rosie Stone (born Rose Stewart, March 21, 1945, Vallejo), Cynthia Robinson (born January 12, 1946, Sacramento, California), Jerry Martini (born

October 1, 1943, Boulder, Colorado), Larry Graham (born August 14, 1946, Beaumont, Texas), and Greg Errico (born September 1, 1946, San Francisco, California).

The band's style combined a range of influences (including rock, funk, jazz, psychedelic rock, standards, and nursery rhymes) with the spirit of a Pentecostal church revival and produced some of the era's most energizing and compelling songs. "Everyday People" and "Thank You (Falletinme Be Mice Elf Agin)"—both of which reached number one on the pop and rhythm-and-blues charts—as well as "Hot Fun in the Summertime" and "I Want to Take You Higher" all became classics of popular music.

Based in the San Francisco Bay area, the unpredictable and innovative Family Stone was one of the first acts to feature blacks and whites and men and women all performing and singing simultaneously. The loud colours and individualistic dress of the players reflected and influenced the counterculture of the 1960s; musically, Sly and the Family Stone laid the foundation for much of the street funk, soul, and disco music of the 1970s.

Raised in a churchgoing family in Vallejo, the charismatic Sylvester Stewart learned to perform at an early age. He established himself in the Bay Area music industry by working at

Autumn Records producing national pop hits for Bobby Freeman ("C'mon and Swim") in 1964 and the Beau Brummels ("Laugh Laugh") in 1965. He was among the area's top soul music deejays when, adopting his radio name, Sly Stone, he founded the Family Stone in 1967. The group comprised his brother Freddie (guitar) and younger sister Rose (piano), trumpeter Robinson, saxophonist Martini, drummer Errico, and bassist Graham.

Signed to Epic in 1967, the band scored its first charting single with the raucous "Dance to the Music" in 1968. That smash hit led to a national tour and television appearances. In 1969 Sly captured the moods of the nation with the *Stand!* album, which showcased an unprecedented combination of joy, optimism, and rage and established Sly Stone as a lightning rod for social commentary. The band's engaging performance at the Woodstock festival in August 1969 was a high point of the legendary concert and the zenith of Sly's career.

The 1970 release of *Greatest Hits* provided the band's second gold album, but Sly was faltering—delving into drugs and missing concerts. He returned with the single "Family Affair" (number one on the pop and rhythm-and-blues charts) and album *There's a Riot Goin' On* in 1971, which surprised critics with its brooding, introspective tone.

Graham, who had pioneered the funk bass style of "thumping" and "plucking," left the band in 1972 to form his own successful group, Graham Central Station, and later to pursue a solo singing career. With a new bassist, Rusty Allen, Sly produced his final gold album, *Fresh*, in 1973, but thereafter recordings and sales dropped sharply.

Interest in Sly Stone resurfaced with the "sampling" of many of his songs (and Graham's bass lines) by hip-hop producers in the 1990s. Sly and the Family Stone were inducted into the Rock and Roll Hall of Fame in 1993.

THE OHIO PLAYERS

Hailing from Dayton, Ohio, funk pioneers the Ohio Players put an indelible stamp on black music from the urban Midwest in the 1970s. The principal members were Clarence ("Satch") Satchell (born April 14, 1940, Cleveland, Ohio, U.S.—died December 31, 1995, Dayton, Ohio), Leroy ("Sugarfoot") Bonner (born March 14, 1943, Hamilton, Ohio), Greg Webster (born January 4, 1938, Hamilton), James ("Diamond") Williams (born March 27, 1950, Dayton), Marshall Jones (born January 1, 1941, Dayton), Ralph ("Pee Wee") Middlebrook (born August 20, 1939, La Grange, Georgia—died October 13, 1996), Marvin ("Merv") Pierce (born July 13, 1951, Dayton), Walter ("Junie") Morrison, and Billy Beck.

Formed in 1959 as the Ohio Untouchables by singer-guitarist Robert Ward (born October 15, 1938, Luthersville, Georgia—died December 25, 2008, Dry Branch, Georgia)—who departed for a solo career some two years later—the group first recorded as a backing band for the vocal group the Falcons, featuring Wilson Pickett. Having changed their name, the Ohio Players signed to Westbound records in 1971 and fused rhythm and blues, rock, jazz, and eclectic album art to create a regional brand of heavy funk. The band's first national hit was the 1972 novelty song "Funky Worm," which featured the comic vocal characters of keyboardist Morrison (who promptly left the group and later joined Parliament-Funkadelic). With Beck as Morrison's replacement on keyboards, Williams replacing Webster on drums, and guitarist-vocalist Bonner playing an expanded role, the Ohio Players fashioned a sleek yet raucous sound that appealed to fans of soul, rock, and disco. A series of five gold albums followed from 1974 to 1976: *Skin Tight*, *Fire*, *Honey*, *Contradiction*, and *Gold*, including two chart-topping pop hits, "Fire" (1974) and "Love Rollercoaster" (1975).

The Ohio Players enjoyed a glittery high-fashion image and created

133

FUNKYTOWN: DAYTON IN THE 1970S

Dayton, Ohio, the small industrial city of approximately 200,000 people located 50 miles (80 kilometres) north of Cincinnati, produced a series of popular funk bands with a string of national hits during the 1970s. The Ohio Players, Lakeside, Slave (featuring Steve Arrington), Heatwave, Sun, Faze-O, and Zapp (featuring Roger) all claimed Dayton as their home. These bands were among the most prolific hit makers of the era, compiling more than 110 charting rhythm-and-blues singles between 1972 and 1988. Dayton funk bands all featured dance music with an emphasis on heavy bass, aggressive rhythms, complex horn arrangements, ensemble vocals, and showstopping choreography.

During the 1970s, industries such as the Chrysler plant, Harrison Radiator factory, and Wright-Patterson Air Force Base provided a stable income base for a population that was roughly 50 percent African-American. From this base came high-school bands that sought the stardom first achieved by the founders of Dayton funk, the Ohio Players. Their number one pop hits "Fire" and "Love Rollercoaster" set a standard for local bands to aspire to, and six different record labels had signed Dayton bands by 1978. Slave, which had strong ties to the Ohio Players, scored a national hit with "Slide" in 1977 and continued to make hits through 1983. Crosstown rival Lakeside moved to Los Angeles before striking it big with "It's All the Way Live" in 1978. Keith and Johnnie Wilder developed their band, Heatwave, while stationed in West Germany and returned to the United States with a global hit, "Boogie Nights," in 1977. Roger Troutman and his band, Zapp, lasted into the 1990s with a slick, high-tech sound and dynamic show.

a rock controversy with their risqué album covers. Yet their diverse, highly original music was steeped in Midwestern blues and influenced a number of contemporary funk and soul groups. They were the most successful of a series of Ohio-based soul and funk artists in the 1970s that included Lakeside, Slave, and Zapp, featuring Roger Troutman.

KOOL AND THE GANG

Kool and the Gang was one of the first successful self-contained black bands of the 1970s. The principal members were Khalis Bayyan (born Ronald Bell, November 1, 1951, Youngstown, Ohio, U.S.), Robert ("Kool") Bell (born October 8, 1950, Youngstown), Claydes ("Charles") Smith (born September 6, 1948, Jersey City, New Jersey—died June 20, 2006, Maplewood, New Jersey), George ("Funky") Brown (born January 5, 1949, Jersey City), Dennis ("DT") Thomas (born February 9, 1951, Jersey City), Robert ("Spike") Mickens (born 1951, Jersey City—died November 2, 2010, Far Rockaway, New York), Ricky West (born Richard Westfield, Jersey City—died 1985), and James ("JT") Taylor (born August 16, 1953, Laurens, South Carolina).

The group's first charting single, "Kool and the Gang," a horn-driven, highly rhythmic instrumental dance track, was followed by a steady string of similar singles through 1976. The band's commercial breakthrough came in 1973 with the album *Wild and Peaceful*, which featured the singles "Funky Stuff," "Jungle Boogie," and "Hollywood Swinging," all of which reached the rhythm-and-blues Top Ten. Kool and the Gang's sound was an innovative fusion of jazz, African rhythms, and street funk that established the band as an innovator in black music until the onset of the disco era. However, when the group's single "Open Sesame" was reissued on the sound track for the motion picture *Saturday Night Fever* in 1977, Kool and the Gang shifted emphasis toward pop and disco.

In 1979 the band added lead vocalist Taylor and producer Eumir Deodato, which led to a cleaner, pop-driven sound and to the crossover single "Ladies' Night." Numerous hits followed, including the number one hit "Celebration" in 1980, as well as the sentimental pop songs "Joanna" in 1983 and "Cherish" in 1985. Kool and the Gang charted more pop singles than any other act in the 1980s. The band continued to record and tour into the early 21st century.

CHAPTER 9

Sound and Spectacle: Glam Rock

G lam rock began in Britain in the early 1970s and celebrated the spectacle of the rock star and concert. Often dappled with glitter, male musicians took the stage in women's makeup and clothing, adopted theatrical personas, and mounted glamorous musical productions frequently characterized by space-age futurism.

Self-glorifying and decadent, glam rock positioned itself as a backlash against the rock mainstream of the late 1960s; on the periphery of society and rock culture, glam rockers were, as critic Robert Palmer put it, "rebelling against the rebellion." At glam's core musically was a heavy guitar sound shaped by hard-rock and pop styles, though the movement also had heavy metal, art rock, and punk incarnations. David Bowie, one of the movement's principal practitioners, set the standard for showmanship while producing *The Man Who Sold the World* (1970) and *The Rise and Fall of Ziggy Stardust and the Spiders from Mars* (1972). Other members of the British glitterati were Slade, Gary Glitter, and Marc Bolan's T. Rex, whose *Electric Warrior* (1971) and *The Slider* (1972) typified the trashy power-pop version of glam rock. Other performers associated with British glam included Elton John, Queen, Roxy Music, the Sweet, and, in the early

1980s, Culture Club. Lou Reed of the Velvet Underground launched his solo career and American glam with *Transformer* (1972), coproduced by Bowie. In the United States glam gained a harder edge with the proto-punk stylings of the New York Dolls and the glitzy hard rock of KISS and Alice Cooper. By the 1980s glam had devolved into the heavy metal excesses of such American groups as Bon Jovi, Mötley Crüe, and Poison. In the 1990s Marilyn Manson courted controversy with a brand of glam intended to shock conservative Americans.

DAVID BOWIE

To call David Bowie (born David Robert Jones, January 8, 1947, London, England) a transitional figure in rock history is less a judgment than a job description. Every niche he ever found was on a cusp, and he was at home nowhere else—certainly not in the unmoneyed London suburb where his childhood was as reserved as his adult life would be glamorous. Gifted as a musician, actor, writer, and artist (he attended art school from the age of 12), Bowie would ultimately find his place as a performer utilizing all these skills and making the most of his distinctive voice, shifting personae, and prescient sense of musical trends.

Nothing if not an eclectic musician in his own right, Bowie had similarly diverse tastes regarding the work of others, being an admirer of the showmanship of British actor and musician Anthony Newley as well as the romantic lyricism of Belgian musician Jacques Brel.

During the mod era of the 1960s he fronted various bands from whose shadow he—having renamed himself to avoid confusion with the singer of the Monkees—emerged as a solo singer-songwriter. "Space Oddity," the science-fiction single that marks the real beginning of his career, reached the Top Ten in Britain in 1969; the song's well-timed release coming just after the Apollo 11 Moon mission. Bowie's third album, *The Man Who Sold the World* (1970), displaying an unprecedented hybrid of folk, art rock, heavy metal, and Latin sounds, was his first album of note. It was not until *Hunky Dory* (1971) that Bowie became truly popular, the hit single "Changes" being the prime vector of that fame.

The singer's ever-changing appearance, too, created a record-selling buzz. At once light-hearted and portentous, Bowie's dramatic chameleon-like approach was tailor-made for the 1970s, his signature decade. Bowie created a series of inspired, daringly grandiose pastiches that insisted on utopia by

137

A colour-enhanced photograph of David Bowie, 1973. Justin de Villeneuve/
Hulton Archive/Getty Images

depicting its alternative as inferno, beginning with the emblematic rock-star martyr fantasy *The Rise and Fall of Ziggy Stardust and the Spiders from Mars* (1972). In the process he stayed so hard on the heels of the zeitgeist that the doom-saying of *Diamond Dogs* (1974) and the disco romanticism of *Young Americans* (1975) were released less than a year apart.

Bowie's public disclosure of his bisexuality, rather than derailing his growing popularity, boosted his enigmatic allure. Nor did his later recantation of such sexual proclivities negatively affect his career. Yet all this public display of personal matters took a private toll. By 1977 Bowie had decamped, ditching his idiosyncratic version of the mainstream for the avant-garde austerities of the minimalist album *Low*, a collaboration in Berlin with Brian Eno, the influential musician and producer who was a member of Roxy Music and is perhaps best known for his ambient albums. As music, *Low* and its sequels, *Heroes* (1977) and *Lodger* (1979), would prove to be Bowie's most influential and lasting, serving as a blueprint for a later generation of techno-rock. In the short run, the albums marked the end of his significant mass audience impact, though not his sales. In addition to Eno, Bowie also collaborated with guitarists Mick Ronson and Carlos Alomar as well as ace nouveau-funk producer Nile Rodgers for "Let's Dance" (1983).

In the 1980s, despite the impressive artistic resolve of *Scary Monsters* (1980) and the equally impressive commercial success of *Let's Dance* (1983), which produced three American Top 20 hits, Bowie's work seemed to have lost the musical, intellectual, and boundary-pushing edge of his previous efforts. In tandem with an acting career that, since his arresting debut in Nicolas Roeg's *The Man Who Fell to Earth* (1976), largely failed to jell, his vague later albums oscillated between would-be commercial moves for which he did not seem to have the heart (*Never Let Me Down* [1987]) and would-be artistic statements for which he had lost his shrewdness (*Outside* [1995]). Perhaps Bowie's greatest innovation in this era was the creation of Bowie Bonds, financial securities backed by the royalties generated by his pre-1990 body of work. The issuing of the bonds in 1997 earned Bowie $55 million, and the rights to his back catalog returned to him when the bonds' term expired in 2007. His 1970s work including, in addition to his own output, service as a producer on landmark albums from Mott the Hoople, Lou Reed, and Iggy and the Stooges remains a vital and compelling index to a time it did its part to shape. Bowie was inducted into the Rock and Roll Hall of Fame in 1996. Ten years later, he was awarded the Grammy Lifetime Achievement Award.

WEST BERLIN

Isolated by the Cold War and divided by the wall that shaped life in the city until its fall in 1989, Berlin turned in on itself for four decades, looking back to its louche but rich Weimar past and reveling in a cynical present of spies, government subsidies, and anarchic activism. Foreigners who saw their own alienation mirrored in the city's outsider status were deeply affected by or drawn to Berlin. Suffused with the atmosphere of Weimar Berlin, the musical *Cabaret* was a big hit in the 1970s, and Lou Reed recorded his concept album *Berlin* in 1973. The city's defining postwar musical moment came, however, when David Bowie and Iggy Pop brought their drug habits to West Berlin, recording a series of albums primarily at Hansa Studio (or Hansa by the Wall, as Bowie referred to it) beginning in 1977.

In West Berlin, Bowie and Pop were able to distance themselves from British and American presumptions about the content and style of popular music. Caught between addiction and clarity, they made music that echoed the city's world-weary self-regard, creating a thin, alienated sound given extra emptiness on Bowie's records by a third collaborator, Brian Eno. Although relatively unsuccessful at the time, these albums—including Bowie's *Low* (1977) and *Lodger* (1979) and Pop's *The Idiot* (1977)—have become increasingly influential. In particular, Bowie's "Heroes" and Pop's *Lust for Life* (both 1977) became alternative anthems, and in time new standards, and Eno's experimental approach to music making found a wide audience with his work with Talking Heads and later U2.

THE NEW YORK DOLLS

Utilizing a raw brand of glam rock, the New York Dolls revitalized the New York City underground music scene in the 1970s, foreshadowing punk rock by half a decade. The members were lead singer David

Johansen (born January 9, 1950, New York, New York, U.S.), lead guitarist Johnny Thunders (born John Genzale, July 15, 1952, New York—died April 23, 1991, New Orleans, Louisiana), drummer Billy Murcia (born 1951, New York—died November 6, 1972, London, England), guitarist Sylvain Sylvain (born Sylvain Sylvain Mizrahi, February 14, 1951, Cairo, Egypt), drummer Jerry Nolan (born May 7, 1946, New York—died January 14, 1992, New York), bassist Arthur Kane (born New York—died July 13, 2004, Los Angeles, California), and guitarist Rick Rivets (born New York).

Formed in 1971, the New York Dolls first gained notoriety in 1972 for their outrageous performances at the Mercer Arts Center and Max's Kansas City in Lower Manhattan, where they appeared in their signature attire—women's makeup and bizarre clothing. Their glam rock androgyny belied an unpolished

The New York Dolls. Michael Ochs Archives/Getty Images

musical style that combined British Invasion-influenced rhythm and blues with the guitar distortion and booming backbeat of proto-punk bands such as the MC5 and Iggy and the Stooges. The drug-related death of Murcia during the band's tour of England in 1972 further fueled their reputation. The following year they signed with Mercury Records and released *New York Dolls*, produced by Todd Rundgren. Their 1974 follow-up, the aptly named *Too Much Too Soon*, gave title to the band's dissolution as its members struggled with drug and alcohol addictions. Notwithstanding their lack of commercial success, the irreverent Dolls had a lasting influence on a generation of bands—most notably the Sex Pistols, whose founder, Malcolm McLaren, managed the Dolls briefly before their breakup in 1977.

Johansen remained active in the New York music scene, but he enjoyed his greatest commercial success when he reinvented himself as the pompadoured lounge lizard Buster Poindexter. As Poindexter, he crooned pop classics and sipped dry martinis, and his lighthearted tribute to the big band sound anticipated the swing revival of the late 1990s by a full decade. Johansen scored a crossover hit with the party anthem "Hot Hot Hot" in 1987. He also branched into acting, scoring a number of memorable film and television roles throughout the 1980s and '90s.

In 2004, Morrissey, former front man of the Smiths and onetime president of the New York Dolls fan club in the United Kingdom, arranged for the surviving members of the Dolls to reunite for a performance at a New York music festival. The set was well received by fans and critics, and the band was preparing for a full tour when Kane died of complications from leukemia. Kane's distinctly unglamorous post-Dolls life and the reunion are at the centre of the film documentary *New York Doll* (2005).

Johansen and Sylvain, with a collection of accomplished musicians filling in for their departed bandmates, entered the studio to produce *One Day It Will Please Us to Remember Even This* (2006), the first collection of new Dolls material to appear since 1974. The tour that followed demonstrated that this second incarnation of the Dolls had the same sort of the energy as the first, and the concert album *Live at the Fillmore East* (2008) captured a band that embraced its place in rock history without succumbing to the nostalgia that characterized so many high-profile reunions.

CHAPTER 10

Down to Earth: Pub Rock

Pub rock, a British back-to-basics musical movement of the early and mid-1970s, provided an alternative to progressive and glam rock. Although a relatively short-lived phenomenon, pub rock was notable both for returning rock to the small clubs of its early years and as a breeding ground for many of the punk and new-wave artists of the late 1970s.

Practiced in London pubs such as the Tally Ho and the Hope and Anchor and rooted in country and rhythm and blues, pub rock stood in sharp contrast to the baroque flourishes of art rock. Rejecting the flamboyance of glam, pub rockers performed in everyday clothes. While even the best-known pub groups—Brinsley Schwarz, Ducks Deluxe, Dr. Feelgood, Bees Make Honey, and Ace—never achieved widespread popularity, the pub rock scene gave rise to a number of critically acclaimed performers, songwriters, and producers (often in the same person). These included Joe Strummer of the Clash, Nick Lowe, Dave Edmunds, Squeeze (fronted by the deft songwriting team of Chris Difford and Glenn Tilbrook), Dire Straits, and Graham Parker—whose accomplished backing band, the Rumour, included Brinsley Schwarz's namesake guitarist and Martin Belmont, formerly of Ducks Deluxe. Like many onetime pub rockers, the movement's most illustrious alumnus, Elvis Costello, initially recorded on the Stiff label.

DIRE STRAITS

The supple, slightly blues-tinged guitar rock of Dire Straits was popular in the late 1970s and '80s. The original members were Mark Knopfler (born August 12, 1949, Glasgow, Scotland), David Knopfler (born December 27, 1952, Glasgow), John Illsley (born June 24, 1949, Leicester, Leicestershire, England), and Pick Withers (born April 4, 1948). Later members included Hal Lindes (born June 30, 1953, Monterey, California, U.S.) and Alan Clark (born March 5, 1952, Durham, England).

Formed in London in 1977, Dire Straits were led by Mark Knopfler, a onetime journalist and college teacher who polished his musicianship as part of the pub rock movement. Their eponymous debut album (1978), featuring the hit "Sultans of Swing," established the group's commercial

Dire Straits in Amsterdam, the Netherlands, 1978. (Clockwise from top left): *John Illsley, Pick Withers, Mark Knopfler, and David Knopfler.* Gijsbert Hanekroot/Redferns/Getty Images

STIFF RECORDS

Independent labels have given voice to music otherwise ignored or rebuffed by the major labels. Stiff was set up to record pub rock, yet it prospered because of punk, the style that displaced the pub rock movement. This is but one of several paradoxes associated with that label, which started in 1976 with a loan from pub rockers Dr. Feelgood to Jake Riviera, their manager, and Dave Robinson, the manager of ill-fated pub rockers Brinsley Schwartz. Started on a back street in Bayswater, London, Stiff issued the first punk record, by the Damned, but never signed another punk act. It presented itself as a brave new musical world yet had its first success with Elvis Costello, Ian Dury, and Jona Lewie, former pub rockers who reinvented themselves. Moreover, Stiff started Britain's do-it-yourself independent label boom but was never comfortable with the anarchic philosophies or brash recordings favoured by most of its successors, such as Beggar's Banquet's 4AD, Daniel Miller's Mute, and Miles Copeland's Step Forward (the last of which moved quickly from punk to the pop-oriented sound of the Police).

Although Stiff's early productions were mostly overseen by jack-of-all-trades Nick Lowe, its house style was formed not in the studio but in the marketing department, and Stiff's look was the creation of accomplished graphic designer Barney Bubbles. An inspired series of singles by Madness in the early 1980s (all accompanied by witty videos directed by Robinson) epitomized the label's unique flair. But when major labels, which had greater financial resources, realized that success was to be driven by marketing, it transpired that Stiff had provided the blueprint for its own demise in the late 1980s.

appeal on both sides of the Atlantic. *Communiqué* (1979), *Making Movies* (1980), often held to be their finest album, and *Love Over Gold* (1982) continued Dire Straits' run of commercially successful albums, the last spawning the minor hit "Industrial Disease." They became superstars with the multimillion-selling *Brothers in Arms* (1985), which produced several hit singles—including the chart-topping "Money for Nothing," a pointed send-up of rock in the age of music videos. The group disbanded in 1988 but re-formed to release *On Every Street* (1991). Mark Knopfler, Dire Straits' singer and main songwriter and a gifted and influential guitarist, also wrote film scores, participated in numerous side projects, and recorded as a solo artist. Among his better-received later solo efforts were *Sailing to Philadelphia* (2000) and *Get Lucky* (2009).

BILLY THORPE

As front man for the Aztecs, British-born Australian rock icon Billy Thorpe (born March 29, 1946, Manchester, England—died February 28, 2007, Sydney, Australia) was regarded as the father of Australian pub rock. Thorpe was known as much for his showmanship as for his musicianship, and the band's shows were marked by high energy and great volume. Thorpe

formed his first band, the Planets, in 1957 in Brisbane. At the age of 17 he moved to Sydney, where he formed the beat combo Billy Thorpe and the Aztecs; their first major pop hit was a cover of "Poison Ivy" in 1964. The band broke up in 1967 but re-formed one year later, with Thorpe on guitar as well as vocals. During this period, guitarist Lobby Loyde joined the Aztecs, adding a new, harder edge to their music. A high point was the group's performances (1972–73) in Victoria at the Sunbury Music Festival, memorialized in the album *Aztecs Live! At Sunbury*, which contained their biggest hit and Thorpe's signature song, "Most People I Know (Think that I'm Crazy)." He was inducted into the Australian Recording Industry Association (ARIA) Hall of Fame in 1991.

LOBBY LOYDE

Before joining the Aztecs in 1969, Lobby Loyde (born John Baslington Lyde, May 18, 1951, Longreach, Queensland, Australia—died April 21, 2007, Melbourne, Australia) fronted his own alternative bands—Purple Hearts and the psychedelic Wild Cherries. En route to becoming an Australian rock icon in his own right, he championed the loud, aggressive musical style that dominated Australian pub rock and influenced such heavy metal bands as AC/DC and the American punk rockers Nirvana. In 1972 Loyde left the Aztecs to found the more intense Coloured Balls, but two years later he moved to Britain, where he joined the punk rock scene. After returning to Melbourne in the late 1970s, he played with Southern Electric, Rose Tattoo, Dirt, and the re-formed Coloured Balls. Loyde also recorded solo albums, notably *Obsecration* (1976), and in the 1980s served as record producer for the Sunnyboys, Painters and Dockers, and other groups. Loyde was inducted into the Australian Blues Foundation Hall of Fame in 2002 and the Australian Recording Industry Association (ARIA) Hall of Fame in 2006.

CHAPTER 11

Rude Boys: Reggae

Widely perceived as a voice of the oppressed, reggae originated in Jamaica in the late 1960s and quickly emerged as the country's dominant music. By the 1970s it had become an international style that was particularly popular in Britain, the United States, and Africa. According to an early definition in *The Dictionary of Jamaican English* (1980), reggae is based on ska, an earlier form of Jamaican popular music, and employs a heavy four-beat rhythm driven by drums, bass guitar, electric guitar, and the "scraper," a corrugated stick that is rubbed by a plain stick. (The drum and bass became the foundation of a new instrumental music, dub.) The dictionary further states that the chunking sound of the rhythm guitar that comes at the end of measures acts as an "accompaniment to emotional songs often expressing rejection of established 'white-man' culture." Another term for this distinctive guitar-playing effect, *skengay*, is identified with the sound of gunshots ricocheting in the streets of Kingston's ghettos; tellingly, *skeng* is defined as "gun" or "ratchet knife." Thus reggae expressed the sounds and pressures of ghetto life. It was the music of the emergent "rude boy" (would-be gangster) culture.

In the mid-1960s, under the direction of producers such as Duke Reid and Coxsone Dodd, Jamaican musicians dramatically slowed the tempo of ska, whose energetic rhythms reflected the optimism that had heralded Jamaica's independence from Britain in 1962. The musical style that resulted, rock steady, was short-lived but brought fame to such performers as the Heptones and Alton Ellis.

Reggae evolved from these roots and bore the weight of increasingly politicized lyrics that addressed social and economic injustice. Among those who pioneered the new reggae sound, with its faster beat driven by the bass, were Toots and the Maytals, who had their first major hit with "54-46 (That's My Number)" (1968), and the Wailers—Bunny Wailer, Peter Tosh, and reggae's biggest star, Bob Marley—who recorded hits at Dodd's Studio One and later worked with producer Lee ("Scratch") Perry. Another reggae superstar, Jimmy Cliff, gained international fame as the star of the movie *The Harder They Come* (1972). A major cultural force in the worldwide spread of reggae, this Jamaican-made film documented how the music became a voice for the poor and dispossessed. Its sound track was a celebration of the defiant human spirit that refuses to be suppressed.

During this period of reggae's development, a connection grew between the music and the Rastafarian movement, which encourages the relocation of the African diaspora to Africa, deifies the Ethiopian emperor Haile Selassie I (whose precoronation name was Ras [Prince] Tafari), and endorses the sacramental use of ganja (marijuana). Rastafari (Rastafarianism) advocates equal rights and justice and draws on the mystical consciousness of kumina, an earlier Jamaican religious tradition that ritualized communication with ancestors. Besides Marley and the Wailers, groups who popularized the fusion of Rastafari and reggae were Big Youth, Black Uhuru, Burning Spear (principally Winston Rodney), and Culture. "Lover's rock," a style of reggae that celebrated erotic love, became popular through the works of artists such as Dennis Brown, Gregory Issacs, and Britain's Maxi Priest.

In the 1970s reggae, like ska before it, spread to the United Kingdom, where a mixture of Jamaican immigrants and native-born Britons forged a reggae movement that produced artists such as Aswad, Steel Pulse, UB40, and performance poet Linton Kwesi Johnson. Reggae was embraced in the United States largely through the work of Marley—both directly and indirectly (the latter as a result of Eric Clapton's popular cover version of Marley's "I Shot the Sheriff" in 1974). Marley's career illustrates the way reggae was repackaged to suit a rock market whose patrons had used marijuana and were curious about the music that sanctified it. Fusion with other genres was an inevitable consequence of the music's globalization and incorporation into the multinational entertainment industry.

The dancehall deejays of the 1980s and '90s who refined the practice of "toasting" (rapping over instrumental tracks) were heirs to reggae's politicization of music. These deejays influenced the emergence of hip-hop music in the United States and extended the market for reggae into the African American community. At the beginning of the 21st century, reggae remained one of the weapons of choice for the urban poor, whose "lyrical gun," in the words of performer Shabba Ranks, earned them a measure of respectability.

SIR COXSONE DODD

Jamaican record producer and entrepreneur Coxsone Dodd (born Clement Seymour Dodd, January 26, 1932, Kingston, Jamaica—died May 4, 2004, Kingston) was one of the pioneers of modern Jamaican popular music and played a pivotal role in the development of ska, a Jamaican amalgam of American rhythm and blues and native mento (folk-calypso) strains, as well as in the emergence of reggae. Though Dodd grew up in Kingston, it was while working as a cane cutter in the U.S. South that he was exposed to both outdoor dance parties and rhythm and blues. Returning to Jamaica, he became one of the originators of the huge portable sound systems that became a sensation on the island in the 1950s,

providing a movable feast of mostly American rhythm-and-blues records. An outstanding cricket player, Dodd was nicknamed Coxsone after a well-known English cricketer from the 1940s, and Dodd's famous sound system was christened Sir Coxsone's Downbeat. Dodd was at the centre of the creation of Jamaica's native ska, whose prime movers included the Skatalites, the house band at Studio One, the legendary recording studio Dodd established (1963) in Jamaica. As ska progressed toward reggae in the 1960s, Dodd introduced the world to reggae king Bob Marley (a singer with the Wailers), Toots and the Maytals, and later (1970s) Dennis Brown, Burning Spear, and Sugar Minott; in the process, rhythm tracks were developed that became essential elements of Jamaican music. From the 1980s Dodd divided his time between Kingston and New York City, where he operated a record shop. In 1991 Dodd was the recipient of Jamaica's third highest honour, the Order of Distinction.

TOOTS AND THE MAYTALS

Formed in 1962 as a ska group fronted by the charismatic Toots Hibbert (born Frederick Hibbert, 1946, Maypen, Jamaica), the Maytals (originally known as the Vikings, then as the V. Maytals) quickly became the

STUDIO ONE

Founded in 1963, Coxsone Dodd's Studio One, a crude, tiny one-track studio and pressing plant, produced hits for the vocal group that later became Toots and the Maytals and employed the talents of the young Bob Marley as writer, performer, and artists-and-repertoire man. In the early ska years the Studio One house band recorded under various individual and collective guises, most successfully as the Skatalites with "Guns of Navarone" (1964). It was the Rastafarian-influenced rhythm created by drummer Leroy ("Horsemouth") Wallace on 1969's "Things a Come Up to Bump," however, that pointed the label toward its peak in the 1970s, when it established reggae's distinctive granite-and-custard sound with productions that pushed the lurching rhythm to the front while leaving the lead vocal piping out from somewhere deep in the mix.

By this point, blessed with an eight-track recorder and an Echo-phlanger—which created phasing and echo—Studio One was nicknamed "the Academy" and became a prime source of "roots rockers"—quasi-religious, bottom-heavy, hip-grinding records by the likes of the Abyssinians, Burning Spear, Dennis Brown, and the Heptones. Studio One's influence is easily tracked: the Clash's cover of Willie Williams's "Armagideon Time" helped to establish reggae as a minority taste with white fans in the United States; the Papa Michigan and General Smiley duets of the late 1970s, among the label's last great moments, are clear precursors of later trends in American hip-hop; and echoes of Studio One's distinctive rumbling sound can be clearly heard in the British group Massive Attack and all who followed in their wake.

top group in Jamaica on the strength of Hibbert's hearty, exuberant vocals, often compared to those of Otis Redding. Other band members included Nathaniel ("Jerry") Matthias (or McCarthy; born c. 1945, Jamaica) and Henry ("Raleigh") Gordon (born c. 1945, Jamaica). In 1968, with Leslie Kong as the producer, the Maytals released their first recording in the emerging style of reggae, "54-46 (That's My Number)." A pumping, frantic account of Hibbert's term in prison on a marijuana charge, it is considered one of reggae's greatest songs. Subsequent hits included "Do the Reggay" (thought to be the first explicit use of the term), "Monkey Man," "Sweet and Dandy," and "Pressure Drop." The last two songs were included in the landmark film *The Harder They Come* (1972), which helped bring the group international renown. Unlike Bob Marley and the Wailers, the Maytals' music is largely apolitical, upbeat, and full of unabashedly joyous singing. In 1982 Hibbert became a solo performer; his subsequent forays into nonreggae styles failed to capture a mainstream audience outside Jamaica.

BOB MARLEY

Jamaican singer-songwriter Bob Marley (born February 6, 1945, Nine Miles, St. Ann, Jamaica—died May 11, 1981, Miami, Florida, U.S.)

distilled early ska, rock steady, and reggae forms into an electrifying rock-influenced hybrid that made him an international superstar. Marley—whose parents were Norval Sinclair Marley, a white rural overseer, and the former Cedella Malcolm, the black daughter of a local *custos* (respected backwoods squire)—would forever remain the unique product of parallel worlds. His poetic worldview was shaped by the countryside, his music by the tough West Kingston ghetto streets. Marley's maternal grandfather was not just a prosperous farmer but also a bush doctor adept at the mysticism-steeped herbal healing that guaranteed respect in Jamaica's remote hill country. As a child Marley was known for his shy aloofness, his startling stare, and his penchant for palm reading. Virtually kidnapped by his absentee father (who had been disinherited by his own prominent family for marrying a black woman), the preadolescent Marley was taken to live with an elderly woman in Kingston until a family friend rediscovered the boy by chance and returned him to Nine Miles.

By his early teens Marley was back in West Kingston, living in a government-subsidized tenement in Trench Town, a desperately poor slum often compared to an open sewer. In the early 1960s, while a schoolboy serving an apprenticeship as a welder (along with fellow aspiring

Bob Marley, c. *1974.* Gary Merrin/Hulton Archive/Getty Images

singer Desmond Dekker), Marley was exposed to the languid, jazz-infected shuffle-beat rhythms of ska (the aforementioned blend of Caribbean and jazz rhythms) then catching on commercially. Marley was a fan of Fats Domino, the Moonglows, and pop singer Ricky Nelson, but, when his big chance came in 1961 to record with producer Leslie Kong, he cut "Judge Not," a peppy ballad he had written based on rural maxims learned from his grandfather. Among his other early tracks was "One Cup of Coffee" (a rendition of a 1961 hit by Texas country crooner Claude Gray), issued in 1963 in England on Chris Blackwell's Anglo-Jamaican Island Records label.

Marley also formed a vocal group in Trench Town with friends who would later be known as Peter Tosh (born Winston Hubert MacIntosh) and Bunny Wailer (born Neville O'Reilly Livingston, April 10, 1947, Kingston). The trio, which named itself the Wailers (because, as Marley stated, "We started out crying"), received vocal coaching by noted singer Joe Higgs. Later they were joined by vocalist Junior Braithwaite and backup singers Beverly Kelso and Cherry Green.

In December 1963 the Wailers entered Coxsone Dodd's Studio One facilities to cut "Simmer Down," a song by Marley that he had used to win a talent contest in Kingston.

Unlike the playful mento music that drifted from the porches of local tourist hotels or the pop and rhythm and blues filtering into Jamaica from American radio stations, "Simmer Down" was an urgent anthem from the shantytown precincts of the Kingston underclass. A huge overnight smash, it played an important role in recasting the agenda for stardom in Jamaican music circles. No longer did one have to parrot the stylings of overseas entertainers; it was possible to write raw, uncompromising songs for and about the disenfranchised people of the West Indian slums.

This bold stance transformed both Marley and his island nation, engendering the urban poor with a pride that would become a pronounced source of identity (and a catalyst for class-related tension) in Jamaican culture—as would the Wailers' Rastafarian faith. The Wailers did well in Jamaica during the mid-1960s with their ska records, even during Marley's sojourn to Delaware in 1966 to visit his relocated mother and find temporary work. Reggae material created in 1969–71 with producer Lee Perry increased the contemporary stature of the Wailers; and, once they signed in 1972 with the (by that time) international label Island and released *Catch a Fire* (the first reggae album conceived as more than a mere singles compilation), their uniquely

REPRESENTATIVE WORKS

The Wailers
▶ *Catch a Fire* (1973)
▶ *Burnin'* (1973)

Bob Marley and the Wailers
▶ *Natty Dread* (1974)
▶ *Live!* (1975)
▶ *Rastaman Vibration* (1976)
▶ *Exodus* (1977)
▶ *Kaya* (1978)
▶ *Uprising* (1980)
▶ *Legend* (1984)

rock-contoured reggae gained a global audience. It also earned the charismatic Marley superstar status, which gradually led to the dissolution of the original threesome about early 1974. Although Peter Tosh would enjoy a distinguished solo career before his murder in 1987, many of his best solo albums (such as *Equal Rights* [1977]) were underappreciated, as was Bunny Wailer's excellent solo album *Blackheart Man* (1976).

Eric Clapton's version of the Wailers' "I Shot the Sheriff" in 1974 spread Marley's fame. Meanwhile, Marley continued to guide the skilled Wailers band through a series of potent, topical albums. By this point Marley also was backed by a trio of female vocalists that included his wife, Rita; she, like many of Marley's children, later experienced her own recording success. Featuring eloquent songs such as "No Woman No Cry," "Exodus," "Could You Be Loved," "Coming in from the Cold," "Jamming," and "Redemption Song," Marley's landmark albums included *Natty Dread* (1974), *Live!* (1975), *Rastaman Vibration* (1976), *Exodus*

RASTAFARI

The Rastafari religious and political movement, begun in Jamaica in the 1930s and adopted by many groups around the globe, combines Protestant Christianity, mysticism, and a pan-African political consciousness. Rastas, as members of the movement are called, see their past, present, and future in a distinct way. Drawing from stories in the Hebrew Bible, especially that of Exodus, they "overstand" (rather than understand) people of African descent in the Americas and around the world to be "exiles in Babylon." They believe that they are being tested by Jah (God) through slavery and the existence of economic injustice and racial "downpression" (rather than oppression). Looking to the New Testament book of Revelation, Rastas await their deliverance from captivity and their return to Zion, the symbolic name for Africa drawn from the biblical tradition. Ethiopia, the site of a dynastic power, is the ultimate home of all Africans and the seat of Jah, and repatriation is one goal of the movement. Many (though not all) Rastas believe that the Ethiopian emperor, His Imperial Majesty Haile Selassie I, crowned in 1930, is the Second Coming of Christ who returned to redeem all black people.

Jamaican Rastas are descendants of African slaves who were converted to Christianity in Jamaica by missionaries using the text of the King James Version of the Bible. Rastas maintain that the King James Version is a corrupted account of the true word of God, since English slave owners promoted incorrect readings of the Bible in order to better control slaves. Rastas believe that they can come to know the true meanings of biblical scriptures by cultivating a mystical consciousness of oneself with Jah, called "I-and-I." Rastas read the Bible selectively, however, emphasizing passages from Leviticus that admonish the cutting of hair and beard and the eating of certain foods and that prescribe rituals of prayer and meditation. Based on their reading of the Hebrew Bible, many Rasta men uphold patriarchal values, and the movement is often charged with sexism by both insiders and outsiders. "Iyaric," or "Dread-talk," is the linguistic style of many Rastas, who substitute the sound of "I" for certain syllables.

Rastafari "livity," or the principle of balanced lifestyle, includes the wearing of long hair locked in its natural, uncombed state, dressing in the colours of red, green, gold, and black (which symbolize the life force of blood, herbs, royalty, and Africanness), and eating an "I-tal" (natural, vegetarian) diet. Religious rituals include prayer services, the smoking of ganja (marijuana) to achieve better "itation" (meditation) with Jah, and "bingis" (all-night drumming ceremonies). Reggae grew out of the Rastafari movement and was made popular throughout the world by Bob Marley.

(1977), *Kaya* (1978), *Uprising* (1980), and the posthumous *Confrontation* (1983). Exploding in Marley's reedy tenor, his songs were public expressions of personal truths—eloquent in their uncommon mesh of rhythm and blues, rock, and venturesome reggae forms and electrifying in their narrative might. Making music that transcended all its stylistic roots, Marley fashioned an impassioned body of work that was sui generis.

He also loomed large as a political figure and in 1976 survived what was believed to have been a politically motivated assassination attempt. Marley's efforts to broker a truce between Jamaica's warring political factions led in April 1978 to his headlining the "One Love" peace concert. His sociopolitical clout also earned him an invitation to perform in 1980 at the ceremonies celebrating majority rule and internationally recognized independence for Zimbabwe. In April 1981, the Jamaican government awarded Marley the Order of Merit. A month later he died of cancer.

Although his songs were some of the best-liked and most critically acclaimed music in the popular canon, Marley was far more renowned in death than he had been in life. *Legend* (1984), a retrospective of his work, became the best-selling reggae album ever, with international sales of more than 12 million copies.

LEE ("SCRATCH") PERRY

Jamaican producer, songwriter, singer, and disc jockey Lee "Scratch" Perry (born Rainford Hugh Perry, March 28, 1936, Kendal, Jamaica) helped reshape reggae music. He was among the first Jamaican producer-musicians to use the studio as an instrument, and he pioneered the reggae instrumental form known as dub, in which sections of a rhythm track were removed and others emphasized through echo, distortion, repetition, and backward tape looping.

Perry's debut recording in the early 1960s, "The Chicken Scratch," earned him his nickname. At Studio One, he produced hits for reggae singers such as Justin Hines and Delroy Wilson as well as recording his own material. After scoring an instrumental hit with "The Upsetter" in the late 1960s, he named his label and band after it and played an important part in the early success of Jamaica's biggest group, the Wailers. But his greatest innovations came after he built Black Ark studio behind his home in Kingston in 1974. He began

Lee "Scratch" Perry, c. *1984.* David Corio/Redferns/Getty Images

experimenting with drum machines and space-age studio effects that would usher in the dub era and influence production techniques in reggae, hip-hop, and rock for decades afterward. A legendary eccentric, he was known to blow marijuana smoke on his finished master tapes to give them the proper "vibe," and he reportedly burned down Black Ark in 1980. His increasingly avant-garde albums continued to win critical praise well into the 1990s.

PETER TOSH

Peter Tosh (born Winston Hubert MacIntosh, October 9/19?, 1944, Belmont, Jamaica—died September 11, 1987, Kingston), Bob Marley, and Bunny Wailer formed the Wailers in 1963 in the Kingston ghetto of Trench Town. In addition to his rich baritone, Tosh brought to the Wailers his versatile musicianship and songs such as "Get Up, Stand Up" (written with Marley) and "Stop That Train." An aggressive defender of the principals of Rastafari (Rastafarianism) and a militant opponent of the political establishment, Tosh carried himself with bravado and was long associated with the dignity-demanding song "Stepping Razor." By 1974, jealous of the attention focused on Marley as the Wailers' popularity grew, Tosh, like Wailer before him, left the group to pursue a solo career.

His albums—most notably *Legalize It* (1976), *Equal Rights* (1977), and *No Nuclear War* (1987)—featured uncompromising political messages about subjects ranging from the legalization of marijuana to the abuse of power. His work earned the respect of fans and fellow musicians—he was a favourite of the Rolling Stones and recorded a duet with Mick Jagger, "(You Gotta Walk) Don't Look Back" (1978)—but incurred the enmity of the authorities he criticized. He was badly beaten by police during his arrest for possession of marijuana in 1978. Tosh was murdered in his home in 1987.

JIMMY CLIFF

The star of the landmark film *The Harder They Come* (1972), Jamaican singer and songwriter Jimmy Cliff (born James Chambers, April 1, 1948, Somerton, Jamaica) was instrumental in introducing reggae to an international audience. Just into his teens, Cliff began recording soon after moving from the countryside to Kingston, making several singles before topping the Jamaican charts with his own composition, "Hurricane Hattie," one of his earliest efforts for Leslie Kong's Beverly Records. He had several more hits that combined pop and ska influences.

After relocating to London in 1965 at the behest of Island's Chris

Blackwell, Cliff broadened his musical approach to incorporate soul and rhythm and blues as he moved in the direction of reggae. By the late 1960s he was a favourite in South America (having won a prize at a festival in Brazil with his song "Waterfall"), and his album *Wonderful World, Beautiful People* (1970) was an international hit as well as the record that prompted Paul Simon to investigate reggae. As the star of *The Harder They Come*—he contributed to its sound track the classics "Many Rivers to Cross," "Sitting in Limbo," and the title song—Cliff became reggae's biggest star. Although he never again equaled this success and his popularity in Jamaica, Britain, and the United States was soon eclipsed by Bob Marley, Cliff remained extremely popular in Africa and South America. He was inducted into the Rock and Roll Hall of Fame in 2010.

DESMOND DEKKER

Jamaican singer-songwriter Desmond Dekker (born Desmond Adolphus Dacres, July 16, 1941, Kingston, Jamaica—died May 25, 2006, Thornton Heath, England) was the first Jamaican to become an international pop music star, with hits in three genres: ska, rock steady, and reggae. He was working as a welder in 1961 when his auditions for Jamaica's biggest record producers,

"Coxsone" Dodd and Duke Reid, failed. Two years later, however, he had a hit on Leslie Kong's Beverley Records with "Honour Your Father and Mother." Performing ska, the exuberant music that mirrored the optimism sparked by Jamaica's recent independence, Dekker had a series of national hits, including "King of Ska" (backed by the future Maytals) and "Mount Zion." With his backup group, the Aces, he began celebrating Kingston's "rude boys," the young gangster-inspired hipsters who reflected the increasing disappointment that many Jamaicans felt as the 1960s progressed. Dekker's rock steady rude-boy classic "007 (Shanty Town)" shot into the British charts in 1967, and in 1969 he cracked the American market with "Israelites." The next year, having relocated to Britain, he had a huge reggae hit with the Jimmy Cliff-written "You Can Get It If You Really Want." Dekker's music suffered after Kong died in 1971, although his career experienced a brief upturn during the ska revival of the late 1970s and early '80s. By 1984 Dekker was bankrupt, but he continued to record and perform.

ROOTS OF REGGAE: SKA

Pioneered by the operators of the powerful mobile-disco sound systems, ska, as noted earlier, evolved in the late 1950s from an early

Jamaican form of rhythm and blues that emulated American rhythm and blues, especially that produced in New Orleans, Louisiana. A new beat emerged that mixed the shuffling rhythm of American pianist Rosco Gordon with Caribbean folk influences, most notably the mambo of Cuba and the mento, a Jamaican dance music that provided the new music's core rhythm. The boogie-woogie piano vamp characteristic of New Orleans-style rhythm and blues was simulated by a guitar chop on the offbeat and onomatopoeically became known as ska. The beat was made more locomotive by the horns, saxophones, trumpet, trombone, and piano that played the same riff on the offbeat. All the while the drums kept a $^4/_4$ beat with bass drum accents on the second and fourth beats.

Because the history of Jamaican popular music is largely oral, contending claims of authorship were inevitable, but guitarist Ernie Ranglin's claim that he invented the ska chop is generally regarded as plausible. Singers Derrick Morgan, Prince Buster, Toots Hibbert, Justin Hinds, and the Dominoes became stars, but ska was primarily an instrumental music. Jamaica's independence from British rule in 1962 left the country and ska in a celebratory mood. The music's dominant exponents were the Skatalites—Don Drummond, Roland Alphonso, Dizzy Johnny Moore, Tommy McCook, Lester Sterling, Jackie Mittoo, Lloyd Brevette, Jah Jerry, and Lloyd Knibbs. The Skatalites' most distinctive musical presence was trombonist, composer, and arranger Drummond. A colourful figure who grappled with mental instability (he was institutionalized after murdering his girlfriend and died in confinement), Drummond was the central musician of the era, as essential to the development of ska as Marley was to reggae.

Ska has had several international waves. The first began in the early 1960s and is remembered for "My Boy Lollipop" by Millie Small, a Jamaican singer based in London, and for hits by Prince Buster and by Desmond Dekker and the Aces. In the 1970s ska was a significant influence on British pop culture, and so-called 2-Tone groups (whose name derived from both the suits they wore and their often integrated lineups) such as the Specials, Selector, and Madness brought punk and more pop into ska. Madness's music crossed the Atlantic Ocean and contributed to the success of ska's third wave of popularity, in the mid-1980s in the United States, where another British group, General Public, had hits. The music's fourth wave came in the mid-1990s as American groups such as No Doubt, Sublime, and the Mighty Mighty Bosstones brought ska into the mainstream of pop music, and

Madness, in a signature, humorous pose, c. 1979. Virginia Turbett/
Redferns/Getty Images

ska pioneers such as the Skatalites and Derrick Morgan found a new audience.

DANCEHALL MUSIC

Dancehall music—also called ragga or dub—had its genesis in the political turbulence of the late 1970s and became Jamaica's dominant music in the 1980s and '90s. Central to dancehall is the deejay, who raps, or "toasts," over a prerecorded rhythm track (bass guitar and drums), or "dub."

The seductive chant of the dancehall deejay—part talking, part singing—came to prominence in the late 1970s but dates from as early as 1969, when U-Roy experimented with talking over or under a "riddim" (rhythm). This multimodal African diasporic style also is evident in the hip-hop music of North America, and the origins of both can be traced to West African performance modes.

The rise of deejay Yellowman in the early 1980s marked the transition from mainstream reggae to

2-TONE RECORDS

In several regional British cities, the distinct late 1970s combination of economic turmoil, unemployment benefits (effectively an arts subsidy), and art school punks resulted in a generation of eccentric talent. In Coventry, the southernmost centre of Britain's Midlands engineering belt, the outcome was 2-Tone, a mostly white take on ska, which had been brought to Britain by Jamaican immigrants in the mid-1960s and was favoured by English mods of the period; it was those mods whose two-tone Tonik suits gave the latter-day movement its name. In 1977 art student Jerry Dammers founded the Specials, a self-consciously multiracial group—both in composition and rhetoric—whose initial hit, "Gangsters" (1979), gave them the clout to demand every punk's dream, their own record label. The sound of that label, 2-Tone, was thin and sharp, dominated by whiny vocals and the kerchunk-kerchunk of the rhythm guitar. After an impressive run of hits by several seminal groups, 2-Tone folded, but not before the Specials had their second British number one hit with "Ghost Town" (1981), which evocatively addressed racial tension and whose timely release coincided with riots in Liverpool and London.

Among 2-Tone's alumni, Madness developed into a very English pop group (on the Stiff label), and the Beat (called the English Beat in the United States) split to become General Public and the Fine Young Cannibals. The legacy of 2-Tone would be explored during the American ska revival of the late 1990s. During the heyday of 2-Tone, and a little farther north, in Birmingham, another multiracial group, UB40, laced Midlands diffidence with reggae rhythms and achieved international success over a 15-year period on its own DEP International label, licensed through Virgin.

dancehall music that took place in Jamaican nightclubs. In addition to the explicitly political lyrics of songs of the early 1980s such as "Operation Eradication" and "Soldier Take Over," Yellowman incorporated into his repertoire salacious lyrics that became widely known as "slackness," a Jamaicanism for licentiousness. Drawing on the raunchy tradition of mento, the aforementioned earlier form of Jamaican dance music that barely disguised sexual discourse in metaphor, and on the spirit of the Caribbean calypso folk song, to which mento is kin, Yellowman teasingly addressed both sex and politics in his radical critique of society in the wake of the failure of Jamaica's experiment with socialism under Prime Minister Michael Manley.

In the 1980s and '90s, computer-generated rhythms mechanized and sped up the dancehall beat. From the 1980s to the mid-1990s, slackness and gun talk dominated the lyrics of dancehall deejays, the most notable of whom were Shabba Ranks, Ninjaman, Bounty Killer, Lady Saw, and Lovindeer (who composed in a calypso idiom). In the late 1990s, however, a resurgent Rastafarian consciousness was exemplified in the work of Buju Banton, Anthony B, and Sizzla, who built upon the earlier examples of Tony Rebel and Josey Wales. There was also a new wave of born-again Christian performers, including Lieutenant Stichie, Papa San, and Carlene Davis. The eclecticism of contemporary Jamaican dancehall music is perhaps best characterized by the iconoclastic Beenie Man.

CHAPTER 12

Dance Fever: Disco

D isco was the preeminent form of dance music in the 1970s. Its name was derived from *discotheque*, the name for the type of dance-oriented nightclub that first appeared in the 1960s. Initially ignored by radio, disco received its first significant exposure in deejay-based underground clubs that catered to black, gay, and Latino dancers. Deejays were a major creative force for disco, helping to establish hit songs and encouraging a focus on singles: a new subindustry of 12-inch, 45-rpm extended-play singles evolved to meet the specific needs of club deejays. The first disco qua disco hit was Gloria Gaynor's "Never Can Say Goodbye" (1974), one of the first records mixed specifically for club play. While most of disco's musical sources and performers were African American, the genre's popularity transcended ethnic lines, including both interracial groups (e.g., KC and the Sunshine Band) and genre-blending ensembles (e.g., the Salsoul Orchestra).

As disco evolved into its own genre in the United States, its range of influences included upbeat tracks from Motown, the choppy syncopation of funk, the sweet melodies and polite rhythmic pulse of Philadelphia soft soul, and even the most compelling polyrhythms of nascent Latin American salsa. Its lyrics generally promoted party culture. As the dance-floor mania developed into a more upscale trend, the cruder sensuality of funk was eclipsed by the more polished Philadelphia sound and the controlled energy of what came to be known as Eurodisco.

European disco—rooted in Europop, with which it is largely synonymous—evolved along somewhat different lines. In Europe producers such as (Jean-Marc) Cerrone (*Love in C Minor*) and Alec Costandinos (*Love and Kisses*) made quasi-symphonic disco concept albums, while Giorgio Moroder, working primarily at Musicland Studios in Munich, West Germany, conceived of whole album sides as a single unit and arrived at a formula that became the standard approach to European dance music in the 1980s and '90s. These continental differences did not prevent intercultural collaborations such as that between Moroder and American singer Donna Summer, nor did they close off input from other sources: Cameroonian artist Manu Dibango's "Soul Makossa," first a dance-floor hit in Paris, helped usher in the disco era in 1973.

Disco moved beyond the clubs and onto the airwaves in the mid-1970s. From 1976 the U.S. Top 40 lists burst with disco acts such as Hot Chocolate, Wild Cherry, Chic, Heatwave, Yvonne Elliman, and Summer. Key to the commercial success were a number of savvy independent labels

REPRESENTATIVE WORKS

▶ Manu Dibango, "Soul Makossa" (1973)
▶ Gloria Gaynor, "Never Can Say Goodbye" (1974)
▶ MFSB, "TSOP (The Sound of Philadelphia)" (1974)
▶ KC and the Sunshine Band, "Get Down Tonight" (1975)
▶ The O'Jays, "I Love Music" (1975)
▶ Donna Summer, "Love to Love You Baby" (1975)
▶ The Bee Gees and various artists, *Saturday Night Fever* (1977)
▶ Cerrone, "Love in C Minor (Part 1)" (1977)
▶ The Tramps, "Disco Inferno" (1977)
▶ Kool and the Gang, "Ladies Night" (1979)
▶ Donna Summer "Bad Girls" (1979)

such as TK in Miami, Florida, and Casablanca in Los Angeles. In 1977 the Bee Gees-dominated *Saturday Night Fever* sound track on the RSO label made disco fully mainstream and inspired forays by rock musicians such as Cher ("Take Me Home"), the Rolling Stones ("Miss You"), and Rod Stewart ("D'Ya Think I'm Sexy?"). Its popularity was matched by an equally ferocious criticism as the genre's commercialization overwhelmed its subversively homoerotic and interracial roots.

As a result, in the 1980s disco returned to its club roots, with a few performers such as Madonna providing radio listeners with glimpses of its continuing development. In the clubs it mutated into house and techno and by the mid-1990s even began to resurface once again.

DONNA SUMMER

Dubbed the "Queen of Disco," Donna Summer (born Donna Adrian Gaines, December 31, 1948, Boston, Massachusetts, U.S.—died May 17, 2012, Naples, Florida) was also successful in rhythm and blues, dance music, and pop in the 1970s and '80s. An admirer of gospel singer Mahalia Jackson, Summer sang in church and later in clubs in Boston. At age 18 she joined the German production of the musical *Hair*. While in Europe she studied with the Vienna Folk

Donna Summer in the arms of body builder and future movie star and politician Arnold Schwarzenegger, posing at her home in Los Angeles, California, 1977. Michael Ochs Archives/Getty Images

Opera and performed in productions of *Godspell* and *Showboat*. She also married actor Helmut Sommor, keeping his name after their divorce but Anglicizing it for the stage. While doing session work at Musicland studios in Munich, Summer met producer-songwriters Giorgio Moroder (an Italian synthesizer player) and

167

Pete Bellotte (an Italian guitarist and lyricist). The three collaborated on several Europop hits before creating the historic single "Love to Love You Baby" (1975), the first of more than a dozen hits in the United States for Summer, most on Casablanca. Nearly 17 minutes long, the club version of the erotically charged song introduced the 12-inch disco mix.

Over the next 14 years Summer wrote or cowrote most of her material, including "I Feel Love," "Bad Girls," and "She Works Hard for the Money." She also scored big hits with "MacArthur Park"; "Hot Stuff"; "No More Tears (Enough Is Enough)," a duet with Barbra Streisand; and her signature song, "Last Dance," from the film *Thank God It's Friday* (1978).

MUSICLAND STUDIOS

Like Berlin, Munich is the cosmopolitan capital of a more parochial hinterland, but, unlike Berlin, postwar Munich seemed oblivious to the Iron Curtain—less than 100 miles (60 km) away. The city's concerns were commercial and artistic. The centre for German pop music television, it was also home to Musicland, the only major recording studio in the 1970s between Paris and Tokyo, used by such stars as the Rolling Stones and Elton John. Like all major cosmopolitan cities, Munich drew talent from around the world. Enabled by

the development of the synthesizer, electro-disco was dreamed up at Musicland in the mid-1970s by producer Giorgio Moroder, his partner Peter Bellotte, and Donna Summer.

While other German musicians such as Kraftwerk and Can experimented with the avant-garde and ironic possibilities of machine-made music, the Musicland crew fused the synthesizer's precise, unearthly rhythms with the blatant eroticism inspired by "Je t'aime moi non plus" ("I love you me neither")—the 1969 groundbreaking hit for Paris-based Serge Gainsbourg and Jane Birkin. Summer's "Love to Love You Baby" (1975) was the first international hit made in Munich. By the end of the 1970s, the Moroder-Bellotte-Summer partnership was based in Los Angeles, and the production duo brought their aseptic sound to records by Blondie and a series of movie sound tracks— *American Gigolo* (1980), *Flashdance* (1983), and *Top Gun* (1986)—that helped define a style of hyperprofessional, emotionally detached '80s pop.

THE BEE GEES

In becoming one of the best-selling recording acts of all time, the Bee Gees (short for the Brothers Gibb) adapted to changing musical styles while maintaining the high harmonies, elaborate melodies, and ornate orchestrations that were their

FRANKIE CROCKER

Frankie Crocker was the flamboyant kingpin of disco radio, though he had never singled out dance music as a specialty. He played rhythm and blues and jazz on the radio in his hometown of Buffalo, New York; in Pittsburgh, Pennsylvania; and in Los Angeles before joining WMCA in New York as one of the "Good Guys" in 1968. He was the Top 40 station's first African-American deejay. "New York was alive with rock and roll as well as soul and R&B, and everybody went to see everybody else," he said. "The only place it was segregated was on the radio, and so that became my desire: to mix it together."

In 1972 Crocker moved to New York City's WLIB, which, with a change of call letters to WBLS, became a disco powerhouse beginning in the late 1970s, following the lead of WKTU. He immersed himself in the culture of the New York City club scene and reflected that culture on the radio. He also worked in television, including a stint as one of the first "video jockeys" on the cable music station VH1.

trademark. The principal members were Barry Gibb (born September 1, 1946, Isle of Man), Robin Gibb (born December 22, 1949, Isle of Man—died May 20, 2012, London, England), and Maurice Gibb (born December 22, 1949, Isle of Man—died January 12, 2003, Miami, Florida, U.S.).

After emigrating to Australia with their parents, the Gibb brothers returned to England in the mid-1960s to further their singing careers. Their early recordings, including dramatic hits such as "Massachusetts" (1967), drew comparisons with the Beatles. The trio reached the Top Ten with "I've Gotta Get a Message to You" and "I Started a Joke" (both 1968) but split briefly after the relative failure of their concept album

MIAMI: SOUNDS OF SUNSHINE

In the 1970s Miami, Florida, boomed economically, and its downtown filled with thin white skyscrapers. At ground level the city developed an infrastructure of recording studios and distributors that by the early 1990s had made it the capital of the Latin-American music business. The foundations were laid by veteran record men Henry Stone and Jerry Wexler. A goateed hustler, Stone had launched and distributed rhythm-and-blues labels since the 1950s. He finally hit the jackpot with productions by Willie Clarke, often featuring drum machines (then a new technology), such as George McCrae's gently swinging disco anthem "Rock Your Baby." After licensing hits to Atlantic (notably Betty Wright's 1971 hit "Clean Up Woman"), from 1972 Stone released them on his own TK label. TK topped the pop chart with five boisterous dance tunes by KC and the Sunshine Band—a band led by two local session players, Harry Wayne Casey ("KC") and Rick Finch.

Meanwhile, Atlantic's Wexler moved to sunny Florida and brought his work with him. Basing himself at the white beach villa at 461 Ocean Boulevard that housed Criteria Studios, he imported two former Atlantic cohorts, arranger Arif Mardin and engineer Tom Dowd, as his coproducing team and recruited the house band from American Sound Studios in Memphis, Tennessee, renaming them the Dixie Flyers. Fifteen years before South Beach became a trendy hub of activity, the relative isolation of Criteria worked well for such troubled talents as Aretha Franklin and Eric Clapton, whose Derek and the Dominos album with Duane Allman was produced at Criteria by Dowd. Two studio hands—Karl Richardson and Albhy Galuten—went on to work with Mardin as engineers on the Bee Gees' early disco hits, culminating in their world-beating *Saturday Night Fever* sound track (which also featured KC and the Sunshine Band's "Boogie Shoes").

Odessa (1969). Once reunited, they had hits with "Lonely Days" (1970) and "How Can You Mend a Broken Heart" (1971), but there were several hitless years before they returned to the charts with *Main Course* (1975). Recorded in Miami, grounded in rhythm and blues, and typified by the chart-topping single "Jive Talkin'," it put the Bee Gees at the forefront of the disco movement, which their work on the sound track album *Saturday Night Fever* (1977) would popularize and in many ways define. Besides writing their own hits, such as "Stayin' Alive," the brothers composed tracks for other artists on the album, which would eventually sell 40 million copies. Subsequent albums, however, failed to match the success of their earlier work. In 1997 the band was inducted into the Rock and Roll Hall of Fame.

RAK RECORDS

For a long time, London pop was cynical, inept, or ironic. In the early 1970s a new generation of producers—heedful of Phil Spector's description of his work as "little symphonies for the kids"—injected a new sense of market-driven buoyancy into the pop single. Mickie Most was a North Londoner, but he learned the business in the 1950s in South Africa. He spent the 1960s producing acts such as Herman's Hermits, Donovan, and the Animals but really came into his own in the 1970s, with a run of brisk, optimistic hits for his own RAK label, recorded at his studio in the Inner London suburb of St. John's Wood. Together with songwriting producers Nicky Chinn (from Bristol) and Mike Chapman (from Australia), Most worked in a variety of styles: Suzi Quatro's innocent take on stadium rock ("Can the Can"), Mud's winking nods to the 1950s ("Lonely This Christmas"), and Hot Chocolate's populist rhythm and blues ("You Sexy Thing"). What his productions had in common was an unwavering sense of irony-free confidence.

Chinn and Chapman also worked at Utopia Studios, where they perfected the raucous teen beat of the Sweet with coproducer Phil Wainman before Chapman moved to New York City to produce most of Blondie's biggest hits. Elsewhere in central London, Mike Leander put together the infectious dance pop of Gary Glitter's "Rock and Roll, Part Two," and Tony Visconti produced Marc Bolan (of T. Rex) and David Bowie (in his Ziggy Stardust phase) at Trident Studios in Soho.

CASABLANCA RECORDS

Even in the bacchanal of 1970s Los Angeles, the drug and promotional excesses of Casablanca Records stood out. In a period when cocaine use

THE OTHER SIDE OF THE VELVET ROPE

To be on the club side of the rope that regulated entrance to Studio 54 was to be in a heaven of sorts. On 54th Street in midtown Manhattan, Steve Rubell created the most chic disco of the 1970s, taking the energy of earlier underground New York City clubs such as the Haven and the Sanctuary and mixing it with the 1960s European concept of *le discotheque*, the classy nightspot where one danced to records rather than live bands. At Studio 54 the beautiful and the damned gathered to take drugs and dance to the new post-Philadelphia soul groove that came to be known as disco. Meanwhile, out in Brooklyn at Odyssey 2000, a younger, less affluent crowd danced to the same music. This was the scene depicted—with forgivable exaggerations—in the motion picture *Saturday Night Fever* (1977).

Populism in $^4/_4$ time, disco was studio music that capitalized on the first fruits of the electronic revolution. Suppleness and drive of the rhythmic base nearly always took precedence over lyrical or vocal subtlety. While tracks such as the Village People's "YMCA" and the Jacksons' "Blame It on the Boogie" (both 1978) became mainstream pop hits, Chic's sardonic "Good Times" (1979) laid the basis for rap and the surge of 12-inch singles that fostered the development of hip-hop via new underground clubs (Galaxy 21 and Paradise Garage). At those clubs a new wave of deejays (including Larry Levan, Walter Gibbons, and David Mancuso) began to remix live, creating ever longer percussive dreamscapes that would recast popular music by the end of the next decade.

was probably at its peak in the music business, Casablanca set the pace. Its offices on Sunset Boulevard were decorated like Rick's Café in the motion picture from which the label took its name, and it was run by Neil Bogart (who had changed his name from Bogatz). The son of a Brooklyn postal worker, he reinvented himself via New York's School of the Performing Arts, had a minor recording hit as Neil Scott, and served an apprenticeship in payola as a record label promotion man. Eventually he found success with Buddah Records as the king of late 1960s bubblegum pop. In many ways Casablanca was the epitome of music business cynicism, typified by the costumed heavy-metal theatrics of KISS. Yet the label was also the centre of some of the most significant dance music of the era. It issued the Village People's "YMCA" (1978), a huge hit by a French-produced American group that set its double-entendre message against the updated grooves of Philadelphia soul; popularized electro-disco with Donna Summer's "I Feel Love" (1977); and supported George Clinton's experiments with Parliament-Funkadelic. Fiscal irresponsibility ensured Casablanca's demise in the 1980s.

BARRY WHITE

American rhythm-and-blues singer Barry White (born Barry Eugene Carter, September 12, 1944, Galveston, Texas—died July 4, 2003, Los Angeles, California) possessed one of the most recognizable bass-baritone voices in the musical world. Especially popular during the disco-era 1970s—an era he helped set in motion with his Love Unlimited Orchestra's "Love's Theme" instrumental (1973)—he half sang and half spoke romantic ballads in velvety sensual tones that, in combination with lush orchestrations, created an intimate, seductive mood. Among White's numerous hit songs were two—"Can't Get Enough of Your Love, Babe" and "You're the First, the Last, My Everything"—that propelled the album they were on, *Can't Get Enough* (1974), to the top of the charts, and his album *Staying Power* (1999) won two Grammy Awards.

EUROPOP

Europop hits contain traces of their national origins and often gain international attention via the dance floor, but the genre generally transcends cultural borders in Europe without crossing the Atlantic Ocean. The first major Europop hit is generally considered Los Bravos' "Black Is Black," a million-seller in 1966. Los Bravos was a Spanish group with a German lead singer and a British producer. Their success was a model for both cross-European collaboration and commercial opportunism. The skill of the Europop producer (and this is a producer-led form) is both to adapt the latest fashionable sounds to "Euroglot" lyrics that can be followed by anyone with high-school-level comprehension of the language in question and to incorporate these sounds in a chorus that can be sung collectively in every continental disco and holiday resort.

Other early successes in the genre were Middle of the Road's "Chirpy Chirpy Cheep Cheep," which sold 10 million copies in 1971, and Chicory Tip's 1972 hit, "Son of My Father," the English-language version of a German-Italian song originally recorded by one of its writers, Giorgio Moroder. Moroder's work with Donna Summer (a Europop star before her success in the United States), especially on her 1975 hit "Love to Love You Baby," had a major impact on New York City studios that were producing disco music and consolidated the dance-floor influence of the German trio Silver Convention. Following Moroder's lead, European dance producers in the 1980s and '90s absorbed the various influences of house and techno music and sampling (composing with music and sounds electronically extracted from other recordings) technology. Their recordings emphasized the contrast between emotionless electronic instrumentation (originally influenced by art rock studio musicians

such as Kraftwerk) and emotive soulful voices (usually black and female); their dance-floor appeal rested on the balance between hard, mechanical repetition and melodic tricks and hooks, and their mass impact was best seen in Mediterranean beach clubs over a long August night. In the late 1980s clubs on the Spanish resort island of Ibiza thus became the inspiration for the British rave scene.

The most influential Europop acts of the 1970s, though, had a broader appeal. Boney M, a foursome from the Caribbean (via Britain and the Netherlands) brought together by German producer Frank Farian, sold 50 million records in 1976–78; the Swedish group ABBA had 18 consecutive European Top Ten hits following their 1974 victory in the Eurovision Song Contest (the annual competition sponsored by state-run European television stations to determine the best new pop song). Both groups appealed (particularly through television) to listeners older and younger than the dedicated dancers, combining child-friendly choruses with slick choreography and a tacky erotic glamour that gave ABBA, in particular, a camp appeal that was a major influence on late 1970s gay music culture. The most successful British pop production team of the 1980s—Mike Stock, Matt Aitken, and Pete Waterman—was clearly influenced by this pop genre and by the promotion processes that supported it. It took itself less seriously than Eurodisco and, as vacation music, could bring a smile to even the most jaded rock fan, as did Aqua's "Barbie Girl," which became Europop's greatest global success to date when it was released in the late 1990s.

ABBA

The Swedish Europop quartet ABBA was among the most commercially successful groups in the history of popular music. In the 1970s it dominated the European charts with its catchy pop songs, and the group's presence in popular culture remained strong in the 21st century. Members included songwriter and keyboard player Benny Andersson (born December 16, 1946, Stockholm, Sweden), songwriter and guitarist Björn Ulvaeus (born April 25, 1945, Gothenburg), and vocalists Agnetha Fältskog (born April 5, 1950, Jönköping) and Anni-Frid Lyngstad (born November 15, 1945, Narvik, Norway).

The group began to take shape in 1969, when Andersson and Ulvaeus, who had previously collaborated on a number of folk and pop projects, met Lyngstad and Fältskog. In addition to working together musically, the four paired off romantically, with Andersson becoming involved with Lyngstad and Ulvaeus dating Fältskog.

The quartet debuted as the cabaret act Festfolk, a name chosen to play on two words with nearly identical pronunciations in Swedish: festfolk, meaning "party people," and fästfolk, a 1970s slang term for "engaged couples." Ulvaeus and Fältskog were married in 1971, and Andersson and Lyngstad followed suit in 1978. While Festfolk failed to gain a following in Sweden, the song "People Need Love," which the group recorded as Björn & Benny, Agnetha & Anni-Frid, was a modest hit in 1972. The following year the foursome finished third in the Swedish qualifying round of the Eurovision Song Contest, with the single "Ring, Ring." Encouraged by that success and dubbed ABBA—an acronym derived from the members' first names—by the group's manager, Stig Anderson, the band returned to Eurovision in 1974 and captured the top prize with the song "Waterloo." The resulting single served as the anchor for the album of the same name, released that year.

More than a year after the triumph at Eurovision, *ABBA* (1975) truly established the group as a global pop phenomenon. The singles "Mamma Mia" and "S.O.S." were massive hits in Europe, Australia, and North America, and the band embraced the emerging music video format to capitalize on the quartet's shared charisma. ABBA's 1977 release, *Arrival*, reached the United

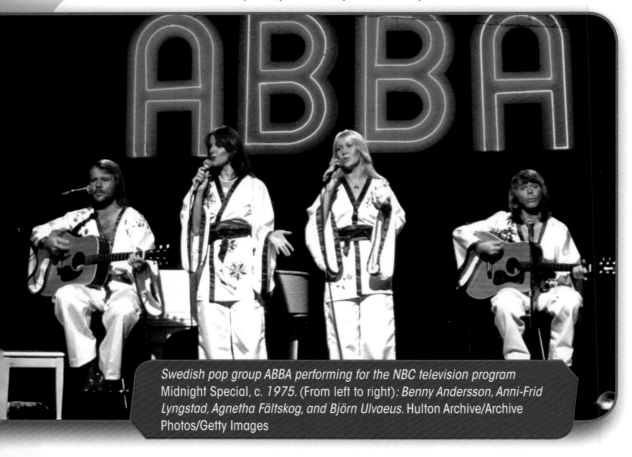

Swedish pop group ABBA performing for the NBC television program Midnight Special, c. 1975. (From left to right): Benny Andersson, Anni-Frid Lyngstad, Agnetha Fältskog, and Björn Ulvaeus. Hulton Archive/Archive Photos/Getty Images

States at the height of the disco craze, and it provided the group with its sole American number one single—the catchy and undeniably club-friendly "Dancing Queen." *The Album* (1978) marked a departure of sorts: although its standout single, "Take a Chance on Me," was a brilliant, if straightforward, pop anthem, other tracks hinted at an art rock influence, and the album's second side was dominated by a "mini-musical" titled "The Girl with the Golden Hair."

While *The Album* marked an artistic progression for ABBA, personal relations within the band suffered when Ulvaeus and Fältskog divorced prior to the release of *Voulez-Vous* (1979). The pair vowed that their breakup would not affect the band's output, but *Super Trouper* (1980) featured a collection of songs, most notably "The Winner Takes It All" and "Lay All Your Love on Me," that betrayed a melancholic undercurrent that was absent in previous recordings. Andersson and Lyngstad divorced during the recording of *The Visitors* (1981), and the reggae rhythms of "One of Us" did little to conceal the prevailing mood of the band. This second breakup proved to be too much for the group, which disbanded in 1982.

After the demise of ABBA, Fältskog and Lyngstad embarked on moderately successful solo careers, and Ulvaeus and Andersson collaborated with lyricist Tim Rice to create *Chess* (1984), a concept album and stage musical that produced the surprise radio hit "One Night in Bangkok." Although the band frequently quashed rumours of a possible reunion over the following years, ABBA's music never truly left the popular consciousness. Other groups performed ABBA songs with varying degrees of faithfulness, and British dance pop band Erasure devoted an entire EP (appropriately titled *ABBA-esque* [1992]) to ABBA covers. The music of ABBA was also a fixture on the big screen, playing a central role in both the plots and sound tracks of such films as *The Adventures of Priscilla, Queen of the Desert* (1994) and *Muriel's Wedding* (1994). Ulvaeus and Andersson merged their shared love of musical theatre with the ABBA back catalog to produce *Mamma Mia!*, a romantic comedy that debuted on London's West End in 1999 and was subsequently seen by millions of people worldwide. A film version of the play, starring Meryl Streep, was one of the top global box office draws of 2008. The group was inducted into the Rock and Roll Hall of Fame in 2010.

CHAPTER 13

DIY: Punk and New Wave

The do-it-yourself ethic of the late 1970s and early '80s manifested itself musically in a pair of related but distinct trends. Punk generally embraced a more confrontational, frequently political, tone, with a guitar-heavy hard rock edge. Lyrically, punk ranged from the fevered poetry of Patti Smith to the anarchic howl of the Sex Pistols' Johnny Rotten. New wave drew upon the sensibilities of '60s pop with a nod to the electronic sounds innovated by art rockers such as Brian Eno. Less overtly cynical than punk, new wave lyrics were suffused with a clever playfulness that managed to remain one step removed from novelty. It was not uncommon for groups to drift from one genre to the other between albums—and sometimes between songs. For both punk and new wave, however, look was almost as important as sound. Thanks to the success of television programs such as Tony Wilson's *So It Goes* and the advent of the music video, the fashion of punk and new wave was perhaps more pervasive than the music itself.

PROTO-PUNK IN THE MOTOR CITY

In the late 1960s Detroit was the breeding ground for the influential proto-punk bands Iggy and the Stooges and the MC5. They practiced their loud, hard-rocking style on the stage of the Grande (pronounced "Grandee") Ballroom, which had been created in the image of San Francisco's psychedelic rock ballrooms.

THE MC5

The MC5 were one of the most controversial and ultimately influential bands of the late 1960s. The principal members were vocalist Rob Tyner (born Robert Derminer, December 12, 1944, Detroit, Michigan, U.S.— died September 17, 1991, Royal Oak, Michigan), lead guitarist Wayne Kramer (born Wayne Kambes, April 30, 1948, Detroit), rhythm guitarist Fred ("Sonic") Smith (born August 14, 1948, West Virginia—died November 4, 1994, Detroit), drummer Dennis Thompson (born Dennis Tomich, September 7, 1948), and bassist Michael Davis (born June 5, 1943, Detroit—died February 17, 2012, Chico, California).

Formed in suburban Detroit in 1965 as a bar band that played mostly cover versions of other performers' songs, the MC5 (Motor City Five) developed a chaotic, heavy, explosive sound that borrowed from avant-garde jazz, rock, and rhythm and blues. Along with the music came a heavy dose of left-wing radical politics, largely through the influence of the band's manager, John Sinclair. Sinclair was the founder of a political group patterned after the Black Panthers, the White Panther Party, for which the MC5 became the ministers of information. (In that capacity they performed outside the 1968 Democratic National Convention in Chicago.) Their first album, *Kick Out the Jams* (1969), a live recording named after their signature song, captures the loud, raw turbulence that characterized their powerful performances. Two more albums followed, including the Jon Landau-produced *Back in the U.S.A.* (1970), before the band broke up in 1972. Louder and brasher than the other political bands of their era, the MC5 were extremely influential despite their limited popularity, and their sound can be heard in heavy metal, punk rock, and grunge.

IGGY AND THE STOOGES

Iggy and the Stooges helped define punk music, and front man Iggy Pop had a far-reaching influence on later performers. The principal members of the band were vocalist Iggy Pop (born James Jewel Osterberg, April 21, 1947, Ypsilanti, Michigan, U.S.), bassist Dave Alexander (died 1975), guitarist Ron Asheton (born July 17, 1948, Washington, D.C.—found dead January 6, 2009, Ann Arbor, Michigan), and drummer Scott Asheton (born 1949, Ann Arbor, Michigan).

In 1967 Osterberg formed the Psychedelic Stooges, taking the name Iggy Stooge. In 1969, its name shortened to the Stooges, the band released its eponymic first album, produced by the Velvet Underground's John Cale. "I Wanna Be Your Dog" and "No

Fun" became proto-punk classics, mixing raw, abrasive rock with insolent lyrics. Destructively energetic and furious, the debut and the band's second album, *Funhouse* (1970)—along with Iggy's outrageous onstage performances, in which he smeared himself with peanut butter and rolled on broken glass—secured the band's cult status. In 1973 the group released *Raw Power*, a collaboration with David Bowie, before disbanding the following year.

In 1977 Iggy—renaming himself Iggy Pop—released two solo albums, *The Idiot* and *Lust for Life*, both produced and cowritten by Bowie in Berlin. The albums, which revealed a new maturity, were praised by critics and gave Iggy his first commercial success. He continued recording through the 1980s and '90s, scoring hits with the new wave-influenced *Blah Blah Blah* (1986) and the unabashedly pop *Brick by Brick* (1990). The latter included "Candy," a duet with Kate Pierson of the B-52s and Iggy's first Top 40 single. Iggy also made minor forays into acting, appearing in a number of independent films and lending his trademark drawl to animated characters on television and the big screen.

In 2003 he reunited the Stooges at the Coachella Valley Music and Arts Festival, with former Minutemen bassist Mike Watt filling in for the late Dave Alexander. The enthusiastic reception that greeted the band prompted a three-year tour of festivals in Asia, Europe, and North America. A performance in Tokyo was captured for the live album *Telluric Chaos* (2005). The Stooges returned to the studio for the first time in more than three decades to record *The Weirdness* (2007). While the album met with disappointing reviews, the resulting world tour presented the classic Stooges to a new generation of fans. The group was inducted into the Rock and Roll Hall of Fame in 2010.

ROCK REBELS AGAINST ITSELF: PUNK

Often politicized and full of vital energy beneath a sarcastic, hostile facade, punk—an aggressive form of rock music that coalesced into an international movement in the late 1970s—spread as an ideology and an aesthetic approach, becoming an archetype of teen rebellion and alienation. Borrowed from prison slang, the word *punk* was first used in a musical context during the early 1970s, when compilation albums such as Lenny Kaye's *Nuggets* (1972) created a vogue for simple mid-1960s garage rock by groups such as the Seeds, the 13th Floor Elevators, and ? (Question Mark) and the Mysterians. Meanwhile, other American groups such as the MC5, Iggy and the

Stooges, and the New York Dolls had begun to use hard rock to reflect and define youthful angst. By 1975 punk had come to describe the minimalist, literary rock scene based around CBGB, the New York City club where the Patti Smith Group and Television performed. The Ramones also performed there, and their self-titled 1976 debut album became the blueprint for punk: guitar as white noise, drums as texture, and vocals as hostile slogans.

After the pastoral concerns of the hippies, punk was a celebration of urbanism, a reclaiming of the inner city. The term spread to Britain, where the Sex Pistols were packaged by Malcolm McLaren to promote his London store, Sex, which sold fetishistic clothing daubed with slogans from the farthest reaches of 1960s radical politics—e.g., the Paris-based Situationist International. Announced by their manifesto, the single "Anarchy in the U.K.," the Sex Pistols established punk as a national style that combined confrontational fashions with sped-up hard rock and allusive, socially aware lyrics that addressed the reduced expectations of 1970s teens. Armed with a critique of the music industry and consumerism—embodied in songs such as the Sex Pistols' "EMI" and X-Ray Spex's "Identity"—early British punk spawned a resurgence of interest in rock. Mirroring social upheaval with a series of visionary songs couched in black humour, groups such as the Buzzcocks ("Orgasm Addict"), the Clash ("Complete Control"), and Siouxsie and the Banshees ("Hong Kong Garden") scored hits in 1977–78. Anarchist, decentralizing, and libertarian, U.K. punk was drawn into the polarized politics of British society and by 1979 had self-destructed as a pop style. Postpunk groups such as Public Image Ltd. and Joy Division replaced punk's worldliness with inner concerns, matching rock with the technological rhythms of disco. Nevertheless, punk's influence could be seen throughout British society, notably in mass media shock tactics, the confrontational strategies of environmentalists, and the proliferation of independent record labels.

Although the Sex Pistols' 1977 chart successes (principally "God Save the Queen" and "Pretty Vacant") made Britain the hotbed of the new youth movement, similar developments had occurred in France, Australia, and the United States (notably in Cleveland, Ohio, where the band Pere Ubu played a prominent role). Visits by British groups such as the Damned and the Sex Pistols later fueled prominent regional punk scenes in Seattle, Washington; San Francisco (the Dead Kennedys); and Los Angeles (X and Black Flag). In the late 1970s, however, punk in the United States was eclipsed by disco and went underground in movements such as hardcore, which flourished from the early to mid-1980s and further accelerated punk's breakneck tempo. Punk's full impact came only after the success of Nirvana in 1991, coinciding with the ascendance of Generation X—a new, disaffected generation born in the 1960s, many members of which identified with punk's charged, often contradictory mix of intelligence, simplicity, anger, and powerlessness.

ANARCHY IN THE U.K.

As Britain's finances spiraled downward and the nation found itself suppliant to the International Monetary Fund, the seeming stolidity of 1970s London concealed various, often deeply opposed, radical trends. The entrepreneurial spirit of independent record labels anticipated the radical economic policies of Margaret Thatcher, whereas punk spoke in tongues with protomillennial fervour. The aftershocks of the collapse of the British Empire transformed London for the first time into a truly cosmopolitan city. Its pop music was flavoured by a new generation of immigrants and people on the margins of society. Pop svengali Mike Chapman arrived from Australia, and English expatriate Mickie Most returned from South Africa. Stiff Records' Dave Robinson was Irish, and the Sex Pistols' Johnny

Rotten grew up in London in a transplanted Irish family. From the late 1950s Caribbean immigration had produced its own music scene and business, based on clubs and small labels. American exiles included producer Tony Visconti from New York City and the Pretenders' Chrissie Hynde from Akron, Ohio. To this mix was added the influence of the art school (the Sex Pistols' manager and three-fourths of the Clash had been art students) and assorted pseudonymous refugees from the suburbs (Siouxsie and the Banshees, Adam Ant, and Rat Scabies).

THE SEX PISTOLS

The Sex Pistols created the British punk movement of the late 1970s and, with the song "God Save the Queen," became a symbol of the United Kingdom's social and political turmoil. The original members were Johnny Rotten (born John Lydon, January 31, 1956, London, England), Steve Jones (born May 3, 1955, London), Paul Cook (born July 20, 1956, London), and Glen Matlock (born August 27, 1956, London). A later member was Sid Vicious (born John Simon Ritchie, May 10, 1957, London—died February 2, 1979, New York, New York, U.S.).

Thrown together in September 1975 by manager Malcolm McLaren, the Sex Pistols began mixing 1960s

English pop music influences (the Small Faces, the Who) with those of 1970s rock renegades (Iggy and the Stooges, the New York Dolls) in an attempt to strip rock's complexities to the bone. By the summer of 1976 the Sex Pistols had attracted an avid fan base and successfully updated the energies of the 1960s mods for the malignant teenage mood of the '70s. Heavily stylized in their image and music, media-savvy, and ambitious in their use of lyrics, the Sex Pistols became the leaders of a new teenage movement—called punk by the British press—in the autumn of 1976. Their first single, "Anarchy in the U.K.," was both a call to arms and a state-of-the-nation address. When they used profanity on live television in December 1976, the group became a national sensation. Scandalized in the tabloid press, the Sex Pistols were dropped by their first record company, EMI, in January 1977; their next contract, with A&M Records, was severed after only a few days in March.

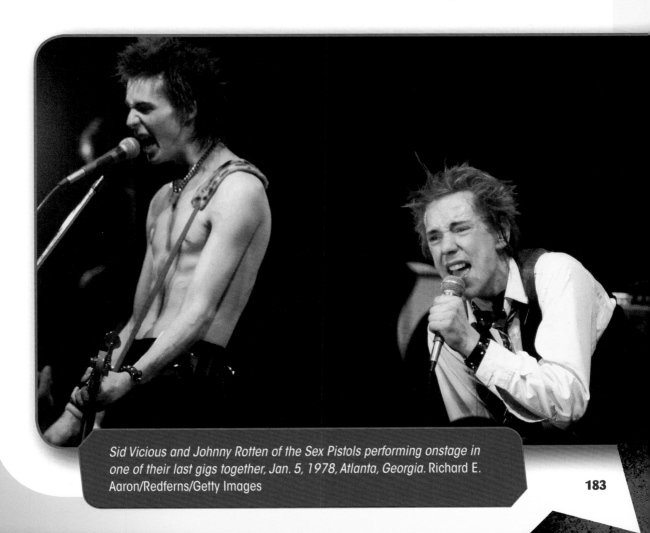

Sid Vicious and Johnny Rotten of the Sex Pistols performing onstage in one of their last gigs together, Jan. 5, 1978, Atlanta, Georgia. Richard E. Aaron/Redferns/Getty Images

Signing quickly with Virgin Records, the Sex Pistols released their second single, "God Save the Queen," in June 1977 to coincide with Queen Elizabeth II's Silver Jubilee (the 25th anniversary of her accession to the throne). Although banned by the British media, the single rose rapidly to number two on the charts. As "public enemies number one," the Sex Pistols were subjected to physical violence and harassment.

Despite a second Top Ten record, "Pretty Vacant," the Sex Pistols stalled. Barely able to play in the United Kingdom because of local government bans, they became mired in preparations for a film and the worsening drug use of Rotten's friend Vicious, who had replaced Matlock in February 1977. Their bunker mentality is evident on their third Top Ten hit, "Holidays in the Sun." By the time their album *Never Mind the Bollocks, Here's the Sex Pistols* reached number one in early November, Rotten, Vicious, Jones, and Cook had recorded together for the last time.

A short, disastrous U.S. tour precipitated the group's split in January 1978 following their biggest show to date, in San Francisco. Attempting to keep the Sex Pistols going with the film project that became *The Great Rock 'n' Roll Swindle* (1980), McLaren issued records with an increasingly uncontrollable Vicious as the vocalist. A cover version of Eddie Cochran's "C'mon Everybody" became the group's best-selling single following Vicious's fatal heroin overdose in New York City in February 1979 while out on bail (charged with the murder of his girlfriend, Nancy Spungen). That same month McLaren was sued by Rotten, and the Sex Pistols disappeared into receivership, only to be revived some years after the 1986 court case that restored control of their affairs to the group. A reunion tour in 1996 finally allowed the original quartet to play their hit songs in front of supportive audiences. This anticlimactic postscript, however, did not lessen the impact of their first four singles and debut album, which shook the foundations of rock music and sent tremors through British society. In 2006 the Sex Pistols were inducted into the Rock and Roll Hall of Fame.

MALCOLM MCLAREN

Before acting as a sort of midwife to the punk rock movement, the Sex Pistols' colourfully provocative manager Malcolm McLaren (born January 22, 1946, London, England—died April 8, 2010, Switzerland) attended a number of art schools in England, where he was drawn to the subversive Marxist-rooted philosophy of the Situationist International movement and its leading figure, Guy Debord. With his girlfriend, fashion designer Vivienne

THE LONDON PUNK SCENE

In the mid-1970s punk began by sending messages from an underworld—posters that aped the style of ransom notes, gigs in Soho strip clubs, and a two-night "festival" in the 100 Club (a bleary basement off London's main shopping boulevard, Oxford Street). The two main London clubs for punk were the Roxy (in Covent Garden) and the Vortex (in Soho), both belowground sweat pits. Tellingly, the *Live at the Roxy* album (1977), which documents the period, begins with the sound of Shane McGowan (of the Pogues) stealing the microphone hidden in the restroom, the centre for the evening's chemical and sexual experimentations. Punk reveled in a taste for slumming that was almost heroic in its intensity— arguably suitable for a city where World War II bomb sites still gaped like missing teeth. Yet, when the major London punks came to record, most chose to work with major labels, surrendering to the professional expertise of the previous generation and to producers who had created the records that the punks had obsessed over as teenagers.

The Sex Pistols signed first to the British-based major EMI and were produced by Chris Thomas, who gave Roxy Music their neurotic timbre and went on to create a lush new-wave sound for Chrissie Hynde's popular Pretenders. The Clash signed to the local arm of the American giant CBS and, between bouts with bona fide eccentrics, including Guy Stevens and Lee Perry, worked with American Sandy Pearlman (producer of Blue Oyster Cult) and Glyn Johns (who had engineered for the Beatles, the Rolling Stones, and the Faces). From an international perspective, punk seemed at the time to be a storm in a British teacup, and only the Clash achieved significant success in the United States; but its message did have a lasting impact elsewhere, notably in Europe and on the West Coast of the United States.

Westwood, he opened the avant-garde clothing boutique Let It Rock, in 1971, but he soon became more interested in rock music as a means to enact his radical aesthetic ideas.

After a brief stint managing and costuming the New York Dolls, in 1975 he began to work with the Sex Pistols—in a cross-marketing ploy with the clothes shop, which had been rebranded as Sex. By the following year the raucous punk group had become a cause célèbre in the United Kingdom, and McLaren eagerly fueled the controversy with stunts such as having the band play its anti-authoritarian anthem "God Save the Queen" aboard a boat outside the Houses of Parliament in London.

Following the Sex Pistols' collapse in 1978, McLaren guided the image and career of new-wave band Adam and the Ants and formed a spin-off act, Bow Wow Wow. In 1983 he released his own solo album, *Duck Rock*, an eclectic fusion of hip-hop and world music that spawned two British top 10 hits: "Buffalo Gals" and "Double Dutch." Several other albums followed, including the opera-inspired *Fans* (1984), *Waltz Darling* (1989), and *Paris* (1994).

PUNK FASHION: DAME VIVIENNE WESTWOOD

British fashion designer Vivienne Westwood (born Vivienne Isabel Swire, April 8, 1941, Glossop, Derbyshire, England) was known for her provocative clothing. With her partner, Malcolm McLaren, she extended the influence of the 1970s punk music movement into fashion.

She was a schoolteacher before she married Derek Westwood in 1962 (divorced 1965). A self-taught designer, in 1965 Westwood met and moved in with McLaren. Together they pursued a career in fashion. Initially, they operated Let It Rock, a stall selling secondhand 1950s vintage clothing along with McLaren's rock-and-roll record collection. Westwood produced clothing designs based on his provocative ideas. Their customized T-shirts, which were ripped and emblazoned with shocking anti-establishment slogans and graphics, and their bondage trousers—black pants featuring straps inspired by sadomasochistic costume—flew out of the London shop of which the couple became proprietors in 1971. Their boutique—variously named Too Fast to Live, Too Young to Die; Sex; and finally Seditionaries—was a youth fashion mecca. Their erotically charged fashion image enraged Britain's right-wing press, however. Soon after Westwood and McLaren staged Pirates, their first commercial ready-to-wear collection, in 1981, they ended their personal relationship. They remained professional partners for an additional five years, but Westwood soon established her

Vivienne Westwood and Malcolm McClaren posing with three fashion models in London, c. 1985. David Montgomery/Hulton Archive/Getty Images

identity as a leading independent designer.

Westwood's "mini-crini" design—a thigh-grazing crinoline produced in both cotton and tweed that debuted as part of her spring-summer 1985 collection—marked a turning point.

For the next two decades she created collections that took inspiration from classical sources, notably the paintings of Jean-Honoré Fragonard, François Boucher, and Thomas Gainsborough, as well as historical British dress, including the 19th-century bustle, which

Westwood incorporated under elaborate knitwear dresses and tartan miniskirts.

Independently, Westwood built her own eponymous mini fashion empire, operating numerous boutiques and producing two menswear and three women's wear collections annually as well as bridal clothes, shoes, hosiery, eyewear, scarves, ties, knitwear, cosmetics, and perfumes. On April 1, 2004, a retrospective devoted to her creations opened at the Victoria and Albert Museum in London. "Vivienne Westwood: 34 Years in Fashion" was the largest exhibition the museum had ever dedicated to a British designer. She was made an Officer of the Order of the British Empire (OBE) in 1992 and advanced to Dame Commander of the Order of the British Empire (DBE) in 2006.

THE CLASH

Of the many punk bands formed in mid-1970s London as a direct result of the catalytic inspiration of the Sex Pistols, the aptly named Clash came closest to rivaling the Pistols' impact. However, whereas the Pistols were (ostensibly at least) nihilists come to destroy rock, the Clash were activists come to save it—rabble-rousing street populists waging a rock-and-roll class war. The principal members were Joe Strummer (born John

Mellor, August 21, 1952, Ankara, Turkey—died December 22, 2002, Broomfield, Somerset, England), Mick Jones (born Michael Jones, June 26, 1955, London, England), Paul Simonon (born December 15, 1955, London), Terry ("Tory Crimes") Chimes (born London), and Nick ("Topper") Headon (born May 30, 1955, Bromley, Kent). Their explosive debut single, "White Riot," and eponymous first album (both 1977) were tinny and cranked-up in volume and tempo—the perfect aural signature for scrappy underdogs in stenciled, paint-spattered thrift shop clothes whose credo was "The truth is only known by guttersnipes." Their stage shows—spearheaded by Strummer's teeth-clenched, raw-throated passion—were as galvanic as anything else available in a decidedly galvanic era.

The Clash was considered so rough, so raw, and so wrong-kind-of-English by the band's American record company that it was not even released in the United States until 1979. Its successor, *Give 'Em Enough Rope* (released in Britain in late 1978 and in the United States in spring 1979), was overseen by American producer Sandy Pearlman in an attempt to capture the American market. However, that breakthrough did not come until the eclectic, sophisticated double album *London Calling* (1980); steeped in reggae and rhythm and blues, it brought the Clash their first American hit single with Jones's composition "Train in Vain (Stand by Me)"—an afterthought added to the album so late that it was not even listed on the cover. By this time the band's hard-won professionalism, rapidly developing musical skills, and increasing fascination with the iconography of classic Americana had distanced them from the punk faithful in Britain, who were still singing along to "I'm So Bored with the U.S.A." from the first album.

Perpetually in debt to their record company and compelled by their punk ethic to give their all for their fans, the Clash tried to satisfy both constituencies with *London Calling's* follow-up, *Sandinista!* (1980), a triple album that unfortunately produced no hits. *Combat Rock* (1982), the

The Clash, c. 1983. Hulton Archive/Getty Images

REPRESENTATIVE WORKS

▶ *The Clash* (U.K. 1977, U.S. 1979)
▶ *Give 'Em Enough Rope* (U.K. 1978, U.S. 1979)
▶ *London Calling* (U.K. 1979, U.S. 1980)
▶ *Combat Rock* (1982)
▶ *Clash on Broadway* (1991)

last album to feature the classic triumvirate of Strummer, Jones, and Simonon, yielded the hit "Rock the Casbah," which ironically was later appropriated as an American battle anthem during the Persian Gulf War.

Internal tensions brought about by the contradictions within the Clash's stance—between their revolutionary rhetoric and their addiction to the macho posturing of rock stardom—led to the firing of Jones (who went on to found his own group, Big Audio Dynamite). Unfortunately, this left the Clash a very ordinary punk band with an unusually charismatic front man. They recorded one more, poorly received album without Jones and then disbanded in 1986.

Long after the Clash had broken up, their "Should I Stay or Should I Go" became a number one hit in the United Kingdom when it was featured in a commercial in 1991. Despite that success and lucrative offers to reunite, the group refused to do so—unlike the Sex Pistols. One of the Clash's most memorable stage numbers was their version of the Bobby Fuller Four's rockabilly classic "I Fought the Law" (its chorus: "I fought the law / And the law won"); a substitution of the words "the music business" or "capitalism" for "the law" hints at the perennial dilemma for the Clash. However, in its time the Clash pushed its contradictions to the limit and in doing so became for many the most exciting rock band of its era.

ARI UP AND THE SLITS

Ari Up (born Arianna Forster, January 17, 1962, Munich, Germany—died October 20, 2010, Los Angeles, California) founded the influential punk band the Slits when she was just 14 years old. The daughter of a music promoter, Ari Up spent much of her early life surrounded by some of the biggest names in the industry. Joe Strummer of the Clash taught her to play guitar, and John Lydon—better known as the Sex Pistols front man Johnny Rotten—would one day become her stepfather. Despite having virtually no formal musical training, Ari Up and her bandmates opened for the Clash in 1977 and released their debut album, *Cut*, two years later. The record was a triumph of the late punk era, combining reggae beats with a brash, feminist attitude. The band's second album, *Return of the Giant Slits* (1981), was more experimental than its predecessor, but it retained much of the group's signature sound. Although the Slits broke up shortly after this release, the band's punk feminist ethic laid the groundwork for the riot grrrl movement of the 1990s.

THE JAM

The Jam emerged at the height of the British punk rock movement, but their sound and image were greatly influenced by the British mod bands of the early 1960s. The principal members were Paul Weller (born May 25, 1958, Woking, Surrey, England), Rick Buckler (born December 6, 1955, Woking), and Bruce Foxton (born September 1, 1955, England).

Formed in 1973 in Woking, near London, the Jam gained popularity on the English club circuit. Their energetic shows and sound drew comparisons with the early Who, and that band's influence is evident in the Jam's first album, *In the City* (1977), which solidified the group's guitar-bass-drums lineup. Later records, particularly *All Mod Cons* (1978) and *Setting Sons* (1979), reflected more influences, which eventually included those of the Kinks, the Beatles, Motown, and soul. Those albums also showcased the band's growing social awareness, with politically charged songs such as "Down in the Tube Station at Midnight," about xenophobic violence, and "Eton Rifles," steeped in class conflict. Always a peculiarly English band in both their outlook and their lyrics, the Jam never gained international popularity to match their success in the United Kingdom, where they were huge stars and where songwriter and driving force Weller was, for a time, regarded as a spokesman for his generation. The Jam broke up in 1982 as Weller went on to form the Style Council and later embarked on a solo career.

JOY DIVISION/NEW ORDER

Joy Division refined the external chaos of 1970s punk into a disquieting inner turmoil, ushering in the postpunk era. After the death of their iconic lead singer, Ian Curtis, the remaining band members continued as New Order, and they subsequently pioneered the successful fusion of rock and 1980s African-American dance music styles. The principal members were Curtis (born July 15, 1956, Macclesfield, Cheshire, England—died May 18, 1980, Macclesfield), Bernard Albrecht (later Bernard Sumner, born January 4, 1956, Salford, Manchester), Peter Hook (born February 13, 1956, Manchester), Stephen Morris (born October 28, 1957, Macclesfield), and Gillian Gilbert (born January 27, 1961, Manchester).

Inspired by seeing the Sex Pistols perform in Manchester, guitarist Albrecht, bassist Hook, and vocalist Curtis formed Warsaw in the spring of 1977 to play thrashing punk music. By early 1978 they had replaced their original drummer with Morris and changed the band's name to Joy Division (slang for female concentration camp prisoners forced into prostitution by the Nazis). Their trademarks were already in place: prominent, melodic bass; guitar and drums as rhythm and texture; complex, literary lyrics; and mediumistic live performances (Curtis's spastic hyperactivity was sometimes actually the result of onstage epileptic seizures). The group's debut album, *Unknown Pleasures* (1979), was produced by Martin Hannett for Manchester's Factory Records with a prescient ambience and sonic atmosphere that anticipated production conventions to come. It marked the viability of the independent bands and labels that had arisen in response to punk and made Joy Division one of the hottest live draws in the United Kingdom. Later covered by disco diva Grace Jones, "She's Lost Control," from *Unknown Pleasures*, became their signature tune.

Working at a dizzying pace, the group incorporated drum machines and synthesizers in their move from rock to a measured European electronic sound influenced by Kraftwerk and producer Giorgio Moroder. In concert Curtis held nothing back, giving nightmare visions such as "Dead Souls" and "Atrocity Exhibition" an existential authority. Along with a troubled private life and worsening epilepsy, this intensity drove Curtis to the brink. On the eve of Joy Division's first U.S. tour in 1980, he committed suicide at the home of his estranged wife. Success followed tragedy; the single "Love Will Tear Us Apart" and the band's second album, *Closer*, made the Top Ten and Top 20, respectively, in the United Kingdom.

Following Curtis's death, the three remaining band members—joined by keyboardist Gilbert—continued as New Order, with Sumner (formerly Albrecht) becoming the vocalist. With singles such as "Everything's Gone Green" (1981) and the best-selling "Blue Monday" (1983), New Order moved toward a more thorough exploration of dance music. Their 1989 single "Fine Time" incorporated elements of the then-current U.K. club sound called acid house, and "World in Motion," the official national theme for the 1990 World Cup, gave them their first U.K. number one hit. "Regret," released in 1993, was New Order's last significant single.

After an eight-year hiatus from recording, New Order returned with *Get Ready* (2001), a solid collection of guitar-driven tracks that eschewed the dance anthem model that had typified their later releases. Less well-received was *Waiting for the Sirens' Call* (2005), an unremarkable return to the disco sound of the mid-1990s that proved to be the band's final studio album. Bassist Hook, who had drifted apart from his bandmates over the years, announced in 2008 that New Order had broken up. Other members disagreed, and they continued to write new material without him. In 2009 founding members Sumner and Morris retired the name New Order and recruited Blur bassist Alex James to record as Bad Lieutenant.

TONY WILSON

British music industry entrepreneur Tony Wilson (born February 20, 1950, Salford, Lancashire, England—died August 10, 2007, Manchester) cofounded Factory Records and founded the Hacienda nightclub in Manchester. He was the ringleader of the so-called "Madchester" postpunk music and club scene of the 1980s and early '90s.

Wilson was a cultural reporter for Manchester's Granada Television when in the mid-1970s he was given his own pop music show, *So It Goes*. He was galvanized by a 1976 Sex Pistols concert and booked the band on his show. In 1978 he cofounded the record label Factory Records, signing Durutti Column, Happy Mondays, Orchestral Manoeuvres in the Dark, and Joy Division (later New Order), which released its first album with the company. In 1983 New Order released on the Factory label "Blue Monday," which became the best-selling 12-inch single ever released in the United Kingdom. Wilson opened the Hacienda in 1982 to showcase local music as well as dance music;

FACTORY RECORDS

Factory Records emerged in the punk moment of the late 1970s and was the heart of Manchester's music scene until its collapse in the early 1990s. Like his Mancunian contemporaries, the Buzzcocks, Factory cofounder Tony Wilson (who presided over the influential pop music television program *So It Goes*) learned from the Sex Pistols, then struck off in a quite different direction, aided by graphic artist Peter Saville, whose neoclassic designs gave Factory packaging a signature. First came the Durutti Column's quietly arty guitar-based mood music. Then came the edgy electronic pop of Orchestral Manoeuvres in the Dark and the sonorous, doom-laden anxieties of Joy Division, given shape and tone by the city's preeminent producer, Martin Hannett. Joy Division's biggest hit, "Love Will Tear Us Apart" (1980), was released after singer Ian Curtis's suicide. The survivors reemerged as New Order, who provided the sound track to Factory's other great project of the 1980s, the Hacienda, the club where dance music was coupled with postpunk. From that arty mélange came Simply Red, the Happy Mondays, the Stone Roses, and the manic-depressive rants of the Smiths, though only the Happy Mondays recorded on Factory.

it was the first British venue to play American house music. Wilson's lack of interest in profits was among the factors that led to Factory Records' bankruptcy in 1992; the Hacienda closed in 1997. Wilson's life and the rise and fall of Factory Records were the subjects of the fictionalized biography *24 Hour Party People* (2002).

THE MEKONS

The Mekons exemplified British punk's do-it-yourself ethos. Principal members were Jon Langford (born October 11, 1957, Newport, Gwent [now in Newport], Wales), Tom Greenhalgh (born November 4, 1956, Stockholm, Sweden), Sally Timms (born November 29, 1959, Leeds, West Yorkshire, England), Susie Honeyman, Steve Goulding, Sarah Corina, Lu Edmonds, and Rico Bell (born Erik Bellis).

Founded in Leeds in 1977 by art students Langford and Greenhalgh and part of the scene that gave rise to the Gang of Four, the Mekons were amateurs even by punk rock standards, as evidenced by the uneven quality of their first albums. More important than their musical ability, however, was the egalitarian philosophy that the band espoused. Virtually anyone with an interest was allowed to play with the Mekons. With a lineup that sometimes swelled to more than a dozen members around the nucleus of guitarist-vocalists Langford and Greenhalgh, the Mekons became, almost despite themselves, more musically sophisticated, exploring a variety of genres—most importantly, country music. Benefiting from the contributions of vocalist Timms and violinist Honeyman, the Mekons produced such critically acclaimed albums as *Fear and Whiskey* (1985) and *The Mekons Rock'n'Roll* (1989), featuring songs informed by leftist political sentiments and laced with sardonic humour. The Mekons (some of whom relocated to the United States) continued to record and perform into the 21st century, making them one of the last original punk bands to remain active. Among their significant later releases were *OOOH! (Out of Our Heads)* (2002) and *Natural* (2007).

Several of the group's members also recorded and performed independently, most notably Langford (primarily on his own and as part of the Waco Brothers), Timms, and Bell. Both Langford and Bell (as Erik Bellis) also exhibited their paintings, and the group mounted collective art exhibitions both in the United States and in Britain. In 1996 they collaborated with author Kathy Acker on *Pussy, King of the Pirates*, a performance art piece.

THE GANG OF FOUR

Formed in Leeds, West Yorkshire, England, in 1977 by a group of leftist university students and taking its name from the Chinese ruling cadre led by Mao Zedong's widow, the Gang of Four forged a distinctive sound that incorporated elements of punk, disco, and Jimi Hendrix-influenced guitar distortion. The principal members were Jon King (born June 8, 1955, London, England), Andy Gill (born January 1, 1956, Manchester), Hugo Burnham (born March 25, 1956, London), and Dave Allen (born December 23, 1955, Kendal, Cumbria).

The band made its recording debut in 1978 with *Damaged Goods*, an extended-play record that featured

KATHY ACKER

American novelist Kathy Acker (born April 18, 1948, New York, New York, U.S.—died November 30, 1997, Tijuana, Mexico) chose a writing style and subject matter that reflected the so-called punk sensibility that emerged in the 1970s. Acker studied classics at Brandeis University and the University of California, San Diego. Her early employment ranged from clerical work to performing in pornographic films. In 1972 she began publishing willfully crude, disjointed prose that drew heavily from her personal experience and constituted a literary analog to contemporary developments in music, fashion, and the visual arts.

From the outset, Acker blatantly lifted material from other writers, manipulating it for her own often unsettling purposes. In the early novel *The Childlike Life of the Black Tarantula* (1973), this process of appropriation is central to the narrator's quest for identity. The book's themes of alienation and objectified sexuality recur in such later novels as *Great Expectations* (1982), *Blood and Guts in High School* (1984), *Don Quixote* (1986), and *Empire of the Senseless* (1988). In 1991 a collection of some of Acker's early works were published under the title *Hannibal Lecter, My Father*. This was followed by *My Mother: Demonology* (1993), which consists of seven love stories. Her 1996 novel, *Pussy, King of the Pirates*, was adapted for the stage by the seminal punk band the Mekons. The band and Acker released a CD under the same title.

Her works elicited frequent comparison with those of William S. Burroughs and Jean Genet, and Acker herself cited the influence of the French nouveau roman, or antinovel.

Gill's stuttering, jerky guitar; it was followed in 1979 by *Entertainment!*, which continued the group's movement toward the dance floor, propelled by bassist Allen and drummer Burnham. The Gang of Four's songs, often of an ironic and theoretical bent, focused on sexual politics and the bleakness of consumerism. The group's third album, *Songs of the Free*, released during the Falkland Islands War (1982), was more accessible and even more dance-oriented than its predecessors but included the antimilitarist "I Love a Man in Uniform" and the dour "We Live as We Dream, Alone." Critically but not commercially successful, the group broke up in 1984 and was re-formed by Gill and vocalist King in 1990 and again in 1995.

TELEVISION

The American rock group Television played a prominent role in the emergence of the punk–new-wave movement. With Television's first single, "Little Johnny Jewel" (1975), and much-touted debut album, *Marquee Moon* (1977), the extended guitar solo found a place in a movement that generally rebelled against intricate musicianship. The principal members were Tom Verlaine (born Thomas Miller, December 13, 1949, Mount Morris, New Jersey, U.S.), Richard Hell (born Richard Myers, October 2, 1949, Lexington, Kentucky), Billy Ficca (born 1949), Richard Lloyd (born October 25, 1951, Pittsburgh, Pennsylvania), and Fred Smith (born April 10, 1948, New York, New York).

Guitarist Verlaine (who took his name from the French Symbolist poet Paul Verlaine) and bassist Hell, former boarding-school roommates, formed the Neon Boys with drummer Ficca in New York City in the early 1970s. In 1973 guitarist Lloyd joined them; as Television they helped establish CBGB-OMFUG, a club in New York City's Bowery, as the epicentre of a burgeoning punk scene. Principal songwriter Verlaine delivered his surreal lyrics with an elasticity that stretched from somber declarations to unearthly squeals, but what set Television apart from other punk–new-wave groups was the improvisational interplay of Verlaine and Lloyd's guitars, which borrowed from avant-garde jazz and psychedelic rock. Patti Smith, with whom Verlaine wrote poetry and on whose debut single he played, described his guitar playing as the sound of "a thousand bluebirds screaming."

Released on Elektra, *Marquee Moon* caused a stir among American critics but, like its more polished follow-up, *Adventure* (1978), sold much better in Britain. Prior to *Marquee Moon*, Hell left to form the Heartbreakers (with ex-New York

CBGB-OMFUG

New York City's proto-punk new wave was a downtown thing, crawling out of the damp stonework in yet-to-be-gentrified area in the general vicinity of Soho and the Lower East Side well before the trendy clothing stores and art galleries arrived. The first generation of musicians emerged from the rubble left by the collapse of the scene surrounding Andy Warhol. Many played at his former hangout, Max's Kansas City; all drew inspiration both from his Pop-art irony and the distinct Manhattan-ness of his former associates, the Velvet Underground.

First came the New York Dolls, a raucous gang of Rolling Stones wanna-bes in stack heels whose greatest moments were live shows at the Mercer Arts Center on the edge of Washington Square and who established a style of short and simple guitar-based songs. Then came the poetic Patti Smith and the guitar exercises of Television, whose Richard Hell took to tearing his T-shirt, inspiring Malcolm McLaren to have the Sex Pistols do the same a few years later in London. The vital gig was Hilly Kristal's CBGB-OMFUG (Country, Bluegrass, Blues, and Other Music for Uplifting Gourmandisers), better known as CBGB, a dank tunnel of a bar on the corner of Bleecker Street and the Bowery that opened in 1973 and always seemed far more dangerous than it really was. Talking Heads, Blondie, and the Ramones all used it as a launching pad. As with London's later punk scene, New York City's new wave was a collision of sensibilities as influenced by suburban refugees as it was by art students—part genuine roughneck and part dilettante.

Doll Johnny Thunders), then fronted the Voidoids. Television disbanded in 1978, reuniting briefly in 1992 for an eponymous album and tour. The group reunited again in 2001, performing a series of live dates in the United Kingdom, before once again splitting up. Interest in the band was rekindled in 2003 when remastered recordings of Television's back catalog were released, along with *Live at the Old Waldorf*, a concert album that captured the group at the end of its 1978 tour. Verlaine also pursued a solo career.

PATTI SMITH

Although she never topped the charts, Patti Smith (born December 30, 1946, Chicago, Illinois, U.S.) precipitated punk rock in New York, London, Los Angeles, and beyond. A pioneer in the fusion of the bohemian sensibility with rock, she was able to translate the incantatory power of Beat writers such as Allen Ginsberg and William S. Burroughs into the rock mainstream. Her compelling charisma, chantlike but hoarsely compelling musical declamation, visionary texts, and simple but ingenious rock music won an intense cult following.

Growing up in New Jersey, Smith won an art scholarship to Glassboro State Teachers College. In 1967 she moved to New York City, where she became active in the downtown Manhattan arts scene, writing poetry and living with the photographer Robert Mapplethorpe. Her performance-driven poetry readings soon took on a musical component, and from 1971 she worked regularly with the guitarist and critic Lenny Kaye. By 1973 they had formed a band and began performing widely in the downtown club scene.

Signed to a contract with Arista Records, she released her first album, *Horses*, in 1975; it was produced by John Cale, the Welsh avant-gardist and cofounder (with Lou Reed) of the Velvet Underground. Her purest, truest album, it replicated her live shows better than any subsequent LP. Later albums of the 1970s moved in a more commercial direction, with a pounding big beat that bludgeoned away some of her subtlety; at the same time, her concerts often became sloppy and undisciplined. After *Radio Ethiopia* (1976) she released her most commercially successful album, *Easter*, in 1978. It included a hit single, "Because the Night," written with Bruce Springsteen.

Following the album *Wave* in 1979, Smith disbanded her group and retired to Detroit, Michigan, where she raised a family with Fred ("Sonic") Smith, founder of the band MC5. Although she recorded an album with her husband in 1988 (*Dream of Life*) and began working on new songs with him a few years later, it was only after his sudden death from a heart attack in 1994 that her comeback began in earnest. *Gone Again*, her first solo album in 17 years, appeared in 1996 and was followed by *Peace and Noise* (1997) and *Gung Ho* (2000). She continued releasing new work in the 21st century. If

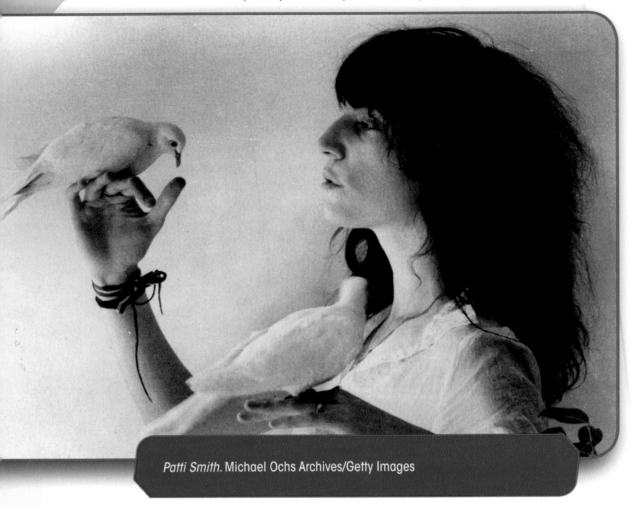

Patti Smith. Michael Ochs Archives/Getty Images

anything, this late work showed her stronger than ever, full of the old fire but purged of her more extreme excesses. In 2007 Smith was inducted into the Rock and Roll Hall of Fame, and in 2010 she published the memoir *Just Kids*, which focused on her relationship with Mapplethorpe. The critically acclaimed work won the National Book Award for nonfiction.

JIM CARROLL

American poet and rock musician Jim Carroll (born August 1, 1949, New York, New York—died September 11, 2009, New York City) wrote several acclaimed collections of poems but was best known for *The Basketball Diaries* (1978; filmed 1995), an unvarnished account of his drug-addled

ROBERT MAPPLETHORPE

American photographer Robert Mapplethorpe (born November 4, 1946, New York, New York, U.S.—died March 9, 1989, Boston, Massachusetts) was noted for austere photographs of flowers, celebrities, and male nudes; among the latter were some that proved controversial because of their explicitly homoerotic and sadomasochistic themes. Mapplethorpe attended the Pratt Institute in New York City (1963–70). After experimenting with underground filmmaking in the late 1960s, by 1970 he was creating photographs using a Polaroid camera, often arranging them into collages or showing them as series. By the mid-1970s he received critical attention for his elegant black-and-white photographs. He experimented with different techniques, including using a large-format press camera, combining photographic images printed on linen, and designing his own wooden frames.

During this period he pursued what were to remain his favourite subjects throughout his career: still lifes, flowers, portraits of friends and celebrities (such as Patti Smith), and homoerotic explorations of the male body. His compositions were generally stark, his combination of cold studio light and precise focus creating dramatic tonal contrasts. While these effects rendered still lifes with an almost Vermeer-like coolness, these same techniques rendered homosexual imagery in a manner that some found shocking. His muscular male models were generally framed against plain backdrops, sometimes engaged in sexual activity or posed with sadomasochistic props such as leather and chains. His clear, unflinching style challenged viewers to confront this imagery. Moreover, the combination of his choice of subject matter with the photographs' formal beauty and grounding in art-historical traditions created what many saw as a tension between pornography and art.

continued on page 202

continued from page 201

Mapplethorpe's reputation grew in the 1980s, and he began to focus more on flowers and celebrity portraits than on the overtly sexual subject matter of his earlier output. Still, Mapplethorpe managed to impart a sensual energy to the folds of one of his favourite subjects, the calla lily, that many would argue equalled the impact of his nudes. Mapplethorpe extended his interest in form in a series of portraits of female bodybuilder Lisa Lyon. His work was exhibited internationally, with major shows at the Whitney Museum of American Art in New York City and the National Portrait Gallery in London (both 1988), and his photographs were featured in such books as *Robert Mapplethorpe Photographs* (1978), *Lady: Lisa Lyon* (1983), *Robert Mapplethorpe: Certain People* (1985), *The Black Book* (1988), and *Flowers* (1990), with an introduction by Patti Smith. When he contracted the AIDS virus, Mapplethorpe chronicled his illness in a harrowing series of self-portraits.

A posthumous retrospective exhibition, "Robert Mapplethorpe: The Perfect Moment," was planned for the Corcoran Gallery in Washington, D.C., but stirred a political debate in 1990 that caused the museum to cancel the show. Because the exhibition—which featured Mapplethorpe's still lifes as well as his nudes—was partly funded by a grant from the National Endowment of the Arts (NEA), the exhibit sparked a debate about government subsidies of "obscene" art and provoked Congress to enact restrictions on future NEA grants. Also in 1990, Dennis Barrie, the director of the Contemporary Arts Center in Cincinnati, Ohio, was arrested but later acquitted of obscenity charges for displaying the same Mapplethorpe exhibition. The exhibition was shown with little to no controversy in other cities, including Chicago, Berkeley (California), and Boston.

Mapplethorpe's reputation as one of his era's most talented—and most provocative—photographers continued to rise at the turn of the 21st century. Important monographs of his work were published posthumously, including *Some Women* (1995), with an introduction by Joan Didion, and *Robert Mapplethorpe: Pictures* (1999), with an introduction by editor Ingrid Sischy.

adolescence in 1960s New York City. Carroll began his journal at the age of 12 as a budding basketball star (he eventually received a basketball scholarship to Trinity, a private high school in Manhattan) but not long after was vividly chronicling his descent into heroin addiction and prostitution. His first book of poetry, *Organic Trains* (1967), won him the admiration of the New York bohemian art scene, including the Beat writer Allen Ginsberg and the artist Andy Warhol, for whom he briefly worked; excerpts of his diaries published in the *Paris Review* in 1970 gained him a wider audience. In the 1970s Carroll's friendship with poet and punk-rock singer Patti Smith inspired him to form his own punk band, and the Jim Carroll Band's debut recording, *Catholic Boy* (1980), featuring the iconic single "People Who Died," was met with praise from the rock cognoscenti. Though several albums and books of poetry followed, Carroll never replicated his early success. A posthumous novel, *The Petting Zoo*, was published in 2010.

THE RAMONES

The Ramones influenced the rise of punk rock on both sides of the Atlantic Ocean. The original members were Joey Ramone (born Jeffrey Hyman, May 19, 1951, New York, New York, U.S.—died April 15, 2001, New York), Johnny Ramone (born John Cummings, October 8, 1951, New York—died September 15, 2004, Los Angeles, California), Dee Dee Ramone (born Douglas Colvin, September 18, 1952, Fort Lee, Virginia, U.S.—died June 5, 2002, Los Angeles), and Tommy Ramone (born Tommy Erdelyi, January 29, 1952, Budapest, Hungary).

Founded in New York City in 1974, the Ramones cultivated a simple three-chord sound that became the foundation of punk rock. Played at a blistering tempo, frequently lasting little more than two minutes, and with catchy, often willfully inane lyrics (so stupid they were smart, according to some critics), Ramones songs such as "I Wanna Be Sedated" contrasted sharply with the complex, carefully orchestrated mainstream rock of the era. In ripped jeans and black leather jackets, the Ramones made their reputation with almost-nonstop touring and energetic live performances, notably at CBGB. Their tour of England in 1976 proved a major inspiration for the punk movement in Britain, where they enjoyed greater commercial success than at home. Influenced by the rebelliousness of their contemporaries the New York Dolls and by 1960s pop music (especially bubblegum and surf music), the Ramones brought their back-to-basics approach to such albums as their eponymous debut (1976) and *Rocket to Russia* (1977). With a shifting lineup, they continued to record and perform into the 1990s, disbanding in 1996. In 2002 the Ramones were inducted into the Rock and Roll Hall of Fame.

LUX INTERIOR AND THE CRAMPS

American punk musician Lux Interior (born Erick Lee Purkhiser, October 21, 1946, Stow, Ohio—died February 4, 2009, Glendale, California) fronted the legendary "psychobilly" rock band the Cramps, which he and his wife, guitarist Poison Ivy (Kristy Wallace), founded in 1976. With a style informed by B horror movies, trashy comic books, early rockabilly, and raw garage-band rock and roll, the Cramps gained a following in the mid- to late 1970s at the New York City punk clubs CBGB and Max's Kansas City. A 1979 tour of Britain opening for the Police brought the Cramps even more devoted fans. Interior's performances were notorious for their menacing and extreme theatricality. The Cramps released their first album, *Songs the Lord Taught Us*, in 1980, and, with assorted personnel behind Interior and Ivy, went on to make 13 more recordings.

X

X delivered tales of urban decay, corruption, and sleaze with skilled musicianship and unique vocal harmonies, marking them as important contributors to the punk movement. The original members were Exene Cervenka (born Christine Cervenka, February 1, 1956, Chicago, Illinois, U.S.), John Doe (born February 25, 1953, Decatur, Illinois), Billy Zoom (born Ty Kindell, February 20, 1948, Illinois), and D.J. Bonebrake (born December 8, 1955, North Hollywood, California). Later members included Dave Alvin (born November 11, 1955, Los Angeles, California) and Tony Gilkyson.

Formed in 1977, X released *Los Angeles* in 1980. That effort and the follow-up albums *Wild Gift* (1981) and *Under the Big Black Sun* (1982) drew critical raves, as X broadened punk's do-it-yourself ethos with excellent musicianship (guitarist Zoom, who had once played with rock-and-roll pioneer Gene Vincent, blazed through country, rockabilly, heavy metal, and punk licks with dispassionate aplomb, while drummer Bonebrake added a background in jazz), the unusual harmonies and sophisticated songwriting of onetime husband and wife Doe and Cervenka (the latter an active poet), and careful production by Ray Manzarek, formerly of the Doors. In the process, X became prime movers of the Los Angeles punk scene chronicled in the documentary *The Decline of Western Civilization* (1981). Capable of matching the fury of other punk bands, X also excelled at melancholy ballads and flirted with pop music throughout its career, though its efforts to reach a broader audience on a major label were largely unsuccessful.

The band toured and recorded sporadically throughout the 1980s and '90s, but members were increasingly occupied by side projects and solo efforts. Doe, Cervenka, Alvin, and Bonebrake formed the Knitters in 1985. Intended as a one-time project, the Knitters performed a selection of folk and country tunes, along with acoustic versions of songs from the X catalog. Cervenka dedicated much of her time to poetry, publishing numerous collections and recording a series of solo albums. Doe turned to Hollywood, scoring small parts in films such as *Road House* (1989) and *Boogie Nights* (1997) and landing a recurring role in the supernatural television series *Roswell* (1999–2002). Alvin earned a Grammy Award for his traditional folk album *Public Domain: Songs from the Wild Land* (2000). The original X lineup reunited for a pair of concerts in 2004 (later collected in the album *Live in Los Angeles* [2005]), and the Knitters re-formed to record *The Modern Sounds of the Knitters* (2005).

BLACK FLAG

Extensive touring and prolific recording helped Black Flag to popularize hardcore punk, the genre that arose in California in the early 1980s in response to the punk movement of the 1970s. The original members were guitarist Greg Ginn (born June 8, 1954), bassist Chuck Dukowski (born February 1, 1954), lead singer Keith Morris, and drummer Brian Migdol. Later members included Henry Rollins (born Henry Garfield, February 13, 1961, Washington, D.C.), Chavo Pederast, Dez Cadena, Kira Roessler, and Anthony Martinez.

Founded in 1977 in Los Angeles, Black Flag focused on themes such as boredom and the banality of suburban life and accelerated punk's blistering tempo to an even more breakneck pace, helping to establish many of the conventions of hardcore. Appealing to a largely white male audience that made "slam dancing" (the purposeful collision of bodies) in the "mosh pit" (the clump of audience members in front of the bandstand) a ritual at live performances, Black Flag brought a fury and aggression to its music and performance seldom equaled by other hardcore bands.

In 1978 Ginn and Dukowski founded SST Records to distribute the band's music, and the label's first release was the single "Nervous Breakdown." Along with Slash Records, SST became the avatar of the West Coast punk scene, and its early roster included seminal hardcore acts the Minutemen, the Meat Puppets, and Hüsker Dü. After settling on Rollins as its vocalist, Black Flag released *Damaged* (1981), its first full-length album. Later recordings flirted with heavy metal, and the band also provided musical accompaniment to Rollins's poetry before breaking up in 1986.

With the demise of Black Flag, Ginn and Dukowski devoted their time to the management of SST, and they signed such acts as the punk reggae combo Bad Brains and the New York art rock band Sonic Youth. As the focus of the American independent music scene shifted to the Pacific Northwest in the 1990s, SST lost much of its cachet. Rollins continued performing as the lead singer of the Rollins Band, but he later turned his attention to acting and spent much of his time delivering spoken-word monologues and managing his publishing house, 2.13.61.

HENRY ROLLINS

Henry Rollins's tenure as the lead vocalist of Black Flag made him one of the most recognizable faces in the 1980s punk scene. Rollins was an avid fan of hardcore music, and as a teenager he performed with a number of bands in the Washington, D.C., area. During a performance by Black Flag in New York City, Rollins, who was in the audience, climbed onstage and sang along with the group. Dez Cadena, then Black Flag's front man, had been considering a move from vocals to guitar, and Rollins joined the band and took over as lead singer. The band encountered legal trouble with its label, MCA, but it nevertheless maintained a relentless touring schedule and produced a number of notable albums throughout the 1980s, including *Damaged* (1981) and *In My Head* (1985).

When Black Flag disbanded in 1986, Rollins continued performing, recruiting a revolving stable of musicians to join him in the Rollins Band. The Rollins Band recorded a string of solid hard-rock albums through the 1990s and early 2000s, and *Weight* (1994) featured Rollins's first Top 40 single, "Liar." However, Rollins was perhaps best known for his nonmusical endeavours. While still a member of Black Flag, he had established 2.13.61, a publishing house that released books of his own poetry, as well works by Nick Cave, Hubert Selby, Jr., and others. He also proved himself to be a gifted monologuist, and his performances often

Henry Rollins. Michael Ochs Archives/Getty Images

blended self-deprecating humour and political commentary with the rage and intensity befitting a former punk front man. Rollins earned a Grammy Award for best spoken word album for *Get in the Van: On the Road with Black Flag* (1994). His popular *Harmony in My Head* radio show, which debuted in 2004, served as an outlet for his eclectic taste in music, and *The Henry Rollins Show* (2006–07) was a unique twist on the traditional television talk show. Rollins also worked as an actor, with parts in films such as *Heat* (1995) and *Lost Highway* (1997) and a recurring role in the television series *Sons of Anarchy* (2009).

HÜSKER DÜ

Hüsker Dü melded pop melodies and lyricism with punk music, helping to set the stage for the alternative rock boom of the 1990s. The members were Bob Mould (born October 12, 1960, Malone, New York, U.S.), Greg Norton (born March 13, 1959, Rock Island, Illinois), and Grant Hart (born March 18, 1961, St. Paul, Minnesota).

Taking the name of a 1950s Scandinavian board game, Hüsker Dü ("Do you remember?") formed in St. Paul, Minnesota, in 1979, when the Minneapolis area was becoming a hotbed of pop music. They won a loyal following by touring steadily, recording frequently, and gaining college radio airplay. Although the band's musical style on early recordings, such as their debut album, *Land Speed Record* (1981), was aggressively hardcore punk, their later music revealed the influence of jazz, pop, and psychedelic rock; their *Zen Arcade* (1984) was one of the few punk-oriented double albums. Celebrated for maintaining their artistic integrity even after moving to a major label with *Candy Apple Gray* (1986), Hüsker Dü disbanded in 1988 after having produced a string of critically acclaimed albums including *New Day Rising* (1985), *Flip Your Wig* (1985), and *Warehouse: Songs and Stories* (1987).

Hart subsequently pursued a solo career and recorded as a member of the Nova Mob. Mould's post-Hüsker Dü years were a more varied affair. He scored success with solo projects and as a member of Sugar; that group's 1992 debut, *Copper Blue*, was an alternative rock smash, and it was widely regarded as one of the best albums of the 1990s. Mould also pursued an interest in professional wrestling, working as a script writer for World Championship Wrestling in 1999. In the 21st century, Mould branched into electronic music, hosting a live DJ party, and he penned the memoir *See a Little Light* (2011).

FUGAZI

American hardcore punk band Fugazi was known as much for its anticorporate politics as for its intense, dynamic music. The members were drummer Brendan Canty (born March, 9, 1966, Teaneck, New Jersey, U.S.), bass player Joe Lally (born December 3, 1963, Rockville, Maryland), vocalist-guitarist Ian MacKaye (born April 16, 1962, Washington, D.C.), and vocalist-guitarist Guy Picciotto (born September 17, 1965, Washington, D.C.).

Formed in 1987, the band emerged from the Washington, D.C., punk scene. All four members had already played in local bands; MacKaye had been a member of influential hardcore band Minor Threat and cofounded the independent label Dischord Records in 1980. By the time Fugazi had released its full-length debut, *13 Songs*, in 1989, it had established a unique sound: building from the raw energy of 1980s hardcore bands such as Black Flag, Fugazi created its own brand of intricate song structures and stop-and-start dynamics, often fueled by call-and-response exchanges between dual singers MacKaye and Picciotto.

The group quickly developed a reputation for its integrity and its grassroots ethos. Despite lucrative offers from major labels, Fugazi remained self-managed and self-produced, releasing all its albums on Dischord. The band refused to charge more than $6 for admission to its exclusively all-ages shows and kept the price of its CDs under about $12—gestures intended to keep Fugazi accessible to its loyal fan base. Especially in light of the popular explosion of alternative and punk bands in the 1990s, Fugazi's adherence to the punk movement's original do-it-yourself populist stance earned the band a great deal of respect among its peers.

Over the course of the 1990s, on albums such as *Repeater* (1990), *Steady Diet of Nothing* (1991), *In on the Kill Taker* (1992), *Red Medicine* (1995), and *End Hits* (1998), Fugazi retained its churning rhythms and raw emotion, but its song structures became more varied and its lyrics more oblique and less overtly political (the band had sometimes been criticized for being too didactic and politically correct in its earlier efforts). Fugazi became known for its intense live performances, marked by consistently tight sets and the magnetic stage presences of MacKaye and Picciotto. Onstage, the band utilized its trademark sound—the buildup of extreme tension followed by calm—to draw its audience into a visceral, emotional experience. Yet Fugazi stood out among its contemporaries in its opposition to slam dancing (the aggressive body-jarring collisions that were the preferred dance form of fans of hardcore).

In 1999 a documentary about the band, titled *Instrument*, was released, followed in 2001 by both a full album, *The Argument*, and an extended-play CD, *Furniture*.

ROMANTICS, POSTPUNKS, AND MISERABILISTS: NEW WAVE

Taking its name from the French New Wave cinema of the late 1950s, the catchall classification *new wave* was defined in opposition to punk (which was generally more raw, rough edged, and political) and to mainstream "corporate" rock (which many new wave upstarts considered complacent and creatively stagnant). The basic principle behind new wave was the same as that of punk—anyone can start a band—but new wave artists, influenced by the lighter side of 1960s pop music and 1950s fashion, were more commercially viable than their abrasive counterparts.

New wave music encompassed a wide variety of styles, which often shared a quirky insouciance and sense of humour. In the United States this broad spectrum included the B-52s, leading lights of an emerging music scene in Athens, Georgia, whose hybrid dance music mixed girl group harmonies with vocal experimentation such as that of Yoko Ono; Blondie, with its sex-symbol vocalist Deborah Harry; the tunefulness of Jonathan Richman and the Modern Lovers; the Go-Go's, whose debut album, *Beauty and the Beat*, reached number one in 1982; the Cars, who found immediate Top 40 success with "Just What I Needed"; and an artier avant-garde that included Devo and Talking Heads.

In Britain new wave was led by clever singer-songwriters such as pub rock veterans Nick Lowe, Graham Parker, and Elvis Costello; Squeeze and XTC, whose songs were sophisticated and infectious; ska revivalists such as Madness and the Specials; genre-hopping Joe Jackson; synthesizer bands such as Human League, Heaven 17, and A Flock of Seagulls; and the so-called New Romantics, including the cosmetics-wearing Duran Duran, Adam and the Ants, and Culture Club. As the mid-1980s approached, the line separating new wave from the corporate mainstream blurred, especially for bands such as the Pretenders (fronted by former rock journalist Chrissie Hynde), the Police, and U2, who became hugely popular. Although punk was pronounced dead (though it later would inspire grunge and alternative), the music and fashion sensibilities of new wave continued to influence pop music through the 1990s.

ELVIS COSTELLO

British singer-songwriter Elvis Costello (born Declan Patrick McManus, August 25, 1954, London, England) extended the musical and lyrical range of the punk and new-wave movements. The son of musicians, Costello was exposed to a mix of British and American styles—dance-hall pop to modern jazz to the Beatles—from a young age. During the early 1970s he lived in London, recording demos and performing locally while working as a computer programmer. He befriended Nick Lowe, bassist for the pub rock band Brinsley Schwarz, who brought him to the attention of Jake Riviera, one of the heads of the independent label Stiff Records. In 1977 Lowe produced Costello's first album, *My Aim Is True*. A critical and commercial success, it aligned the cynicism and energy of punk bands such as the Sex Pistols and the Clash with the structures of a more literate songwriting tradition, weaving complex wordplay through a set of clever pop tunes and moving easily among varied melodic styles.

After the success of *My Aim Is True*, Costello formed a strong backing band, the Attractions, with Steve Nieve on keyboard, Pete Thomas on drums, and Bruce Thomas on bass. On the early albums with the Attractions—*This Year's Model* (1978), *Armed Forces* (1979), and *Get Happy!!* (1980)—Costello and Lowe developed a distinctive guitar and keyboard mix that was influenced by a variety of 1960s artists, including Booker T. and the MG's. The most notable work of this early period—rockers such as "This Year's Girl" and "Lip Service," deceptively upbeat pop tunes such as "(The Angels Wanna Wear My) Red Shoes," and rapid-fire, soul-inflected songs such as "Black and White World"—featured appealing melodic bass lines that complemented an energetic rhythm guitar and a stylized, almost awkward vocal style. Through densely constructed thematic puns, Costello explored the intersection of power and intimacy, often from the perspective of a rejected lover.

During the 1980s Costello broadened his range, working with various producers who developed more layered arrangements. The hit "Everyday I Write the Book" (1983) was composed during this period, and albums such as *Trust* (1981) and *Imperial Bedroom* (1982) won critical acclaim. However, the early 1980s were also a time of creative inconsistency, as Costello experimented with the country genre in *Almost Blue* (1981) and released *Goodbye Cruel World* (1984); both albums had only limited critical and commercial success. In 1985 Costello divorced his wife, and he married Cait O'Riordan, the bassist of the British band the Pogues, the following year. Following their wedding, Costello recorded *King of America* (1986), a radical stylistic departure. Produced by T-Bone Burnett, King of America featured spare acoustic arrangements and a more direct lyrical style. Costello continued to explore new sounds on his next album, *Spike* (1989). In both of these works, Costello wrote about the role of the artist in popular culture, blending contemporary cultural imagery with modern and classical literary allusions. He developed a fragmented, dissonant lyrical style; the influence of modern poets such as T.S. Eliot was evident on visionary songs such as "…This Town…" from *Spike* and "Couldn't Call It Unexpected #4" from *Mighty Like a Rose* (1991).

In the 1990s he released a mixed set of recordings, ranging from straightforward, well-crafted rockers to experimental works such as the song cycle *The Juliet Letters* (1993), recorded with a string quartet, and *Painted from Memory* (1998), written with the composer Burt Bacharach. In 2003 Costello married Canadian jazz musician Diana Krall; the two collaborated on Krall's *The Girl in the Other Room* (2004). Costello continued to develop musically and lyrically and remained one of rock's most respected songwriters into the 21st century.

THE SMITHS

Prime exponents of British alternative rock, the Smiths were one of the most popular and critically acclaimed English bands of the 1980s. The original members were lead singer Morrissey (born Steven Patrick Morrissey, May 22, 1959, Manchester, England), guitarist Johnny Marr (born John Maher, October 31, 1963, Manchester), bassist Andy Rourke (born 1963, Manchester), and drummer Mike Joyce (born June 1, 1963).

The creative engine of the group was the unlikely partnership of singer-lyricist Morrissey (a reclusive bookworm inspired as much by Oscar Wilde as by his glam-rock heroes the New York Dolls) and budding guitar hero Marr. With drummer Joyce and bassist Rourke completing the lineup, the band burst on the Manchester scene and quickly won a cult following with sessions recorded for BBC radio, live shows, and the plangent folk-punk of their debut single, "Hand in Glove." Signed to the prominent independent label Rough Trade, the Smiths scored several U.K. hits, notably "This Charming Man" and "What Difference Does It Make?" Morrissey's flamboyant stage presence, forlorn croon, and compellingly conflicted persona (loudly proclaimed celibacy offset by coy hints of closeted homosexuality) made him a peculiar heartthrob, and songs such as "Still Ill" sealed his role as spokesman for disaffected youth. But Morrissey's "woe-is-me" posture inspired some hostile critics to dismiss the Smiths as "miserabilists."

After their brilliant eponymous debut and the sparkling radio-session collection *Hatful of Hollow* (both released in 1984), the Smiths released *Meat Is Murder* (1985), an uneven album ranging from the ponderous title track's vegan rage to the poignant "Well I Wonder." The group's marked shift from the personal to the political, combined with Morrissey's carefully fashioned outsider image, made the Smiths into champions for those alienated by Tory materialism and disgusted by its pop music reflection (glossy, lyrically inane funk and soul). The Smiths' non-rhythm-and-blues, whiter-than-white fusion of 1960s rock and postpunk was a repudiation of contemporary dance pop, a stance emblazoned in the hit single "Panic," with its controversial chorus, "Burn down the disco / Hang the blessed DJ." After 1986's *The Queen Is Dead*, their most perfect balance of private angst and public anger, the Smiths—frustrated at the failure of their singles to hit the Top Ten—abandoned Rough Trade for the marketing muscle of the major label EMI (in the United States they remained with Sire Records). Shortly before the release of their last album for Rough Trade, *Strangeways, Here*

We Come (1987), the group broke up unexpectedly.

Morrissey's solo career started promisingly with 1988's *Viva Hate* (on which guitar virtuoso Vini Reilly proved a capable Marr surrogate); however, on subsequent singles and *Kill Uncle* (1991), Morrissey, backed by an undistinguished rockabilly band, dwindled into tuneless self-parody. His muse rallied with the glam-rock-influenced *Your Arsenal* (1992) and the delicate *Vauxhall and I* (1994). These albums, and the less impressive *Southpaw Grammar* (1995) and *Maladjusted* (1997), testified to a growing homoerotic obsession with criminals, skinheads, and boxers, a change paralleled by a shift in the singer's image from wilting wallflower to would-be thug sporting sideburns and gold bracelets. A seven-year hiatus followed, and fans and critics warmly greeted the politics and pathos of *You Are the Quarry* (2004), the solid craftsmanship of *Ringleader of the Tormentors* (2006), and the self-assured *Years of Refusal* (2009). Despite Morrissey's aesthetic fluctuations in the decades following the demise of the Smiths, the cult of this true pop original endured.

Marr's post-Smiths career was equally productive, even if it lacked the theatricality of Morrissey's. Drawn once again to a charismatic vocalist with a penchant for dark lyrics, Marr joined Matt Johnson in

The The, where his signature sound drove two of that band's most successful albums—*Mind Bomb* (1989) and *Dusk* (1991). Marr teamed with Bernard Sumner of New Order in the supergroup Electronic. Although Marr and Sumner had initially conceived their partnership to be temporary, the success of the 1989 single "Getting Away with It" inspired the pair to record three well-received dance albums. More than a decade after the demise of the Smiths, Marr formed his own group, the Healers. Distribution issues plagued the band's debut effort, however, and three years passed before it hit stores as *Boomslang* (2003). In 2007 Marr joined alternative rock act Modest Mouse on the group's *We Were Dead Before the Ship Even Sank*.

LIVERPOOL'S SECOND COMING

A decade and a half after the Beatles emerged from the Cavern (a below-ground musical venue in Liverpool, England, that bills itself as "the cradle of British pop music"), a new generation of Liverpudlian music arose from the subterranean shabbiness of Eric's Club, run by Roger Eagle from 1976 until it closed in 1980. Less a distinctive sound than an attitude, the Liverpool beat of the late 1970s and '80s first took shape on the local Zoo label, run by Bill Drummond.

Both Echo and the Bunnymen and the Teardrop Explodes (whose respective leaders, Ian McCulloch and Julian Cope, had been members of the punk group the Crucial Three) had a languid style and a sense of self-adoration that looked back to punk and glam rock and forward to the New Romantic movement led by Duran Duran. Both groups moved on from Zoo to major labels.

Another Merseyside group, A Flock of Seagulls, had some international success in the early 1980s, but the biggest act to come out of Liverpool during this period was Frankie Goes to Hollywood ("Relax," "Two Tribes"), whose front man Holly Johnson had worked with Drummond in the art-punk group Big in Japan. Scottish-born Drummond, who managed both the Bunnymen and the Teardrop Explodes, later cofounded KLF (Kopyright Liberation Front), the "group" whose experimental approach to music making resulted in several British number one hits constructed wholly by sampling—that is, by creating a pastiche of sounds from other recordings.

THE POLICE

Five best-selling albums, a bevy of hits, and aggressive touring—including stops in countries usually overlooked by Western pop musicians—combined to make the

SHEFFIELD: A NEW WAVE HOTBED

Sheffield, England, is the heartland of Britain's rust belt. Built on coal and steel industries, it was devastated by the tsunami of world economic change in the 1980s. The contemporaneous wave of innovative music produced in the city owed far less to local traditional music—e.g., brass bands—than it did to the musical possibilities offered by the very electronic technology that contributed to the closing of the city's factories, mills, and mines. Because of its size and regional significance, this hilly Yorkshire city has long had a substantial local music scene—including the rock blues of Joe Cocker and the archetypal steel-city heavy metal of Def Leppard. But what united the Sheffield music of the early 1980s was that it was all, in various ways, a response to the anarchic call of punk.

Although they never sold many records, Cabaret Voltaire welded punk's fury to electronic rhythms, creating experimental dance music whose influence was still being felt at the end of the century. ABC, led by Martin Fry, united punk sloganeering with lushly romantic lyrics and strings. The most successful locals, however, were the Human League, who started as an avant-garde electronic group in 1977 before splitting in two in 1980. Martyn Ware and Ian Craig Marsh (who achieved their greatest success as producers, notably by resuscitating the career of Tina Turner in 1983) went on to jointly form the British Electric Foundation and Heaven 17. Meanwhile, those who remained in the Human League defined technopop (electronic pop) through the early 1980s; both "Don't You Want Me" (1982) and "Human" (1986) were major hits in the United States. Formed in 1978, Pulp, with its eccentric front man, Jarvis Cocker, waited 15 years to achieve national recognition in Britain with "Common People" (1995), though its success was not mirrored in the United States.

Police the world's most popular band in the early 1980s. The members were Sting (born Gordon Sumner, October 2, 1951, Wallsend, Tyne and Wear, England), Stewart Copeland (born July 16, 1952, Alexandria, Virginia, U.S.), and Andy Summers (born Andrew Somers, December 31, 1942, Poulton-le-Fylde, Lancashire).

Unlike most of their punk contemporaries, the Police were skilled musicians when they came together in London in 1977. Drummer Copeland played with the progressive rock band Curved Air, bassist-vocalist-songwriter Sting performed with jazz combos in his native Newcastle, and Summers (who replaced the group's original guitarist, Henri Padovani) was a veteran of numerous British rhythm-and-blues and rock bands. Having dyed their hair blond to play a punk band in a commercial and thereby established their signature look, the Police charted in both Britain and the United States with the reggae-imbued albums *Outlandos d'Amour* (released in late 1978 in Britain and in early 1979 in the United States) and *Regatta de Blanc* (1979). *Zenyatta Mondatta* (1980) and the synthesizer-rich *Ghost in the Machine* (1981) saw a marked evolution from the stripped-down arrangements of their early work to a more layered but still tightly focused sound. The group reached its commercial and critical peak with the multiplatinum album *Synchronicity* (1983). On all their work, Summers's evocative guitar playing and Copeland's polyrhythmic virtuosity provided a solid foundation for Sting's impassioned vocals and sophisticated lyrics (which included references to writers Vladimir Nabokov and Arthur Koestler).

In 1985, at the peak of their popularity, the Police dissolved. Copeland went on to score numerous motion pictures, while Summers recorded adventurous music, including two albums with fellow guitarist Robert Fripp. Sting became an extremely popular soloist, revisiting his jazz roots (accompanied by such accomplished musicians as saxophonist Branford Marsalis and keyboardist Kenny Kirkland) and later incorporating Latin and folk influences. He also continued an uneven acting career, which began with *Quadrophenia* (1979) and included *Dune* (1984) and *Stormy Monday* (1988). The Police were inducted into the Rock and Roll Hall of Fame in 2003. The trio reunited for a performance at the 2007 Grammy Awards and followed it with a highly successful world tour.

BLONDIE

Blondie incorporated varied influences, including avante garde, reggae, and hip-hop, into the new wave sound of the 1970s and '80s.

The band was formed in 1974 by vocalist Deborah Harry (born July 1, 1945, Miami, Florida, U.S.) and guitarist Chris Stein (born January 5, 1950, Brooklyn, New York). The pair—also longtime romantic partners—recruited drummer Clem Burke (born Clement Bozewski, November 24, 1955, Bayonne, New Jersey), bassist Gary Valentine (born Gary Lachman, December 24, 1955), and keyboardist Jimmy Destri (born April 13, 1954, Brooklyn). Later members included bassist Nigel Harrison (born April 24, 1951, Stockport, England) and guitarist Frank Infante (born November 15, 1951).

The band played New York punk clubs such as CBGB alongside contemporaries such as Talking Heads, Television, and Patti Smith, and released its self-titled debut album on Private Stock Records in 1976. Major label Chrysalis Records released *Plastic Letters* the following year, earning the group a following in the United Kingdom. *Parallel Lines* (1978) broke the band into the rock mainstream thanks to hits such as "Picture This," "One Way or Another," and the disco-influenced "Heart of Glass." *Eat to the Beat* (1979) was similarly successful.

The group's image was always defined by bleach blonde Harry's sly streetwise vocal delivery and sexually charged public persona. A collaboration with producer Giorgio Moroder led to the single "Call Me," which topped the charts in 1980 and served as the theme for the film *American Gigolo*. By the time of *Autoamerican* (1980), the other members' creative contributions had waned, even as the group's style grew more adventurous, encompassing the reggae hit "The Tide Is High" and introducing the nascent genre of hip-hop to rock audiences with the single "Rapture." *The Hunter* (1982) represented a downturn in record sales. After Stein became seriously ill that year, Blondie disbanded.

In 1998 original members Harry, Stein, Burke, and Destri reunited for a European concert tour, and they released a new album, *No Exit*, the following year. Blondie continued to tour sporadically and record throughout the following decade, and in 2006 the group was inducted into the Rock and Roll Hall of Fame.

DEVO

Devo took its name from *devolution*, the theory of mankind's regression that informed the band's music and stage act. The band members were Mark Mothersbaugh, Jerry Casale, Bob Mothersbaugh, Bob Casale, and Alan Myers. (Biographical information on the group's members was withheld by Devo to reinforce its mechanistic image.)

Formed in Akron, Ohio, in 1972 by art students Mark Mothersbaugh

BRIAN ENO

British producer, composer, keyboardist, and singer Brian Eno (born May 15, 1948, Woodbridge, Suffolk, Enland) helped define and reinvent the sound of some of the most popular bands of the 1980s and '90s. He also created the genre of ambient music.

While an art student in the late 1960s, Eno began experimenting with electronic music, and in 1971 he joined the fledgling band Roxy Music as keyboardist and technical adviser. A rivalry with singer Bryan Ferry led Eno to leave the group in 1973, whereupon he launched a solo career. *No Pussyfooting* (1973), a collaboration with guitarist Robert Fripp, used tape-echo and tape-delay techniques to create new sounds and reached the Top 30 in Britain. Eno's next album, *Here Come the Warm Jets* (1973), was soon followed by the proto-punk single "Seven Deadly Finns." In the mid-1970s Eno began developing his theory of ambient music, creating subtle instrumentals to affect mood through sound. Albums such as *Discrete Music* (1975), *Music for Films* (1978), and *Music for Airports* (1979) exemplified this approach.

During this period Eno also began producing albums for other artists, and his experimental approach to music making was well suited to such alternative performers as Devo, Ultravox, and David Bowie (especially on Bowie's trilogy of albums recorded primarily in Berlin). Although Eno's work was influential, it was not until his collaborations with Talking Heads and U2 that mainstream listeners became familiar with his sound, most notably on Talking Heads' Top 20 album *Remain in Light* (1980) and U2's chart-topping albums *Unforgettable Fire* (1984), *The Joshua Tree* (1987), and *Achtung Baby* (1991).

Throughout the 1990s, Eno joined a number of visual artists to provide sound tracks to installation pieces, and in 1995 he worked with Laurie Anderson on *Self Storage*, a series of installations housed in individual lockers at a London storage facility. Anderson provided the vocals for a track on Eno's electronic album *Drawn from Life* (2000), and Eno followed with a rare vocal album of his own, *Another Day on Earth* (2005). He returned to the producer's chair for Paul Simon's critically lauded *Surprise* (2006) and Coldplay's multi-platinum *Viva la Vida* (2008). In 2008 Eno teamed with former Talking Heads front man David Byrne for their first collaborative effort in nearly three decades. Adopting the self-publishing model popularized by Radiohead, Byrne and Eno released *Everything That Happens Will Happen Today* on the Internet, where listeners could stream the entire album for free or purchase physical or digital copies directly from the artists.

and Jerry Casale (their musician brothers later joined the band), Devo adopted a man-as-machine persona—complete with flowerpot headgear, matching industrial jumpsuits, robotic movements, and a heavy mechanical sound (including pioneering use of a drum machine invented by Bob Mothersbaugh)—to convey the dehumanizing effect of modern technology. Original videos of disturbing images were shown during concerts to underscore their philosophy. Following the success of their first single, "Jocko Homo" (1977), Devo released their debut album, *Q: Are We Not Men? A: We Are Devo!* (1978), to critical success. Produced by Brian Eno, it was considered their best record, featuring a techno-danceable beat and including a staccato cover version of the Rolling Stones' "(I Can't Get No) Satisfaction." Following their hit single "Whip It" (1980), however, the band's popularity declined, though they continued to influence other performers.

TALKING HEADS

In 1974 three classmates from the Rhode Island School of Design moved to New York City and declared themselves Talking Heads. Singer-guitarist David Byrne (born May 14, 1952, Dumbarton, Scotland), drummer Chris Frantz (born May 8, 1951, Fort Campbell, Kentucky, U.S.), and bassist Tina Weymouth (born November 22, 1950, Coronado, California) used the ironic sensibilities of modern art and literature to subvert rock, then embraced dance rhythms to alter it even more. After adding former Modern Lovers keyboardist Jerry Harrison (born February 21, 1949, Milwaukee, Wisconsin) in 1976, Talking Heads spent a decade moving from spare intimacy to rich pan-cultural fluency—and then back again. The enormous popularity of the quartet's records paved the way for other rock adventurers; their videos and film were also influential.

Byrne's anxious lyrics, twitchy persona, and squawky singing dominated *Talking Heads '77* (featuring "Psycho Killer"), a debut album that sold surprisingly well for a group so removed from the musical mainstream. Talking Heads' blend of workable rhythms for dance clubs and brain fodder for hipsters provided an intellectually challenging and creatively adult musical alternative to arena rock, disco, and the commercial impossibility of punk. As the group's music developed, it became a great white answer for an audience whose curiosity about world music and funk was most easily sated under the guidance of white urban intellectuals.

Talking Heads' choice of Brian Eno as producer affirmed their commitment to creative growth. Eno began simply, adding percussion and other elements to the group's own constructs on 1978's *More Songs About Buildings and Food* (ironically, what propelled the album to sell half a million copies was not its visionary originality but a straightforward hit cover version of Al Green's "Take Me to the River"). Over three albums, the application of Eno's inscrutable modus operandi—songwriting and performing as well as production—inspired an organic leap of ambition. With increasing confidence, ambition, and success, the group gathered rhythmic and textural elements into such potent inventions as the African-inflected "I Zimbra" and "Life During Wartime" (both from 1979's *Fear of Music*) and "Once in a Lifetime" and "The Great Curve" (from 1980's *Remain in Light*, Eno's final album with the group).

Following a year of solo projects (during which Frantz and Weymouth, who married in 1977, launched the Tom Tom Club, offering playful dance songs) and a carefully conceived live album (*The Name of This Band Is Talking Heads*, 1982), the group released *Speaking in Tongues* (1983), yielding the Top Ten single "Burning Down the House." *Stop*

Talking Heads (from left to right): *David Byrne, Chris Frantz, Tina Weymouth, and Jerry Harrison.* Echoes/Redferns/Getty Images

Making Sense (1984), the sound track to Jonathan Demme's acclaimed Talking Heads concert film, followed. *Little Creatures* (1985) returned the group to a simpler sound and became its first million-seller. Talking Heads' final album was 1988's *Naked*. The group then ceased to exist, its farewell unannounced.

Thereafter Byrne pursued a fascinating multimedia solo career, including becoming an avid supporter of the bicycle as a central means of transportation. Harrison became a producer; Frantz and Weymouth also kept busy as a production team. Harrison, Weymouth, and Frantz reunited as the Heads for a 1996 album and tour, which Byrne unsuccessfully attempted to block with legal objections to their use of the name.

Conclusion

The development of rock in the 1970s had two major consequences that were to become clearer in the 1980s. First, the musical tension between the mainstream and the margins, which had originally given rock and roll its cultural dynamism, was now contained within rock itself. The new mainstream was personified by Elton John, who developed a style of soul-inflected rock ballad that over the next two decades became the dominant sound of global pop music. But the 1970s also gave rise to a clearly "alternative" rock ideology (most militantly articulated by British punk musicians), a music scene self-consciously developed on independent labels using "underground" media and committed to protecting the "essence" of rock and roll from commercial degradation. The alternative-mainstream, authentic-fake distinction crossed all rock genres and indicated how rock culture had come to be defined by its own contradictions.

Second, sounds from outside the Anglo-American rock nexus began to make their mark on it (and in unexpected ways). In the 1970s, for example, Europop began to have an impact on the New York City dance scene via the clean, catchy Swedish sound of ABBA, the electronic machine music of Kraftwerk, and the American-Italian collaboration (primarily in West Germany) of Donna Summer and Giorgio Moroder. At the same time, Bob Marley's success in applying a Jamaican sensibility to rock conventions meant that reggae became a new tool for rock musicians, whether established stars such as Eric Clapton and the Rolling Stones' Keith Richards or young punks such as the Clash. In addition, reggae played a significant role (via New York City's Jamaican sound-system deejays) in the emergence of hip-hop, a cultural movement that would shape the development of popular music into the 21st century.

Glossary

agitprop Short for agitation-propaganda, a political strategy in which the techniques of both are used to influence and mobilize public opinion.

alumnus One who is a former member of a group.

ambient music Music intended to serve as an unobtrusive accompaniment to other activities (as in a public place) and characterized especially by quiet and repetitive instrumental melodies.

anarchic Of, relating to, or advocating anarchy (lawlessness).

arpeggio Production of the tones of a chord in succession and not simultaneously.

arrhythmic Lacking rhythm or regularity.

aseptic Lacking vitality, emotion, or warmth.

avatar An embodiment (as of a concept, philosophy, or musical movement).

bacchanal Excessive indulgence (named for Bacchus, the Roman god of wine).

bebop Also called bop (its shortened form), an onomatopoeic rendering of a staccato two-tone phrase distinctive in this type of jazz music.

bombastic Pompous, overblown.

braggadocio Boasting; cockiness.

Brill Building Located in New York City, the Brill Building was the hub of professionally written rock and roll. The 1960s equivalent of Tin Pan Alley, it reemphasized a specialized division of labour in which professional songwriters worked closely with producers and artists-and-repertoire personnel to match selected artists with appropriate songs.

canción Spanish for *song*.

circumlocutory Marked by using an unnecessarily large number of words to express an idea.

coterie An intimate, often exclusive, group of persons having a binding common interest or purpose.

cover A song previously recorded by someone else.

culling Hunting or killing (animals) as a means of population control.

declamatory Marked by rhetorical effect or display.

dilettante An admirer or lover of the arts.

elegy Song or poem expressing sorrow or lamentation especially for one who is dead.

eponymous Named after a particular person or musical group; self-titled.

ethereal Unworldly; heavenly.

fabulist A creator or writer of fables especially that carry a moral lesson.

falsetto An artificially high singing voice.

figuration Ornamentation of a musical passage by using decorative and usually repetitive figures.

foursquare Marked by boldness and conviction.

frenesí Spanish for *frenzy*.

fuzztone Distorted effect that can be created on an electric guitar by increasing vibrations or adding overtones.

galvanic Having an electric, intensely exciting effect.

gourmandiser One who appreciates good food and drink.

guttersnipe Homeless vagabond, especially an outcast boy or girl in the streets of a city.

hedonism Doctrine that pleasure or happiness is the sole or chief good in life.

iconography Imagery or symbolism of a work of art, an artist, or a body of art.

keening Mournful; sorrowful.

legato A smooth and connected manner of performance (as of music); a passage of music so performed.

licentiousness Unrestrained by law or general morality.

louche Not reputable.

Mancunian One from Manchester, England.

manifesto A public declaration of the intentions, motives, or views of its issuer.

mediumistic Of, relating to, or having the qualities of a spiritualistic medium.

Mephistophelian Exhibiting behaviour like that of Mephistopheles, a demon in the Faust legend.

modus operandi Latin for a *method of procedure*.

nihilist One who rejects all philosophical or ethical principles.

onomatopoeically Something named in a manner that suggests the sound associated with it.

Pentecostal Any of various Christian religious bodies that emphasize individual experiences of grace, spiritual gifts (such as speaking in tongues and faith healing), expressive worship, and evangelism.

plangent Having an expressive and especially plaintive quality.

polyrhythms Conflicts of rhythm or cross rhythms.

posthumous Following or occurring after death, as in a posthumous award, exhibition, or album.

progression Succession of musical tones or chords.

prolix Long and wordy.

proto- Prefix meaning the first in time (as in proto-punk, which describes an artist or song as being among the first of its kind in punk rock music).

psychobilly Genre of rock music that fuses elements of punk with rockabilly (rockabilly being a form of popular music marked by features of rock and country music).

qua Latin for *as*.

Rastafarian Member of a political and religious movement that originated in Jamaica. Rastafarians believe in the divinity of Emperor Haile Selassie I of Ethiopia and in the eventual return of his exiled followers to Africa.

repatriation To restore or return to the country of origin, allegiance, or citizenship.

riot grrrl An underground feminist punk rock movement begun in the 1990s.

rock steady Jamaican musical genre characterized by offbeat rhythms slower than ska and that would later evolve into reggae.

salacious Arousing or appealing to sexual desire or imagination.

saturnine Having a disdainful, sceptical, or derisively mocking aspect.

schmaltzy Effusively or insincerely emotional; corny.

sideman Supporting instrumentalist in a band or orchestra.

skengay In ska, the sound of a guitar that emulates that of gunshots.

skiffle Form of music formerly popular in Great Britain featuring vocals with a simple instrumental accompaniment.

staccato Marked by short clear-cut playing or singing of tones or chords.

sui generis One of a kind, unique.

svengali Based on a fictional character (the villain of the romantic novel *Trilby* (1894) by British author George du Maurier), the name has come to designate an authority figure or mentor who exerts great influence, often evil, over another person.

thrash metal Also known as speed metal (for its fast tempo), guitar-driven subgenre of heavy metal characterized by aggressive vocals.

timbre The character or quality of a musical sound.

Tin Pan Alley Genre of American popular music that arose in the late 19th century from the American song-publishing industry centred in New York City. The phrase *tin pan* referred to the sound of pianos furiously pounded by the so-called song pluggers, who demonstrated tunes to publishers.

vernacular Characteristic of a period, place, group, or style.

xenophobic Characterized by a fear or dislike of strangers or foreigners.

Bibliography

LED ZEPPELIN

Stephen Davis, *Hammer of the Gods: The Led Zeppelin Saga* (1985, reissued 2008), a sensationalist account, traces the band's history from inception to breakup, as well as post-Zeppelin solo activities by Jimmy Page, Robert Plant, and John Paul Jones. Ritchie Yorke, *Led Zeppelin: The Definitive Biography* (1993), gives a more dispassionate account of the band's history. Chris Welch, "Jimmy Page: Paganini of the Seventies," *Melody Maker*, p. 16 (February 14, 1970), p. 12 (February 21, 1970), and p. 10 (February 28, 1970), is one of the earliest interviews with Jimmy Page, who explains the band's music and philosophy. Cameron Crowe, "The Durable Led Zeppelin: A Conversation with Jimmy Page and Robert Plant," *Rolling Stone*, 182:32–37 (March 13, 1975), is the only interview the band did with *Rolling Stone*.

William Burroughs, "Rock Magic: Jimmy Page, Led Zeppelin, and a Search for the Elusive Stairway to Heaven," *Crawdaddy*, 49:34–40 (June 1975), examines the band's music and live concerts in terms of ritual effect. Dave Lewis, *Led Zeppelin: A Celebration* (1991), presents a track-by-track analysis of each song on each recording, information on concerts the band played and equipment they used, and some insight into their recording process. Charles R. Cross and Erik Flannigan, *Led Zeppelin: Heaven and Hell* (1991), collects essays including an attempt at a complete list of concerts played, treatment of the art of collecting bootleg recordings, and a reprint of one of the few interviews Page gave during the 1970s. Dave Headlam, "Does the Song Remain the Same? Questions of Authorship and Identification in the Music of Led Zeppelin," in Elizabeth West Marvin and Richard Hermann (eds.), *Concert Music, Rock, and Jazz Since 1945* (1995), pp. 313–363, examines the thorny question of Led Zeppelin's "borrowings" from the blues: how much of such songs as "Whole Lotta Love" was borrowed, and how much was original? Steve Waksman, "Every Inch of My Love: Led Zeppelin and the Problem of Cock Rock," *Journal of*

Popular Music Studies 8:5–25 (1996), examines gender issues in the band's music and image.

BRUCE SPRINGSTEEN

The most indispensable Springsteen book is *Bruce Springsteen, Songs,* expanded ed. (also published as *Bruce Springsteen Songs*, 2003), which collects his lyrics from his first album through *Devils and Dust* with limited but important comments from the author. The standard Springsteen biography is Dave Marsh, *Born to Run* (1979, reissued 1996), and its companion volume, *Glory Days* (1987, reissued 1996), published together as *Bruce Springsteen: Two Hearts* (2003), with a foreword and final chapter updating the tale. Dave Marsh, *Bruce Springsteen On Tour: 1968–2005* (2006), a coffee-table book featuring photos from Springsteen's personal collection, takes on the story from another angle. The fan's (and the band's) perspective is exemplified by the stories and memorabilia collected in Bob Santelli, *Greetings from E Street: The Story of Bruce Springsteen and the E Street Band* (2006). Frank Stefanko, *Days of Hope and Dreams: An Intimate Portrait of Bruce Springsteen* (2003), collects the author's photos of Springsteen from the late 1970s and early '80s, offering the most personal visual document of the artist.

June Skinner Sawyers (ed.), *Racing in the Street: The Bruce Springsteen Reader* (2004), is a compilation of significant journalism and criticism, most of it focused on lyrics. Of academic studies, the most interesting is Robert Coles, *Bruce Springsteen's America: The People Listening, A Poet Singing* (2004), which offers interviews with Springsteen fans conducted by someone who knows the artist well. Two simultaneous cover profiles make amusing reading, if only for their contrasting approaches to celebrity journalism and for evidence of how much harm hype can and cannot do to an artist's career: the laudatory Jay Cocks et al., "The Backstreet Phantom of Rock," *Time* (October 27, 1975), pp. 48–58; and the hostile Maureen Orth, Janet Huck, and Peter S. Greenberg, "Making of a Rock Star," *Newsweek* (October 27, 1975), pp. 57–63.

PAUL MCCARTNEY

The Beatles Anthology (2000), an essential reference work assembled by committee from preexisting and new interviews, is the official history of the band, with the self-censorship that implies. Hunter Davies, *The Beatles: The Illustrated and Updated Edition of the Bestselling Authorized Biography* (2006), suffers from the censorship Lennon later regretted imposing in order not to offend his maternal aunt Mimi, who brought him up. Mark Lewisohn, *The Complete Beatles Chronicle* (1992, reissued 2004), offers a detailed description of every Beatles recording session and performance, plus day-by-day details of their lives. Paul McCartney and Linda McCartney, *Paul McCartney Composer/Artist* (1981), collects McCartney's lyrics and drawings; and Brian Clarke et al., *Paul McCartney Paintings* (2000), is the catalogue of McCartney's first show, with many illustrations and scholarly essays. The authorized biography by Barry Miles, *Paul McCartney: Many Years from Now* (1997), based on more than 40 interviews with McCartney and with others, concentrates on McCartney's career up until 1970 and on his relationship with Lennon.

HEAVY METAL

The first attempt to analyze the social meanings of heavy metal was Philip Bashe, *Heavy Metal Thunder* (1985). Mark Hale, *HeadBangers: The Worldwide Megabook of Heavy Metal Bands* (1993), is the best reference work on the subject; Jas Obrecht (ed.), *Masters of Heavy Metal* (1984), provides technical profiles of influential guitarists. Ian Christe, *Sound of the Beast: The Complete Headbanging History of Heavy Metal* (2004), examines the genre's

development and provides a survey of the metal's biggest names. The best scholarly studies of heavy metal are Robert Walser, *Running with the Devil: Power, Gender, and Madness in Heavy Metal Music* (1993), which mixes musicology with cultural studies; and Deena Weinstein, *Heavy Metal: A Cultural Sociology* (1991). Donna Gaines, *Teenage Wasteland: Suburbia's Dead End Kids* (1991), is a sobering and insightful ethnographic study of one group of heavy metal fans.

COUNTRY ROCK

John Rockwell, "The Sound of Hollywood," in Jim Miller (ed.), *The Rolling Stone Illustrated History of Rock & Roll*, rev. and updated (1980), pp. 407–414, is a superb placement of country rock in the larger perspective of Los Angeles pop music, with special emphasis on chief practitioners and concomitant movements of the 1970s and '80s. James Hunter, "The Eagles," in Paul Kingsbury (ed.), *Country on Compact Disc* (1993), pp. 55–56, offers an evaluative sketch of the Eagles' career and recordings and traces the influence of their work on mainstream Nashville country music. "The Eagles," in Patricia Romanowski, Holly George-Warren, and Jon Pareles (eds.), *The Rolling Stone Encyclopedia of Rock & Roll*, rev. and updated (2001), is a good running narrative of country rock's earliest and more commercialized, era-defining days.

SINGER-SONGWRTITERS

Paul Zollo, *Songwriters on Songwriting*, expanded ed. (2003), collects 62 interviews with songwriters about their work and includes conversations with Bob Dylan, Paul Simon, Randy Newman, Leonard Cohen, Laura Nyro, and Jackson Browne.

JOHN LENNON

There is no biography of John Lennon that finds an intelligent, informed middle ground between hagiography and hatchet job. The best of the former is Ray Coleman, *Lennon: The Definitive Biography* (1992). The most fully researched of the latter, Albert Goldman, *The Lives of John Lennon* (1988, reissued 2001), is so transparently spiteful as to be almost useless. Jann S. Wenner, *Lennon Remembers*, new ed. (2001), the *Rolling Stone* interviews; and David Sheff, *The Playboy Interviews with John Lennon and Yoko Ono*, ed. by G. Barry Golson (1981, reissued as *All We Are Saying: The Last Major Interview with John Lennon and Yoko Ono*, 2000), are eloquent interviews. The Editors of *Rolling Stone*, *The Ballad of John and Yoko*, ed. by Jonathan Cott and Christine Doudna (1982); and Elizabeth Thomson and

David Gutman (eds.), *The Lennon Companion: Twenty-five Years of Comment* (1987, reissued 2004), are useful collections. The best academic studies are Anthony Elliott, *The Mourning of John Lennon* (1999), written from a postmodernist perspective; and Jon Wiener, *Come Together: John Lennon in His Time* (1984, reprinted 1991), a political take.

NEIL YOUNG

David Downing, *A Dreamer of Pictures: Neil Young, the Man and His Music* (1994), attempts to put Young's long and varied career in perspective. Michael Heatley (compiler), *Neil Young: In His Own Words* (1997), is a long interview that reveals as much about Young's attitudes as it does facts. Johnny Rogan, *The Complete Guide to the Music of Neil Young*, ed. by Chris Charlesworth (1996), is an exhaustive track-by-track examination of Young's output. Paul Williams, *Neil Young: Love to Burn* (1997), presents an empathetic if somewhat oversensitive portrait. "Neil Young," in Anthony DeCurtis et al. (eds.), *The Rolling Stone Illustrated History of Rock & Roll* (2008), offers a good basic introduction to Young's life and work.

JONI MITCHELL

Brian Hinton, *Joni Mitchell: Both Sides Now* (1996), is a biography.

ART ROCK AND PROGRESSIVE ROCK

Edward Macan, *Rocking the Classics: English Progressive Rock and the Counterculture* (1997), a comprehensive work, discusses the origin of progressive rock, its musical, visual, and lyrical styles, and its critical reception. Bill Martin, *Music of Yes: Structure and Vision in Progressive Rock* (1996), treats Yes's early music, 1970s albums, band members' solo projects, and later manifestations of the band; to a certain extent, the work applies sociocultural theory to Yes by focusing on individual works by the group. Eric Tamm, *Brian Eno: His Music and the Vertical Color of Sound, updated ed.* (1995), systematically accounts for Eno's musical compositions and other activities, including his progressive rock from the mid-1970s, his later ambient style, his collaborations as a cocomposer and producer, and his views on cultural aesthetics; and Tamm's *Robert Fripp: From King Crimson to Guitar Craft* (1990), treats Fripp as a progressive-rock guitarist before, during, and in between his several incarnations of the band King Crimson, his collaborations as a guitarist and producer, his experimental developments of "Frippertronics" and other forms, and his later activities as a music theorist and teacher.

JAZZ-ROCK

Stuart Nicholson, *Jazz Rock: A History* (1998), is a comprehensive study of the genre. Julie Coryell and Laura Friedman, *Jazz-Rock Fusion, the People, the Music* (also published as *Jazz-Rock Fusion*; 1978), discusses the idiom's 1970s stars. Miles Davis and Quincy Troupe, *Miles, the Autobiography* (1989), presents the highly opinionated recollections of the leading jazz-rock figure. Jack Chambers, *Milestones*, 2 vol. (1983–85, reissued in 1 vol., 1998), is a thoroughly researched critical biography of Miles Davis.

FUNK

Rickey Vincent, *Funk: The Music, the People, and the Rhythm of The One* (1996), presents a comprehensive analysis of funk music and its social context. Brian Ward, *Just My Soul Responding* (1998), provides a historical analysis of rhythm and blues, black consciousness, and race relations. Jim Payne, *Give the Drummers Some!: The Great Drummers of R&B, Funk & Soul*, ed. by Harry Weinger (1996), collects interviews with innovators of funk rhythms. Greg Tate, *Flyboy in the Buttermilk: Essays on Contemporary America* (1992), presents interviews and analyzes funk in a social context. S.H. Fernando, Jr.,

The New Beats: Exploring the Music, Culture, and Attitudes of Hip-Hop (1994), examines the influence of funk on rap music.

PARLIAMENT-FUNKADELIC

David Mills, et al., *George Clinton and P-Funk: An Oral History* (1998), is a definitive collection of viewpoints from Parliament-Funkadelic players themselves. Rickey Vincent, *Funk: The Music, the People, and the Rhythm of The One* (1996), explores P-Funk spirituality, style, and influence on black culture. Greg Tate, *Flyboy in the Buttermilk: Essays on Contemporary America* (1992), presents interviews and essays that analyze P-Funk in social context. S.H. Fernando, Jr., *The New Beats: Exploring the Music, Culture, and Attitudes of Hip-Hop* (1994), examines the influence of P-Funk on rap music. Detailed chronologies of P-Funk can be found in Irwin Stambler, *Encyclopedia of Pop, Rock & Soul*, rev. ed. (1989); Colin Larkin (ed.), *The Guinness Encyclopedia of Popular Music*, 2nd ed., vol. 2 and 4 (1995); and Patricia Romanowski, Holly George-Warren, and Jon Pareles (eds.), *The Rolling Stone Encyclopedia of Rock & Roll*, completely rev. and updated (2001). Brian Ward, *Just My Soul Responding* (1998), provides historical analysis of rhythm and blues, black consciousness, and race relations.

SLY AND THE FAMILY STONE

Joel Selvin, *Sly and the Family Stone: An Oral History* (1998), chronicles the rise and fall of Sly Stone through interviews with supporters and members of the band. Rickey Vincent, *Funk: The Music, the People, and the Rhythm of the One* (1996), covers Sly's musical and cultural innovations in terms of funk. Greil Marcus, *Mystery Train: Images of America in Rock 'n' Roll Music*, rev. ed. (2008), discusses Sly Stone's life in a social context. Detailed chronologies of Sly and the Family Stone can be found in Irwin Stambler, *Encyclopedia of Pop, Rock & Soul*, rev. ed. (1989); Colin Larkin (ed.), *The Guinness Encyclopedia of Popular Music*, 2nd ed., vol. 5 (1995); and Patricia Romanowski, Holly George-Warren, and Jon Pareles (eds.), *The Rolling Stone Encyclopedia of Rock & Roll*, rev. and updated (2001).

THE OHIO PLAYERS

The Ohio Players are covered in Rickey Vincent, *Funk: The Music, the People, and the Rhythm of the One* (1996), pp. 195–198; Colin Larkin (ed.), *The Guinness Encyclopedia of Popular Music*, 2nd ed., vol. 4 (1995); and Patricia Romanowski, Holly George-Warren, and Jon Pareles (eds.), *The Rolling Stone Encyclopedia of Rock & Roll* (2001). The recording of their top singles is chronicled in Adam White and Fred Bronson, *The Billboard Book of Number One Rhythm & Blues Hits* (1993).

REGGAE

Stephen Davis and Peter Simon, *Reggae Bloodlines*, rev. ed. (1979, reissued 1992), is an early exploratory account of the evolution of reggae as a sociocultural statement as well as a form of music. Stephen Davis and Peter Simon, *Reggae International* (1982), considers the origins of the music and traces its international dispersal. Steve Barrow and Peter Dalton, *The Rough Guide to Reggae*, 3rd ed., rev. and expanded (2004), presents a thorough account of the evolution of reggae from ska to dancehall. Peter Manuel with Kenneth Bilby and Michael Largey, *Caribbean Currents: Caribbean Music from Rumba to Reggae*, rev. and expanded (2006), is a comprehensive survey of Caribbean music with a substantial consideration of reggae; Dave Thompson, *Reggae & Caribbean Music* (2002), also places reggae in context and includes a discography and bibliography. Kevin O'Brien Chang and Wayne Chen, *Reggae Routes* (1998), is the first comprehensive study of reggae written by Jamaicans. Malika Lee Whitney and Dermott Hussey, *Bob Marley: Reggae King of the World*, 2nd ed. (1994), offers a Jamaican perspective on the international significance of Bob Marley. Chuck Foster, *Roots, Rock, Reggae: An Oral History of Reggae Music from Ska to Dancehall* (1999), re-creates reggae's development from the perspective of the participants.

BOB MARLEY

Timothy White, *Catch a Fire: The Life of Bob Marley*, rev. and enlarged (1989 and 1998), includes an examination of the traditional roots of Marley's work. Adrian Boot and Chris Salewicz, *Bob Marley: Songs of Freedom*, ed. by Rita Marley (1995), is a pictorial work.

SKA

Garth White, *A Definitive Introduction to the Development of Jamaican Popular Music Pt. 2* (1984), provides a comprehensive overview. Steve Barrow and Peter Dalton, *Reggae: the Rough Guide* (1997); and Kevin O'Brien Chang and Wayne Chen, *Reggae Routes* (1998), include informative chapters on ska. Brian Keyo, "A Brief History of the Skatalites," from the liner notes to the *Foundation Ska: The Skatalites CD*, offers a detailed account of ska's origins and development.

DISCO

In a genre with scant scholarship to date, Albert Goldman, *Disco* (1978), essentially a coffee-table book, remains definitive. Barbara Graustark, "Disco Takes Over," *Newsweek*, 93(14):56–64 (April 2, 1979), offers decent reportage of the moment. Good historical accounts of the phenomenon are provided in Reebee Garofalo, *Rockin' Out: Popular Music in the USA* (1997); and Hugh Mooney, "Disco: A Music for the 1980s?," *Popular Music and Society*, 7(2):84–94 (1980). Tom Smucker, "Disco," in Anthony DeCurtis, James Henke, and Holly George-Warren (eds.), *The Rolling Stone Illustrated History of Rock & Roll*, 3rd ed. (1992), attempts to recapture disco as a scene. Aspects of gay culture are covered in Richard Dyer, "In Defense of Disco," in Corey K. Creekmur and Alexander Doty (eds.), *Out in Culture: Gay, Lesbian, and Queer Essays on Popular Culture* (1995); and Walter Hughes, "In the Empire of the Beat: Discipline and Disco," in Andrew Ross and Tricia Rose (eds.), *Microphone Fiends: Youth Music & Youth Culture* (1994).

PUNK

Greil Marcus, L*ipstick Traces: A Secret History of the Twentieth Century* (1989), analyzes the impact of punk music. Jon Savage, *England's Dreaming* (1991), covers the Sex Pistols and the origins of punk music. John Lydon, Keith Zimmerman, and Kent Zimmerman, *Rotten: No Irish,* *No Blacks, No Dogs* (1994), presents the Sex Pistols' Johnny Rotten's varied views on many topics, including punk.

THE CLASH

Marcus Gray, *Last Gang in Town: The Story and Myth of the Clash* (1995, reissued 1997), is a biographical study that examines the Clash in all their contradictions.

JOY DIVISION/ NEW ORDER

Joy Division is discussed in Mark Johnson et al., *An Ideal for Living* (1984); Claude Flowers, *New Order + Joy Division: Dreams Never End* (1995); and Deborah Curtis, *Touching from a Distance: Ian Curtis and Joy Division* (1995), written by Ian Curtis's widow.

PATTI SMITH

Patti Smith, *Patti Smith* (1977), is a collection of poems and sheet music; and *Patti Smith Complete: Lyrics, Reflections & Notes for the Future* (1998) combines all her lyrics to date with her own annotations and photographs by Annie Leibovitz and Robert Mapplethorpe, among others. Dusty Roach, *Patti Smith: Rock & Roll Madonna* (1979), is a popular photo book. Profiles of her may be found in Lucy O'Brien, *She Bop: The*

Definitive History of Women in Rock, Pop, and Soul (1995), pp. 111–117; and Deborah Frost, "Patti Smith," in Barbara O'Dair (ed.), *Trouble Girls: The Rolling Stone Book of Women in Rock* (1997), pp. 269–275.

ELVIS COSTELLO

Brian Hinton, *Let Them All Talk: The Music of Elvis Costello* (1999), considers Costello's life and work, with the emphasis on the latter. James E. Perone, *Elvis Costello: A Bio-Bibliography* (1998), presents a brief biography but, more importantly, compiles more than 800 bibliographic citations and a complete discography.

THE SMITHS

Nick Kent, "Morrissey, the Majesty of Melancholia, and the Light that Never Goes Out in Smiths-dom," in his *The Dark Stuff* (1994), pp. 202–211, examines Morrissey's unhappy childhood and persecuted adolescence in Manchester, the seedbed for the singer's pursuit of fame as a type of revenge. The essay by Simon Reynolds, "Morrissey," in his *Blissed Out: The Raptures of Rock* (1990), pp.15–29, is based on an interview and defends the singer's glamorization of failure, neurasthenia, and unrequited love as a rebellion against the 1980s culture of health and efficiency and compulsory happiness. Jon Savage, "Morrissey: The Escape Artist," in his *Time Travel: Pop, Media, and Sexuality, 1976–96* (1996), pp. 257–264, compares Morrissey to the hero of *Billy Liar*, the 1960s novel and film about a doomed dreamer who never leaves his northern England hometown, and analyzes the singer's love-hate relationship with Manchester and his increasing isolation from contemporary pop culture on the eve of the 1990s. Michael Bracewell, *England Is Mine: Pop Life in Albion from Wilde to Goldie* (1997), celebrates Morrissey, often criticized for his parochial nostalgia for a lost 1960s Britain, as the last of a dying breed of quintessentially English pop aesthetes.

TALKING HEADS

Krista Reese, *The Name of This Book Is Talking Heads* (1982), provides an overview of the band's career.

Index